MANAGEMENT AND UNIONS

by the same author

The Fawley Productivity Agreements

Experiment in Industrial Democracy:
A Study of the John Lewis Partnership
(*with Ruth Pomeranz and Joan Woodward*)

MANAGEMENT AND UNIONS

The Theory and Reform of Industrial Relations

by

Allan Flanders

FABER AND FABER
London

First published in 1970
by Faber and Faber Limited
24 Russell Square London WC1
Printed in Great Britain by
Western Printing Services Ltd, Bristol

ISBN: 0 571 09280 2

© *Allan Flanders 1970*

PREFACE

My appointment to the Commission on Industrial Relations and consequent departure from academic life at the University of Oxford seemed to be a fitting occasion to bring together in a single volume the more important of my recent papers on industrial relations. With one exception they have all been printed before, but I hope there will be an interest in these previously scattered parts appearing as a collected whole. I hope too that this will bring out more clearly both the evolution and unity of my thought on the changing roles and responsibilities of managements, unions and governments in the rapidly changing conditions of the post-war epoch. This at a practical level is a common theme. At a theoretical level most of the papers reflect my concern to analyse industrial relations and, not least, the institution of collective bargaining in terms of systems of job regulation.

Two of the longer essays have already been published separately by Faber and Faber. For the rest I wish to express my thanks to various editors and publishers whose kind permission to reprint particular papers is tacitly acknowledged elsewhere. I am especially indebted to Alan Fox for his agreement to include our joint article. Although some have been shortened, otherwise no attempt has been made to revise any of the papers beyond making minor corrections and deleting what in the present setting would be repetitive passages or references.

ALLAN FLANDERS

CONTENTS

ON TRADE UNIONS

TRADE UNIONS IN THE SIXTIES
(1961)

The public reputation of British trade unionism is under fire. Increasingly the unions are accused of being out of date, of clinging to restrictive practices that have outlived their usefulness, of failing to adapt their organisation to present needs, of being unimaginative in their policy and unresponsive to the challenges that contemporary society presents. Above all the tag 'I am all right, Jack', with all its odium, has attached itself to them more than to managements and employers.

This represents a sharp change as compared with ten years ago. During the years immediately after the war praise heavily outweighed criticism. The unions' sense of responsibility was then being acclaimed on all sides. Bouquets were being handed out for their willingness to undertake wage restraint and to engage in productivity drives. Conservative politicians courted them eagerly, if anything more eagerly than Labour politicians. One might have thought, many did at the time, that the unions had climbed to a pinnacle of respectability from which they could never be shaken.

Looked at from the point of view of any ordinary trade unionist this sudden fall from public favour must appear strangely capricious. His own trade union has not changed appreciably in his eyes. It is providing him with the same services, engaging in the same activities, following to a large extent the same policies. Why, then, all the fuss? Frank Cousins may have replaced Arthur Deakin, but one man could hardly account for it. So the reaction of many trade unionists is to shrug their shoulders and say 'what else can you expect?'. The capitalist leopards have not changed their spots and they no longer bother to conceal their claws. The honeymoon is over. They are up to their old tricks again, trying to discredit the unions in order to weaken them.

Such a reaction is not only understandable, it is in part justified. Many of the criticisms to which trade unions are now subjected are founded either on prejudice or on ignorance. One can see the old cloven hoof projecting prominently when all the blame for rising

13

prices is laid at the unions' door. Attacks on the closed shop itself, as distinct from some of the less pleasant methods that may occasionally be used to attain it, usually betray a lack of knowledge of the real nature of industrial relations as well as the basic norms of working-class morality.

But none of this makes it wise for trade unions to discount their loss of public sympathy. Time and again they have depended on public support for success in their battles for freedom and status. Nor must we forget what has been happening in the courts of law in recent years, where protection that the unions believed they had obtained under the 1906 Act and earlier legislation is being eroded bit by bit. What does this illustrate other than the gradual adaptability of Common Law to trends in public opinion? And how can the unions seek to redress this situation without changes in Statute Law which can only be secured when sufficient public support can be mobilised in their favour?

In a democratic society it is not only undemocratic of democratic organisations to disregard public opinion, it is downright folly. The present movement of opinion against the unions must surely be seen by them as an extremely dangerous threat which urgently needs to be counteracted. But how? There are some who argue that it is all due to the unions' bad public relations. They point to the deeply ingrained indifference within the trade union movement towards publicity, Press relations and other modern methods of communication. Employers, especially the large firms, find it expedient continually to increase their expenditure on public relations in order to create a favourable image of themselves. Why do trade unions not follow their example and make the best of their case?

That trade unions do pay too little attention to their public relations is certainly true. There are exceptions, but it is puzzling why so much wintry gloom should surround the occasional communications made by the unions to the public, when they make them at all. The more the trade unions can do to improve their methods of publicity, the better; nevertheless there are practical limits. Publicity is a very costly affair and trade unions are not wealthy organisations. It would be unrealistic not to recognise that they will always find it hard to compete with their opponents on these terms. In any case I doubt whether the reluctance of the unions to improve their public relations is the main factor accounting for their loss of

14

public sympathy. For not all the criticisms levelled against the unions
are biased and unfair. The unions cannot be judged entirely blameless
for their loss of public sympathy.

In 1948 I wrote a pamphlet on British trade unionism in which I
introduced two quotations in order to pose a problem. One was
taken from a study outline in which the author had written of British
trade unionism:

> To look at externals, it appears lacking in system, in common con-
> sciousness, and in the possibility of consistent action. But there is a
> deeper current that must be noticed: a current drawn from the depths
> of British life, which runs subtly and powerfully through the whole
> record of trade union development. The trade union movement may have
> lacked a coherent set of principles, but it has not lacked a sentiment of
> common purpose. It has generated loyalty, induced sacrifice, deepened
> its grip on the public life because it has dimly sought to be a 'sword
> of justice'.[1]

I compared that passage with an extract from one of the editorial
articles of *The Economist* appearing in the same year:

> it would be . . . wrong for anybody any longer to entertain any notions
> about the trade unions being a force for progressive initiative in the
> nation. They are an incubus, an inertia. So far from representing in some
> special way the noblest instincts of mankind (as Labour mythology has
> so often inferred) they are in reality only the most securely entrenched
> of the vested interests.[2]

An exaggerated statement indicative of that journal's familiar bias,
you may say, but it contains more than a grain of truth.

Trade unions have always had two faces, sword of justice and
vested interest. But it is the second, rather than the first, that is now
turned most frequently to public view. More than that, it has become
accepted as their normal, natural image by the unions themselves.
It is this, more than anything else, which has been ultimately
responsible for their loss of sympathy. The trade union movement
deepened its grip on public life in its aspect as a sword of justice.
When it is no longer seen to be this, when it can no longer count on
anything but its own power to withstand assault, it becomes extremely
vulnerable. The more so since it is as a sword of justice rather than
a vested interest that it generates loyalties and induces sacrifices
among its own members, and these are important foundations of its
strength and vitality.

On Trade Unions

Why has the spirit of materialism so submerged the spirit of idealism within the trade unions today? Or, to put the same question in less abstract terms, why is trade unionism thought of more as a business and less as a cause? Is it, as some would argue, because the workers themselves have been strongly infected by acquisitive values in an affluent society? Is there, as others have suggested, some long-term secular trend in all countries away from labour movement loyalties towards bureaucratic business trade unionism, as the unions gain in age, maturity and security? Neither of these explanations satisfies me, because I do not believe that the present trend is inevitable. What the movement is suffering from today is, quite simply, loss of social purpose. Given the appropriate leadership that malady can be overcome. The real trouble is that such leadership has not been forthcoming in adequate measure.

Let me explain the logic of my diagnosis. I must first distinguish between social purpose and social function. No one seriously disputes that, in one sense, trade unions serve a most valuable, indeed a necessary, purpose in present-day society. They function as an integral part of a complicated yet on the whole smoothly working system of industrial relations. They operate within a framework of rules and conventions, some of them given legal force but most of them voluntary, and they continually participate in adapting this framework to changing needs. Most of their energies are absorbed in these activities, especially in the successive rounds of wage negotiations.

All this is their bread and butter as unions and on it depends the bread and butter of their members. But this social function is not what is usually meant by social purpose. When we speak of trade unions or any other bodies having a social purpose we have in mind their striving to change society. We think of the trade unions acting as a 'sword of justice'. But the processes of social change present us with a paradox. The social purpose of yesterday, once accomplished, becomes the social function of today. Social purpose has, therefore, ever to be created afresh. It is exhausted as much by success as by failure.

For the sake of comparison turn back to the 1930s. What social purposes were in the foreground of union striving at that time? Two overshadowed all others. The first was not new but had been given added point by the experiences of the 1920s, culminating in the great

16

depression of 1929–32. It was to establish the position of the trade unions in industry on firmer foundations–and all that this implied in terms of membership, union recognition by employers, satisfactory machinery for collective bargaining, the observation of agreements, and so on. The demand was for organisation not for its own sake, but as a prerequisite to defend and improve the workers' standards.

The second predominant social purpose of British trade unions in the 'thirties was to gain a consultative relationship with government on an equal footing with employers. In particular they were claiming a voice in national economic policy, which would be theirs of right and not dependent on the changing fortunes of party politics. While the first purpose was pursued mainly by individual unions and their industrial federations, the second was championed by the TUC. Both these purposes could be expressed as demands for improvements in the existing arrangements for negotiation and consultation with employers and the government; behind them both stood the quest for justice.

The achievement of these social purposes of the 'thirties was greatly facilitated by the circumstances of the Second World War. In the annals of British trade unionism the decade 1940–50 is only paralleled by that of 1910–20 for rapid growth and great achievement. But these decades differed significantly in their aftermaths. After 1920 the unions were again under attack and on the defensive. The same type of challenge has not arisen after 1950. There has been no sudden decline in membership, no dismantling of collective bargaining machinery, no open cold-shouldering of the trade unions in the councils of the nation. Even when Conservatives replaced Labour in government in 1951 they were careful to preserve intact all the existing national arrangements for consultation.

This induced a mood of complacency in the trade union world which is only gradually, though by now very perceptibly, being dispelled. My immediate point, however, is that the pre-war social purposes had been exhausted by their transformation into post-war social functions. Much the same thing happened to the Labour Party during its period of office as a majority government after the war. The trade unions and the Labour Party have in fact shared a common problem, the price of their previous success. Both in their several ways had to raise their sights and set them afresh if they were to retain their dynamic. New social purposes, appropriate to the changed situation, had to be formulated and pressed for. Failure to do this has been responsible for the impression that the unions are now more of a vested interest than a sword of justice.

The unions' loss of social purpose has not only affected their public standing but also their internal life. The communist problem is a good illustration. When one looks at the small number of committed Party members in this country the influence they are able to exert on the policy of some unions, and indirectly on the policy disputes within the Labour Party, borders on the fantastic; it is quite disproportionate to their real strength. This is explained as being due to their operating as an organised faction, to the unscrupulousness of their methods and to the apathy of so many union members. But there is nothing new in any of these factors; they have always operated on their side. Why should they be more successful today than they were during the 'thirties when the prevailing conditions were far more likely to make workers take the path towards revolution? My impression is that communists gain support among non-communist militants because they have a cause in which they believe and all too frequently those who oppose them have not.

Another internal consequence of the unions' loss of social purpose is a weakening of the tradition of voluntary service. Men and women may work for a trade union either for love or for money, but British trade unions have always assumed that money would not and should not be the main inducement. They are strongly disinclined to pay their full-time officers salaries in any way comparable with what they would receive outside the movement. They depend on a great army of lay officers who are expected to devote many hours of their spare time on behalf of their fellows with little or no financial reward. Such a position can only be sustained so long as trade unionism has the appeal of a cause worth making sacrifices for. The ultimate logic of a purely business unionism is the logic of business itself–that no one is ready to work for it unless he is paid his full market rate. There may be a case for trade unions becoming better employers than they are today, to improve the wages and working conditions that they offer their own employees, but it is inconceivable that they will ever be able to compete with business on a market basis for the recruitment of talent. Unless they continue to tap the love as well as the money motive in recruiting both their full-time and their lay officers, they are bound to be faced with a progressive decline in

standards of performance. Thus there are good reasons to believe
that their loss of social purpose threatens the trade unions' power
and influence, both by damaging their public reputation and by
weakening their internal loyalties.

It would be wrong to suggest that there has been no awareness of
this problem within the unions or that no attempt has been made to
meet it. One such attempt to find a new social purpose after the war
has been the taking up of the higher productivity objective. We find
this expressed in the association of the TUC with the British
Productivity Council and in industrial agreements such as those made
in the boot and shoe industry to facilitate the introduction of work
study. This, I am convinced, is a false trail. Not because the unions
can afford to be indifferent to the efficiency of industry, any more than
other bodies of responsible citizens can. Not because there is anything wrong in their trading increased earnings for their members
against a better utilization of their labour–that is plain common
sense. Full employment has given them the possibility of changing
practices which they were forced to maintain when many of their
members were unemployed. But what is at stake is not only a more
responsible type of collective bargaining. It is whether higher productivity can furnish the unions with a new social purpose of their own.
I would claim that it cannot on two counts. It is neither in their
power nor in their nature to fulfil this particular purpose.

It is not in their power because the main decisions affecting
productivity lie elsewhere, with managements and boards of directors.
Where trade unions lend support to the impression that they have
parity of responsibility with employers for industrial efficiency and
productivity, they are placing themselves in an invidious position,
since they have not parity of power *to act*. They merely mislead the
public on a point where some sections of it are only too eager to be
misled. How often does one hear that it is all the fault of the unions
that Britain lags behind her competitors?

Equally it is not within the nature of trade unions to accept this
objective as their social purpose. One can understand why governments and employers urge them to do so and why initially trade
unions gain in respectability as a consequence. But this respectability
is, in the end, purchased at the cost of respect. Productivity may be
a national interest, although I doubt whether productivity at any
social cost can be so regarded. But the trade unions exist to represent

a *sectional* interest, which is no more than saying that they have to champion the common interests of certain groups within the community. That is a law of their being which they can never deny in practice, whatever may be said in propaganda. Nor do they need to be apologetic about it. It is the way democracy works. The first concern of trade unions must always be to provide a means of self-protection for those who earn their living as employees. Any new social purposes which they now acquire must grow out of that and not be foreign to their character.

What social purposes should the unions be following today? More than one answer can be given. Some people are deeply concerned that trade unions should take a greater interest in the arts, in cultural issues. I am wholly on the side of those who think they should. It would be a very narrow interpretation of the declared aim of trade unions to improve the living standards of their members, to measure these standards only with an economic yardstick. As economic standards improve and the workers come to enjoy more income and more leisure, the problem of how they spend their income and how they spend their leisure is bound to loom larger. Nor is the problem solved simply by saying that it is a matter of private choice. Of course it is, in the sense that no one is entitled to impose his standards on others in these matters, but what the individual has to choose from is socially determined. At a time when commercial interests are using the mass media so extensively to make money by pandering to the lowest common denominator, the unions have surely a responsibility to cast their weight on the other side, if only to ensure that their members have a real instead of a nominal freedom of choice.

But the main job of trade unions lies in industry. There they must still find at least the greater part of their new social purpose. And there indeed it can be found—in the workshop, or whatever may be its equivalent, the colliery, the office, the site, the depot. We all know that years of full or high employment have given an impetus to works bargaining and that this has brought about some shift of power within the unions from the head office to the shop floor. The extent to which this has happened varies from industry to industry according to many factors peculiar to each. Nevertheless in some degree it has happened in all industries. We have the drift or creep of earnings away from nationally negotiated rates. We have shop stewards or other union workplace representatives engaged, not only in enforcing agreements or in administrative duties, but in negotiations which sometimes seem more important to the union member than those conducted by his full-time officials.

Why this is happening is not in doubt. The change in the state of the labour market has caused employers to compete for labour by bidding up earnings. In many cases this is done by devious devices, such as the provision of contrived overtime. On the other hand with the lessening of the risks of victimisation, militant shop stewards sometimes engage in a constant guerrilla warfare to build up earnings for their members well above rates in collective agreements. More power to their elbow, you may say. They are only trying to get a bigger slice of the cake for the workers by claiming the same freedom as employers for greater flexibility in wage determination.

But this greater flexibility is not without its dangers, and not least dangers for the trade unions. It certainly has something to do with un-official strikes, for which this country holds the world record. It leads to a loss of union control in the regulation of wages and working conditions, and to indiscipline and tensions within the unions. But there is one consequence, more than any other, which calls for attention. Despite the increased strength of the unions under full employment, the status of the workers in industry has not been raised appreciably throughout the post-war years. Union energies have been almost entirely absorbed, either at national or at workshop level, in the struggle for money. The struggle for status has received scant attention.

Status is expressed in rights and their attendant responsibilities. Throughout their history trade unions have fought not only for more income, for more leisure and for more security for their members. They have fought to raise their status by establishing rights for them in industry, the right to a certain wage, the right not to have to work longer than so many hours, the right not to be subject to arbitrary dismissal. That is why trade unions can fairly be described as a 'sword of justice'. That is the continual social purpose which has fired their idealistic motivation. Are they now at the end of this road? Are there no rights for their members, for the workers they represent, which have yet to be established?

Of course there are. At their place of work Britain's workers are still in many respects second-class citizens. They are subjected to treatment which would be considered intolerable in any other walk of life. Perhaps most of them accept it as the natural order of things

21

for the sake of a job and the money it brings in, just as a hundred years ago many of them accepted the absence of rights in industry as a part of the lot they were born to. This was changed by leadership, the leadership of those few among them who had social purpose and were willing to make some sacrifices on its behalf. They were not deterred by the argument that the majority were not on their side, because many were afraid of losing their jobs if they went near a union. They had the courage of their convictions and it was their very determination that changed the minds of their more irresolute fellows.

The problem confronting the unions today is that national negotiations and industry bargaining can only establish a limited framework of rights for the workers in industry, on wages and hours and certain standard conditions of work. To go beyond that, for the workers to acquire rights to settle many other aspects of their working life, the struggle has to be conducted in the individual establishment, at the works level, and the rights themselves have to be embodied in works agreements or understandings. This largely applies to such issues as engagement, discipline, dismissal, promotion, training, welfare in many aspects, fair treatment on the job. But it is a struggle which the trade unions have to lead nationally, even if it is fought locally. These are issues on which they need to develop their policy and give guidance and support, not least support in terms of training and education, to their workplace representatives.

This raises many further and complicated questions about union organisation. I have tried to do no more than show that there is scope for a new social purpose to animate the spirit of the trade union movement in contemporary society, and where it lies. Full employment has also brought new problems for managements by weakening the sanctions on which they have previously relied to maintain their authority. They are compelled to seek for a greater measure of voluntary co-operation since they can rely less on a discipline enforced by the threat of the sack. Consequently, while the unions have been slow in taking any official initiative in improving industrial relations within the workplace, intelligent managements have not. Faced with an urgent need to do something to create goodwill and reduce friction, personnel management has been strongly developed, arrangements for joint consultation have been built up, profit-sharing schemes tried out, communications improved, and all the paraphernalia of 'human relations' has acquired a vogue.

Trade Unions in the Sixties

Much if not all of this is to be welcomed, in so far as it is a sign of an intention to deal fairly with workers as responsible human beings, rather than in terms of that old familiar notice at the works gate–'Hands Wanted'. But managerial initiative, even when it is intelligent and far sighted, is taken to suit the aims of management and these do not necessarily coincide with the aims of unions and of the people they represent.

Where the unions leave a vacuum by their own lack of social purpose, that vacuum will surely be filled by the purposes of other groups, with other interests and other values. Organised workers have to come to terms with management within a business enterprise just as much as trade unions have to come to terms nationally with employers' associations. They have to live together and do so by reaching agreements on the rules which will govern the settlement of their disputes. But trade unions have rightly refused to accept any final definition of exclusive managerial functions. They have recognised that the frontiers of union control are shifting frontiers, that any decision that affects the life and well-being of their members can be their concern. Today they are not using deliberately and effectively the opportunities that full employment has afforded to extend the frontiers of their controls, to enlarge the rights and thus raise the status of the workers in industry. Because of this, they are in danger of allowing the devil to have all the good tunes. Or, since there are no angels or devils in this world, perhaps I should rather say, they are not making the most of their own stirring music, their great theme of the cry for justice, and by default seem only to be listening to the clinking of cash.

TRADE UNIONS AND POLITICS
(1961)

Despite the notable contribution they have made to its development, trades councils are often treated as the cinderellas of the labour movement. Reading about the history of your own council brings the Christian injunction to mind–it is more blessed to give than to receive. It seems to have been your fate again and again to pioneer– with the aid of very limited means–activities which have subsequently been taken over by other bodies within the movement.

I need hardly remind you that, after its formation in 1860, the London Trades Council played an important part, not only as a local, but as a national centre in the trade union world. Ten years later many of these functions were transferred to the newly created Parliamentary Committee of the Trades Union Congress. In 1891 your council decided to raise a fund for running candidates in local and national elections, but that work was soon handed over to the Labour Representation League. About this time, too, separate councils were springing up around the fringes of the Metropolitan area and diverting members from the London Council, a trend which continued somewhat to its detriment. Eventually when the London Labour Party was established as an entirely separate body in 1914, although this cleared up a chaotic situation, once again you had to turn over your political activities to an organisation you had helped to create.

But it is not my intention this evening to talk about the details of labour history. Nor do I want to deal with the various activities of trades councils, where your knowledge is probably greater than mine. Instead I have chosen a subject–Trade Unions and Politics– which will not, I hope, be thought entirely inappropriate. For one thing it is as old, indeed older, than the London Trades Council itself. From their earliest days trade unions have debated it. For another it has been the cause of such great, and at times such bitter, controversy, that trades councils have often been engulfed and even destroyed by it.

Moreover, although the problems my subject raises are both old

24

and controversial, we have good reason to look at them afresh at the present time. The Labour Party is facing a crisis, possibly the greatest crisis in its history. Many factors have brought this about, some long term, some short term. From a long-term point of view I am inclined to think that the most important consideration may be the deep-seated dislike of the whole of the labour movement to adjusting its traditional ideas to social change. This is something it shares with the rest of the British nation with what may yet prove to be perilous consequences. An attachment to tradition, which has been called our greatest strength, now threatens to become our greatest weakness. Not to mince my words, we seem to be suffering from insular smugness, something we can ill afford to cultivate in the present world.

Be that as it may, the immediate crisis within the Labour Party was precipitated at Scarborough, by events closely related to my subject. For the first time in living memory the voting strength of trade unions at Annual Conference was used to carry resolutions contrary to a major statement of policy previously agreed by the Parliamentary Party, the National Executive and the TUC General Council. It was also carried, one gathers, contrary to the votes of the majority of the delegates from Constituency Parties. In consequence during the recent Defence debate in Parliament a substantial section of the Parliamentary Party demonstrated its opposition to the motion put forward in the names of their own Front Bench by abstaining from voting against the Government and remaining seated in the House. The following day *The Times* could write a leader under the heading of 'Two Labour Parties' without anyone feeling that it had departed from its normal sobriety.

I am only stating familiar facts which give us a measure of the present crisis confronting the Labour Party. How we judge them, who we blame for them, whether they cause us to rejoice or to despair is another matter. I am appearing tonight in my professional role as an academic, and, strongly as I feel about the immediate issues, my purpose is to encourage reflection about some of their deeper and broader implications. To this end I have chosen to approach my subject by a path that leads first through the abstract and rather austere realms of theory.

I am convinced that certain propositions can be established about the behaviour of trade unions which are not confined in their application to any one country but have a certain universal validity.

On Trade Unions

There are two such propositions dealing with the relationship of trade unions to politics that I want to put before you this evening. They are derived from studying labour movements, and their history, in a variety of democratic countries. They relate to free trade unions, autonomous bodies ultimately subject to the control of their members, not to those organisations which are an integral part of the machinery of state, such as exist in the communist countries.

The first of these propositions can be formulated as the priority accorded by trade unions to their industrial over their political methods. The second as the lower and upper limits of their political aims. These bald formulations, I know, will not tell you anything. I have to explain the meaning of each of the propositions. Let me start with the first.

You all know that the precise methods used by trade unions to further their aims vary considerably from country to country, even from union to union within the same country. Nevertheless their principal methods fall broadly into two categories, industrial and political. We would include under industrial methods the negotiation of agreements with employers and all that belongs to collective bargaining, grievance procedure, strike action, the use of arbitration and so on. Joint consultation and participation in management would also come within this category. Political methods, on the other hand, cover all types of union participation in party politics, but not only that. No less important are what the modern political theorist terms the 'pressure group' activities of trade unions in relation to the state, whether they be conducted by campaigns, delegations, lobbying or sitting on governmental advisory committees.

To put the distinction in a nutshell, when trade unions use industrial methods they bring their power and influence to bear on employers of labour, be they private or public. When they use political methods they bring their power and influence to bear on parties or governments. In practice the distinction may be difficult to draw at the margins, especially as industry and politics have become increasingly interwoven, but in most cases it is not in doubt. There are some union activities, such as their provision of friendly benefits or their educational schemes, that cannot be readily classified in either of these two categories, but these it will be found are largely auxiliary to their industrial or their political methods.

My first general proposition asserts that, when they have a choice, trade unions invariably prefer to rely on industrial rather than political methods to achieve their aims. This does not mean that they necessarily despise or disparage political action. On the contrary they are as a rule very ready to resort to it as a second string to their bow. What it means is that they are prepared to use political methods to support and to supplement their industrial methods, but never to supplant them.

Sidney and Beatrice Webb, when they wrote their classic study of of trade unions, *Industrial Democracy*, towards the close of the nineteenth century, anticipated a different development. They asserted, to use their terms, that with the inevitable growth of collectivism the method of legal enactment would gradually, if not entirely, replace the method of collective bargaining. That has to be accounted one of their mistaken prophecies. For it can be shown that whenever and wherever trade unions have gained enough strength to regulate wages and conditions of work by direct negotiation with employers they have dispensed with government assistance. In some countries, it is true, unions have demanded and secured a very much stronger legal framework for industrial relations than exists in Britain. But this has not meant that they have preferred state regulation to collective bargaining. Rather has the former been a necessary condition for the growth and maintenance of the latter.

There has been, I would submit, one crucial reason for this order of priority in the choice of trade unions between industrial and political methods–their institutional needs. An institution, like an individual, has needs which must be satisfied if it is to survive, to grow, to gain in strength, power and influence. Its own organisation, for example, must be sustained by adequate sanctions, that is by the rewards of membership and penalties of non-membership. The greater the strength of these membership sanctions, the stronger it becomes and the more it is able to fulfil its purposes. The point I want to make is that trade unions derive their membership sanctions, in other words satisfy this institutional need, primarily through their industrial activities.

You have only to consider why the vast majority of workers belong to their unions to see that this is so. They join and, what is more important, remain in good standing for one of two reasons or, more likely, some combination of both. The one reason is the value to them of the services which unions provide in enlarging and protecting their rights in industry. The other is the disadvantages they would suffer in terms of job opportunities, as the result of a partial or complete 'closed shop' situation, if they failed to maintain their membership. These rewards of membership and penalties of non-membership are the outcome of the industrial activities of trade unions. In contrast how many members would the unions be able to recruit and retain if all that they had to offer were their political activities? No more than a devoted few who were completely identified with the causes for which the unions were fighting. Ignoring as I must some of the finer points of theory, this is why unions prefer industrial to political methods.

So much for the first of my propositions; now let me turn to the second. At first sight it would seem quite impossible to advance any valid generalisation about the political aims of trade unions. Their industrial aims are reasonably specific: better wages and working conditions, greater security of income and employment, protection against arbitrary and discriminatory treatment by management. One can easily begin to list them and expect to find a fair measure of agreement that unions everywhere pursue such aims. In politics, however, union members hold a variety of different opinions. In some countries unions are even divided on political lines. Furthermore a little knowledge of labour history tells us that the political aims of trade unions have changed considerably over time.

At one time the American unions were firmly committed to Samuel Gompers' formula for political barter, 'Reward your friends and punish your enemies,' a so-called non-partisan policy. In recent years they have almost without exception given their wholehearted support to Democratic candidates in Presidential elections. Or to come back to this country, the Webbs, in *Industrial Democracy*, roundly proclaimed that when the Trades Union Congress

> . . . diverges from its narrow trade union function, and expresses any opinion, either on general social reforms or party politics, it is bound to alienate whole sections of its constituents. The trade unions join the Congress for the promotion of a Parliamentary policy, desired, not merely by a majority, but by all of them; and it is a violation of the implied contract between them to use the political force, towards the creation of which all are contributing, for the purposes of any particular political party.[3]

How strangely that passage reads today! It was written, of course, before the Labour Party was formed, and the Webbs' views were revised by the Party's success.

Trade Unions and Politics

Given all the differences and changes to be observed in the political aims of trade unions, can anything more be said about them in general terms other than that they do differ and they do change? More can be said, when we have grasped that the really decisive factor determining the aims of trade unions in politics is once again their institutional needs. To illustrate what I mean, let me quote an American authority, J. B. S. Hardman.

> In the fight for industrial control and in the exercise of that control ... the trade union comes in contact and frequently in conflict with the productive and distributive functions of industrial society–with politics and legislation, finance and education, with theories of law and concepts of ethics, right and justice, with a practically endless variety of matters covered by that all inclusive term, social living. Whatever the reactions of individual trade unionists to these matters ... the trade union as a social body finds itself related to them all by its major task, the achievement of control of the labour supply of the community.[4]

In short, as he said, trade unionism 'cannot accumulate social power outside of an active relation to social issues, and it cannot effectively wield industrial power unless it is socially powerful.'[5]

You will note his words 'whatever the reactions of individual trade unionists.' They stand in opposition to the simple-minded idea that union political attitudes represent the highest common denominator of their members' political opinions. That kind of explanation ignores the effect of the institutional needs of trade unions. They meet these needs, as I have previously argued, largely by extending their control in industry. But they cannot extend their control in industry, as Hardman points out, without becoming involved in politics to secure and defend the necessary social basis for their industrial power.

Admittedly an organisation is not an automaton. Human beings have to ensure that its institutional needs are satisfied. But that is precisely the task of its bureaucracy, the corps of leaders and officials who serve the organisation and have a stake in its stability and permanence. Every organisation, if it is to endure, has to have a bureaucracy that is strong enough to prevent its institutional needs being sacrificed to temporary fluctuations in membership opinions and pressures which would endanger its long-term interests. So with the trade unions. It was only when they acquired a bureaucracy, a responsible leadership, that they could avoid their earlier and oft-repeated fate of a mushroom growth followed by an equally rapid decline, when their members asked for the moon and found they could not get it.

What my second proposition asserts is that the institutional needs of trade unions, as upheld by their bureaucracy, circumscribe their political aims, regardless of their individual members' views on politics. Although these needs do not determine their aims, they set lower and upper limits to them. Let me try to show how.

Everywhere unions have been compelled to engage in political action to obtain enough freedom from legal restraint to exercise their main industrial functions. Freedom of association, the right to strike and to picket, the prevention of undue interference in their internal affairs, all these are familiar objectives at some stage in their development and their achievement has demanded the use of political methods. Not that their interest has been confined to changing resistrictive or oppressive laws. Depending on how much industrial strength they could accumulate without it, they have also fought for legislation that would assist them in collective bargaining and the like. Furthermore their growth has been affected by economic as well as by legal conditions. Here, too, they have had to turn to political action to secure changes in national economic policy or in the structure of their industries which would enhance their bargaining strength.

Much more could be said about this, but these indications should suffice to show that, as a minimum, trade unions must be involved in politics in order to establish and maintain the legal and economic conditions in which they can flourish. That is the lower limit imposed on their political aims by their institutional needs. It makes the term 'non-political union', taken literally, a nonsensical description; there is no such animal. As a matter of fact to be politically effective trade unions obviously cannot make an appeal simply in terms of their own power interests. To rally the active support of their members and to gain the sympathy of the general public they have to broaden their appeal by taking up issues which may have little more than a marginal interest for them as unions.

But if there is a minimum to their political commitments, there is also a maximum, an upper limit to the aims they can follow in politics, which is also set by their institutional needs. They cannot, for example, adopt political aims which would seriously threaten their industrial unity. Their success in industry depends on their ability to organise all, or at least a large proportion, of the employees they claim to represent, regardless of their differences in politics. When political divisions within a trade union become too acute and occupy too much attention, the result is paralysis and possibly disruption. Even where its leadership falls under control of one political party, the doctrines and policies of that party cannot be imposed on the membership beyond the point when they begin to undermine its industrial achievements. One can observe how communist union leaders recognise the limits to which they can push the party line and how on occasions they have had to abandon it when it conflicted with the union's institutional needs.

The lower and upper limits to which I have referred are, as it were, limits of safety. I am not suggesting that they are never transgressed. Unions have been destroyed, or have allowed themselves to be destroyed, by not observing these limits, that is by accepting an inadequate or an excessive political commitment. A good example would be the German trade unions during the last years of the Weimar Republic. It may sound like a paradox but their political commitment was inadequate because it was excessive; they refrained from using their political strength to the full against the Nazis partly because they had been subjected to too much party control. I think it is true, however, that the more trade unions mature as trade unions, gain in stability, strength and independence under a responsible leadership, the more certain it becomes that these limits are respected.

I realise that these abstract propositions may appear rather theoretical to you and possibly of little use in understanding the complexities of practical situations. Perhaps I shall be able to endow them with greater meaning and reality now that I come to their application to the special circumstances in our own country. Here I want to concentrate my remarks on what is only one aspect of my subject, the nature of the relationship which has evolved between the trade unions and the Labour Party. That, of course, by no means exhausts the political activities of trade unions in the British context.

The Trades Union Congress, for example, according to my earlier definitions, is more than anything else a political arm of the unions. The greater part of its work is directed towards influencing governments and public administration, rather than employers and business managements as such. It can plausibly be argued that by and large the unions now attach more importance to this type of 'pressure group' political action than they do to their direct involvement in politics. One indication, in the case of the major unions affiliated to both the Labour Party and the TUC, is that they put forward their second-ranking officers for election to the Party's National Executive, while their General Secretaries stand for the General Council.

From the student's angle, however, it is the association of many of our unions—all of the manual workers' unions of any size—with one political party which raises the most intricate and intriguing problems of analysis. For we have to ask how it is possible for trade unions, which are sectional bodies with limited social functions, to be an integral part of the Labour Party, without either the unions or the Party finding the association too unprofitable. You may not think this is a serious problem. The relationship is now so strongly sanctified by tradition that we take it for granted. But for the outsider, the student, say, who comes from abroad to study the working of the British labour movement it is—I assure you—a perpetual puzzle. And when, as a teacher, one tries to help him unravel it, the difficulties soon emerge.

Put yourself in his position! He reads somewhere that the trade unions control the Labour Party and certain facts seem to support the statement. Apparently they hold most of the purse strings and command an overwhelming majority of votes at Annual Conference. Then he reads somewhere else that the Labour Party controls the trade unions. Perhaps he learns with wonder about the 1948 to 1950 experiment in wage restraint or discovers that there are members of unions affiliated to the Labour Party who pay the political levy but vote Conservative. These facts seem to tell on the other side. Who controls whom? he asks. One has to reply that this question is too simple. But how then does one explain the nature of this exceedingly complex relationship?

History can give us more assistance than logic in providing an explanation, and it is as well to begin at the beginning with the origin of the relationship. In most other countries Socialist or Labour Parties came into being at much the same time as trade unions; in some, as in Germany, they created the unions. In Britain, on the other hand, not only were trade unions firmly and strongly established before the Labour Party was founded in 1900; they also had a previous history of successful political action. Consequently they had to be persuaded that they had more to gain by allying themselves with the young socialist parties than they would lose from severing their ties with the Liberals or the Conservatives. Fortunately for the Labour Party one event following swiftly on its formation. The Taff Vale Judgment of the House of Lords in 1901 proved to be persuasive, especially after the Liberal Government had been compelled by Labour Party pressure to withdraw its own unsatisfactory measure in favour of the Trades Disputes Act in 1906. Even then the powerful Miners' Federation of Great Britain delayed its decision to affiliate until 1910.

The development of socialist ideas and influence within the unions may have contributed to the change, but the decisive factor was undoubtedly the unions' interest in legislation that would give them freedom and support in their industrial activities. The alliance between unions and socialists at this time was also made possible by the predominant attitude of the socialists themselves. This can best be described as ethical but non-doctrinaire. The Independent Labour Party, the one socialist body that counted, had about as much agreed dogma as the Church of England has today. Practically all shades of socialist opinion could be comfortably accommodated within it. That incidentally was its strength, not its weakness as the Marxists thought; it suited the British temperament and accordingly what the unions could understand and appreciate.

The union–socialist alliance started, then, in this country as a marriage of convenience, with both parties adopting a very pragmatic attitude to the advantages which each of them could gain from living together. And so, in its essentials, it has always remained. What marriages in politics are not marriages of convenience? Granted, with the passing of time, loyalties have been strengthened and have come to provide an additional bond in their own right; that happens in other marriages of convenience. Granted, too, that the transformation of the Labour Party in 1918 from a fairly loose federation into an organisation with an individual as well as an affiliated membership and constituency parties of its own, was a far-reaching change in its structure. To stay with my analogy, it virtually banished any prospect of divorce.

The main effect of the 1918 re-organisation on the terms of the alliance was in fact to strengthen the power of the trade unions within the Labour Party. In return for their commitment to an

33

extremely vague expression of socialist aspirations (the famous Clause 4 which was intended to mean all things to all men and for that reason was never debated) they were given effective control over the new party machine at the expense of the Trades Councils and the ILP. From 1918 onwards there can be no doubt that on paper the unions were in a position to dominate the Labour Party. Apart from the significance of the size of their block votes at Annual Conference in the passing of policy resolutions, they were given a majority of seats on the National Executive. Up to 1937, if they had ever chosen to act in unison, they could have filled the Executive exclusively with their candidates.

But the working of democratic organisations often depends less on the formal provisions of their constitutions than on the 'unwritten rules of the game,' those tacit assumptions which everyone recognises should be observed to avoid upsetting the apple-cart. The Labour Party is no exception. I would argue that the relationship between the unions and the Party has been governed far more by unwritten assumptions than by its formal constitution. They are usually covered by some such phrase as 'acting responsibly' and for the unions this has meant that they did not abuse the power that was theirs.

In addressing the 1956 Labour Party Conference, Mr. Frank Cousins said: 'I told you last year not to tell the unions how to do their job, and I am certainly not going to tell the Labour Party how to do its job'[6]

One could not wish for a plainer statement of the basic principle which has broadly governed the role of the unions within the Party. It turns on a distinction, fully understood though logically inexact, between 'industrial' and 'political' issues. Roughly speaking, any issue that the unions consider to lie within their own preserves and to be best dealt with either by themselves or by the TUC General Council is 'industrial'; the rest are 'political'. Wages and strikes obviously belong to the first category and on them the Labour Party is not expected to make any pronouncements beyond giving moral support to the unions' own. Otherwise this would be telling the unions how to do their job.

The second part of this principle, the reciprocal of the first, that the unions should not tell the Party how to do its job, is admittedly less precise and not as stringently observed. Trade unions have always submitted resolutions on political issues to Party Conferences and debated them at their own. Clearly they have never been prepared to practise quite the same non-intervention in this realm that they have insisted that the Party should practise on industrial issues. Nevertheless the assumption has been that the main policy initiative should lie with the Parliamentary Party and its leadership. In other words, that the unions would not use their voting strength at Annual Conference to dominate the Party *against* the leadership on major political issues. In effect it has been tacitly recognised that trade unions should not usurp the functions of a political party.

This brings me to my two general propositions on the theory of trade unionism. The principle which Mr. Cousins so well expressed is very relevant to their application in Britain. The first of them, you will recall, was the priority which trade unions accord to their industrial over their political methods. That is the reason for their insistence within the Labour Party that it should not trespass on their preserves. To admit its right to do so would carry with it the danger that matters now settled by negotiation in industry might be made the subject of political intervention. Some socialists have thought that there is a good case for a national wages policy; that the central planning of wages is a necessary part of socialist economic planning. The unions cannot allow the Labour Party to take such dangerous thoughts too far, as they have made perfectly clear on more than one occasion.

My second proposition regarding the lower and upper limits of the political aims of trade unions has also found expression in their relations with the Labour Party. One could say that it is the lower limits which have been responsible for forging the alliance. I have already referred to the significance of the unions' struggle to change the legal framework of their activities in bringing them to support the Party prior to 1914. During the inter-war years, even though the repeal of the 1927 Act was a constant concern, interest shifted principally to the economic framework and the threat which falling prices and mass unemployment presented to industrial negotiations and the very existence of collective bargaining in some industries. The Trades Union Congress and the Labour Party were used as two complementary political arms in attempts to remedy these disadvantages.

It is the upper limits of their political aims, however, which have been responsible for the observation of that silent self-denying ordinance practised by the unions within the Labour Party. If we ask why they have not in the past used their voting strength to dominate the Party on political issues, part of the answer may have been that they thought it would not be good for the Party because its electoral appeal would be weakened. Sometimes it may have been due to downright indifference; the majority of union members are much less interested in political than in industrial issues. But I suspect that the most important reason has been the intuitive knowledge on the part of trade union leaders that it would not be good for the unions. They have known and recognised, even if they have not openly acknowledged it, that their intervention in party politics should be largely confined to questions on which they had a direct interest as trade unions. To go far beyond that would be to invite interminable political wrangles in their own ranks, which would prevent them from getting on with their real job. For the same reason, it seems to me, trade unions have never tried to keep their sponsored M.P.s on a tight rein, provided they looked after the unions' interests when Bills were before the House that affected them.

To conclude I would like to return to the events at Scarborough and the present crisis within the Labour Party. What bearing has my analysis on these present troubles? It can be stated quite simply. For various reasons, and I do not propose to speculate about them or to distribute any blame, the principle which Mr. Cousins so bluntly and so clearly expressed in 1956 has been violated. The unions, or rather enough of them to command a majority of votes, have told the Labour Party how to do its job on a political issue, the most important political issue of all—the defence of the country. Whatever position one may hold in the great debate on a unilateral versus a multilateral approach to disarmament, whether one favours pacifism, neutralism or support for the Western Alliance, the traditional terms of the marriage between unions and Labour Party have, for the time being, been thrown into the melting pot.

Maybe they can be rescued and restored. Then the crisis will be over, although fierce debates over policy will continue within the Labour Party, as indeed they should. Before the year is out we should know for certain whether that rescue operation is likely to succeed. If not, then no one should deceive himself about the seriousness of the consequences. A marriage can continue very happily for a long time,

36

even a marriage of convenience, as long as each of the parties continues to behave in the way the other expects. But if one of them suddenly breaks their mutual understanding anything can happen. The situation can rapidly go from bad to worse until–who knows?– divorce is the only acceptable solution. Such an outcome would, in my opinion, be a tragedy for Labour. For, though I cannot see a political future for a Labour Party dominated by trade unions, equally I cannot see a political future for one that is separated from them.

WHAT ARE TRADE UNIONS FOR?
(1968)

This question 'What are trade unions for?' might be called the George Woodcock question. He has raised it repeatedly in recent years, but the answer is slow in coming and still remains more of a hope than a happening. There is in fact great confusion today about the purposes of trade unions. This affects attitudes to their future and what should be their legal and social rights and obligations in present-day society, as well as their own decisions on policy and organisation. No less an authority than Professor Galbraith has stated that unions in the future will 'have a drastically reduced function in the industrial system' and will 'retreat more or less permanently into the shadows.'[7] And his is not a lone voice. Trade unions are increasingly made the target of many criticisms. Much of this may be unfair, but the unions themselves rarely bother to state their own case in persuasive terms.

I would like, first, to reject two views of union purpose which merely mislead. They are poles apart but they have this in common. Those who hold them believe they know more about what trade unions are for than the unions and their members know themselves.

The first is the Marxist view. Admittedly it has many different shades and variations and, since all its advocates claim to be offering the one true interpretation of the one true gospel, they are often violently at odds with each other. Most of them, however, would subscribe to a recent exposition by the editor of the *New Left Review*.

> As institutions, trade unions do not *challenge* the existence of society based on a division of classes, they merely *express* it. Thus trade unions can never be viable vehicles of advance towards socialism in themselves; by their nature they are tied to capitalism. They can bargain within society but not transform it.[8]

From this it follows that the inevitable limits of trade union action must be overcome with the help of a revolutionary movement or party which–to continue quoting from the same essay–'must include intellectuals and petit bourgeois who alone can provide the essential *theory* of socialism'. Why? Because: 'Culture in a capitalist society is ... a prerogative of privileged strata; only if some members of these strata go over to the cause of the working class can a revolutionary movement be born.'[9]

Ignoring for a moment the conceit in this statement, I would not dispute the point that trade unions are not a substitute for political parties, be they revolutionary or reformist. Workers do not join unions because they think alike and share the same political outlook. They do so for the sake of gaining immediate improvements in their lot which can only come from collective action. Their unity, that completeness of the organisation of trade unions which is the foundation of their strength, must always be imperilled when they import political faction fights. Unions may decide by a majority to support a particular political party–as many in this country have decided to affiliate with the Labour Party–but this is another matter. It reflects no more than a recognition that they must engage in political as well as industrial action to further their own objectives, and taking sides is the best strategy because it produces the best results.

What I find so objectionable as well as invalid in the Marxist view is its implicit contempt for 'pure and simple' trade unionism. Trade unions, by doggedly sticking to their immediate ends and refusing to be captured and exploited by any political party, have gradually transformed society. Only not according to the sacred texts or the dialectical laws! That they may be right in preferring reform to revolution, and unity to discord, never crosses the mind of those whose theory tells them all the answers.

I do not deny that socialism–as someone once said– has been 'the conscience of the labour movement'.[10] But this is socialism as a set of ideals, as a moral dynamic, not as a particular blueprint for an economic or political system. In this sense it has undoubtedly provided restraints against the emergence of the cruder forms of business unionism that can be found in the United States.

If the first mistaken view of the purposes of trade unions comes from the Left, then the second comes from the Right. The operative word for its expression is *responsible* trade unionism. Michael Shanks has amusingly characterised, and only slightly caricatured, this view.

There has grown up in recent years a widespread superstition that a trade union leader is a sort of *ex officio* civil servant, responsible to the community at large. The trade union leader's main responsibility, to judge from the sort of comment one reads in the press and hears from middle-class lips, is to 'keep his chaps in line' or 'knock some sense into them'. . . . In practical terms, the main function of a union leader according to this view is to deter his members from putting in ambitious wage claims, stop them from going on strike, and behaving in other anti-social ways, and encourage them to work harder and increase their productivity. . . . Having done all that, he can gracefully retire with a peerage. He may even be introduced to the Queen and taken to dine in a West End Club from time to time.[11]

It is interesting to see how in the Conservative Party's industrial relations programme *Fair Deal at Work* references to responsible trade unionism (and naturally, to preserve the balance, responsible management) continually recur. The many new legal restraints on trade unions which they propose to introduce are, they say, 'as much in the interests of wage-earners and responsible trade unions as of employers and the public at large.'[12] In short, they have the good of the unions at heart, and especially their members' good, even if the unions refuse to believe it.

The essence of this view is that trade unions are there to act as a kind of social police force–to keep the chaps in order and the wheels of industry turning. To this there is only one answer. The first and over-riding responsibility of all trade unions is to the welfare of their own members. That is their primary commitment; not to a firm, not to an industry, not to the nation. A union collects its members' contributions and demands their loyalty specifically for the purpose of protecting their interests as they see them, not their alleged 'true' or 'best' interests as defined by others.

Leadership is important, of course. Trade union leaders should be ahead of their members in thinking about their problems. It is their responsibility to point out the further and more far-reaching consequences of decisions which could be regretted later despite their strong immediate appeal. When union leaders seek only to court popularity, and defend this on the grounds that they are 'the servants' of their members, they betray the responsibilities of their office. When the argument is over, however, their principal task must be one of representation. If they fail in this the trade union no longer serves its purpose. No other organisation is there to do this job.

Obviously trade unions cannot reasonably behave as if they were not part of a larger society or ignore the effects of their policies on the national economy and the general public. No voluntary organisations can do that with impunity. If they do, they turn society against them, and society can retaliate. In any case members of trade unions are citizens and consumers as well as producers. Even so, trade unions exist to promote sectional interests–the interests of the section of the population they happen to organise. As do professional associations and many other bodies! There is nothing selfish or slightly disreputable about this; it is an essential part of the democratic process. Indeed, once trade unions appear to be acting as servants of employers or servants of the government, they are bound to be written off by their own members who will turn, as they sometimes do already, to unofficial leaders to take up their demands.

Both of the views I have been attacking belittle the democratic function of trade unions; their function of representation. That is why each in its different way claims to know better than the trade unions themselves where the interests of their members lie. My starting point in defining union purpose is the opposite premise; that the best way of finding the right answer is to look at the behaviour of trade unions; to infer what they are for from what they do.

Here one thing is at once certain, and it applies to all trade unions, and has applied throughout the greater part of their history. The activity to which they devote most of their resources and appear to rate most highly is collective bargaining. So the question we have to ask is what purposes do unions pursue in collective bargaining? The conventional answer is that they defend and, if possible, improve their members' terms and conditions of employment. They are out to raise wages, to shorten hours, and to make working conditions safer, healthier and better in many other respects.

This answer is right as far as it goes, but it does not go far enough. Collective bargaining may be what the words imply–that depends on how we define bargaining– but it is also a rule-making process. The rules it makes can be seen in the contents of collective agreements. In other words, one of the principal purposes of trade unions in collective bargaining is regulation or control. They are interested in regulating wages as well as in raising them; and, of course, in regulating a wide range of other issues appertaining to their members' jobs and working life.

Why do they have this interest in regulating employment relationships, and what social purpose does such regulation serve? It is certainly not a bureaucratic interest in rules for their own sake. Unions and their members are interested in the effect of the rules made by collective bargaining, which is to limit the power and authority of employers and to lessen the dependence of employees on market fluctuations and the arbitrary will of management. Stated in the simplest possible terms these rules provide protection, a shield, for their members. And they protect not only their material standards of living, but equally their security, status and self-respect; in short their dignity as human beings.

One can put the same point in another way. The effect of rules is to establish rights, with their corresponding obligations. The rules in collective agreements secure for employees the right to a certain rate of wages; the right not to have to work longer than a certain number of hours; the right not to be dismissed without consultation or compensation and so on. This surely is the most enduring social achievement of trade unionism; its creation of a social order in industry embodied in a code of industrial rights. This too is the constant service that unions offer their members: daily protection of their industrial rights.

Such rights could be, and to some extent are, established by law. But collective bargaining serves yet another great social purpose. Apart from providing protection, it also permits participation. A worker through his union has more direct influence on what rules are made and how they are applied than he can ever exercise by his vote over the laws made by Parliament. We hear a lot these days about participation, including workers' participation in management. I have yet to be convinced that there is a better method than collective bargaining for making industry more democratic, providing its subjects and procedures are suitably extended. Putting a few workers or union officials on boards of directors only divorces them from the rank-and-file. In collective bargaining trade unions must continually respond to and service their members' interests.

The constant underlying social purpose of trade unionism is, then, participation in job regulation. But participation is not an end in itself, it is the means of enabling workers to gain more control over their working lives. Nothing has happened over the post-war years to change that basic purpose or to lessen its importance. The really remarkable thing about this period has been the slow rate of progress made by trade unions in advancing their social purpose, in spite of incessant activity on wage claims and the seemingly more favourable circumstances resulting from full employment. To account for this we must consider another equally fundamental aspect of trade unionism.

Trade unions are a mixture of movement and organisation, and the relationship between the two is the key to an understanding of the dynamics of their growth. Movement, in the words of G. D. H. Cole, 'implies a common end or at least a community of purpose which is real and influences men's thoughts and actions, even if it is imperfectly apprehended and largely unconscious'.[13] The members of a movement combine because, sharing in some measure the same sentiments and ideas, they want to achieve the same things. The bonds of organisation are different. An organisation must have effective means for ensuring that its members comply with its decisions. These means are its sanctions; the rewards it can offer and the penalties it can impose to uphold its internal discipline. On the strength of its sanctions, rather than on the appeal of its objectives, the unity and power of an organisation depends.

One problem which has always confronted trade unions is how to convert temporary movement into permanent organisation. In their early days they often counted their membership by supporters during a strike rather than the number paying regular contributions. To evolve from loose groups that could be destroyed when the economic tide flowed against them, they had to acquire sanctions strong enough to sustain continuous membership. One way, usually the most important, was to secure recognition from employers so as to build up enduring relations with them in the form of collective bargaining. They could then provide their members with the constant service of advancing their industrial rights. More than that, they could then prevent employers from penalising union membership, perhaps get them to penalise non-membership instead, as under 'closed shop' agreements.

While movement had to be converted into organisation if trade unions were to flourish, they could not subsequently allow it to languish and disappear. Trade unions by their very nature have to be dynamic organisations. They must constantly renew their vigour by keeping the spirit of a movement alive in their ranks. In this respect they differ, for instance, from business organisations. The latter can grow and expand if they have sufficient money to buy command over the material and human resources they need. People will join them, that is to say enter their employment, for the sake of the remuneration offered. Trade unions cannot be run simply as businesses. Many members may join who wish to play no active part in union affairs, who see their contribution, perhaps, as nothing more than payment for a service. Even so, every union must have at least a core of active members who feel some deeper loyalty. A trade union that had none of the characteristics of movement, which was thrown back entirely on the bonds of organisation, would be in a sorry state. To sum up, trade unions need organisation for their power and movement for their vitality, but they need both power and vitality to advance their social purpose.

With this conclusion in mind how are we to assess the position of trade unions in our society over the past two decades, the period since the war? Until recently there was only one word to describe it – it has been by and large a period of stagnation. Only now can one discern important signs of change. Looked at from the point of view of organisation there was no overall union growth. True, total membership figures increased slowly but they have not kept pace with the growing size of the labour force. Density of union organisation, the proportion of actual to potential membership, has declined. This decline was greatest among male manual workers because of the contraction of industries – coal, cotton, railways – that had long been the citadels of union strength. But even among the far less well-organised sections of women and white-collar workers, in spite of some impressive increases in membership, their overall density of organisation has only barely increased.

This has had its counterpart in an absence of movement. Given the inflationary background, unions may have been constantly busy putting in claims for wage increases and negotiating settlements. They had to run fast in order to stay on the same spot. This has become almost a routine; a response to pressures rather than the outcome of campaigns. Where were the new objectives directed towards a further fulfilment of the unions' social purpose, which alone could have generated a genuine movement to capture interest and arouse enthusiasm?

Yet over the post-war years there has been at the same time a great upsurge of union activity *in the workplace*. Bargaining between shop stewards and management has developed on a scale previously unknown. This bargaining is not only about money, though that is an important feature. It is equally associated with demands for a

44

greater say in managerial decisions in such matters as discipline and redundancy, control of overtime and fringe benefits. In general, for a variety of reasons, workers are raising their sights; their level of aspirations and expectations is rising. The increase in workplace bargaining has undermined the regulative effect of industry-wide agreements in many industries, so that much of the old formal system of collective bargaining has become a pretence and is in a state of decay.

This has very important implications for trade unions. In terms of their basic social purpose the upsurge of workplace bargaining represents at once a danger, an opportunity and a responsibility. It is a danger because, although they now rely heavily on the work-place activity of their stewards, this activity in its present form threatens their discipline, cohesion and strength. At the same time it is an opportunity for the trade unions to make the most of a movement already in being. Properly led and directed it could result in a considerable extension of the subjects of collective bargaining and therefore a greater fulfilment of their basic purpose of job regulation. Their responsibility is self-evident once the danger and opportunity have been stated.

If the principal recommendations of the Donovan Report on the reform and extension of collective bargaining are acted upon, they should both assist and induce trade unions to close this chapter of comparative stagnation in organisation and movement and to ad-vance towards a fuller realisation of their social purpose. The formal negotiation of written factory or company agreements, as proposed in the Report, is essential. Only at this level can many of the new issues in collective bargaining be effectively and jointly regulated and the decay of the old system arrested. Similarly there is an urgent need for a body, such as the proposed Commission on Industrial Relations, to promote union recognition much more actively, not least in the white-collar field, so that union membership is increased and union organisation strengthened.

There is, however, another contemporary facet of the question, what are trade unions for, that the controversy over incomes policy throws into sharp relief. Many trade unionists sincerely believe that support for an incomes policy is virtually a betrayal of union purpose. They argue that trade unions should always be fighting for higher wages and therefore should not be confined and crippled by 'norms' or restrictions of any sort. In their eyes restraint and militancy are incompatible. On the other hand, a large section of the general public seems to think that union power and militancy are the main stumbling blocks in making an incomes policy work. These it sees as one of the chief causes of inflation in conditions of full employment and the reason why we will continue to have rising costs and prices until the power of the unions is curbed. Both of these positions I believe to be mistaken.

If the basic social purpose of trade unions is job regulation and control, then the pursuit of this purpose does not stop short at the boundaries of an industry. Regulation is now needed on a national scale, because full employment has generated intense competition among trade unions to get more for their members at the expense – let us face it – of members of other unions. Some attempt must be made to tame this industrial jungle war. There is no prospect of bringing more order and justice into our national pay structure, or even to improve the position of low-paid workers, unless we have some national rules or guidelines to regulate the 'free for all'.

This is what an incomes policy is about. It is not just a device to get us out of our present balance-of-payments difficulties. Even when we are out of pawn to foreign bankers, the need for regulation will remain. We may have a long way to go in producing a viable policy, but it is not an objective which trade unions can spurn and remain true to their own purpose. Only those who hold the Marxist view can brush it aside until – on some glorious but unspecified date in the future – we enter the promised land and the day of a fully socialist planned economy dawns.

The opposite position which sees the country's salvation in curbing the power of trade unions is just as untenable. One of the problems in making an incomes policy work is the weakness, not the strength, of our trade unions. Many people who assert that unions have too much power go on to blame them, when they fail to prevent unofficial strikes, for not exercising enough control over their members. They cannot have it both ways. These same people are usually advocates of responsible trade unionism, in the sense that I have attacked this view of union purpose. They believe that trade unions should subordinate union claims and policies to the national interest, as they define it. They are crying for the moon. The only restraints that trade unions will ever voluntarily accept on the use of their bargaining power are *those which they have agreed.* Incomes policy cannot be treated as if it were simply an exercise in economic engineering. It is pre-eminently a social problem, a problem of finding agreement on national rules which are accepted as reasonable and fair, at least for the time being, and preferable to a continuation of the present 'free for all'.

Here too the only hope I see of further enduring advance turns on the relationship between movement and organisation. The TUC objects to a government-imposed incomes policy and insists that, so far as wages are concerned, a voluntary policy operated by itself is the right answer. Clearly this would be preferable. The doubt is whether the TUC has the necessary power and organisation to make any policy effective. It is more than a doubt. It is certain that the TUC as a central organisation is not yet strong enough. This situation is unlikely to be changed until a movement develops within and among the trade unions, as happened in Sweden, for a concerted wage policy on grounds of social justice. Once there is a will to achieve the end the means will be found.

The creation of that will depends on leadership and the present omens are gloomy. I do not know when it will be forthcoming in the clear and unequivocal terms that are needed to challenge outmoded attitudes and vested interests in the trade unions. But when it does come of this I am sure. It will be a higher expression of their basic social purpose.

ON MANAGEMENT

THE FAWLEY EXPERIMENT
(1963)

What has come to be known as the 'Blue Book' at the Esso refinery at Fawley near Southampton was an elaborate series of proposals put forward by management for negotiation with the unions in February 1960. In the course of the negotiations, one or two of the proposals fell by the wayside, others were whittled down and, again, others modified and extended, but the greater part of the programme did become the subject of two agreements signed in July 1960. The one with the Transport and General Workers' Union, which organises all the non-craft hourly-paid employees on the refinery, and the other with a body known as the Craft Union Committee, which, so far as Esso is concerned, consists of seven unions representing craftsmen in its employment at Fawley.

These agreements had two prominent features which are, I believe, without precedent in the history of collective bargaining in this country. The nearest parallel is the agreement concluded in the United States for the West Coast Longshore industry in October of the same year. That was the one where the union gave the employers freedom to revise many of its previous restrictive practices in exchange for a very substantial trust fund to finance early retirement rights and to provide guarantees against lay-offs for a fully registered labour force.

The first of the arresting features of the Fawley agreements is that they represented a quite specific productivity package deal. The formal title of the Blue Book was 'High Productivity and High Wages'. The Company offered large increases in wage rates for all its employees of the order of 40 per cent–2s. 6d. an hour in the case of craftsmen–in return for the men's and their unions' consent to certain defined changes in their existing working practices. May I stress the word 'defined'? There have been other agreements where the unions gave vague promises about reviewing restrictive practices, as in the engineering settlement of 1957. This is the first agreement, so far as I know, in which the relaxing of practices which management experiences as restrictive was spelled out unambiguously.

51

Before I can explain what those practices were that the unions agreed to change, you will need to know something about the structure of the refinery labour force. In the first place, the greater part of the hourly-paid and the union-organised employees are employed in two departments – Maintenance and Construction, and Process. These two departments, I have often heard it said, are 'two different worlds'.

In Maintenance and Construction the craftsmen are employed, – around 500 when the Blue Book was launched. Most of them were recruited locally, many from the Southampton shipyards, and they brought with them the traditions of that industry. In the non-craft part of the labour force in M & C at that time, there were some 300 craftsmen's mates and another 400 workers employed on various kinds of semi-skilled or labouring work. Most employees in M & C were on day work; there was only a small shift force.

In Process, on the other hand, about 800 operators manned a system of four rotating shift forces. The worlds are quite different, because in Process there are many more opportunities for promotion and the men work together in small teams. In the various Process units there is by comparison a much stronger co-operative attitude towards management.

As for union organisation, the TGWU has two separate Branches – the Day Branch representing mainly the non-craft M & C workers, and the Shift Branch mainly Process workers. Of the seven unions on the Craft Union Committee, four of them on the mechanical side – the Amalgamated Engineering Union, the Plumbing Trades Union, the Electrical Trades Union and the Boilermakers' Society – have the bulk of the membership.

I will pass over the Process part of the Blue Book agreements – not because it is unimportant. The Process workers were asked to make their contribution to higher productivity, as indeed were the workers in all departments, but the changes involved presented no great problems in union negotiations. The Process members of the Transport and General Workers' Shift Branch were pretty solidly behind the Blue Book from the outset, and had every reason to be.

It is the proposals for M & C which asked most of the unions, especially of the unions organising the craftsmen, because some of them disturbed, and might possibly have been regarded as being contrary to, their long-standing principles and traditions. Prominent among these was the proposal to eliminate the occupation of crafts-man's mate and to redeploy the mates on other work. The Blue Book had also suggested the up-grading of 120 of the 300 mates to crafts-men after two years' training, but all the CUC unions, with the sole exception of the ETU, refused to accept that proposal. There was only this small breakthrough of a dozen electricians' mates who have now completed their training to be craftsmen.

Next in importance were a group of proposals all aiming at greater flexibility of working by a relaxation of existing demarcation practices. This meant a relaxation of craft demarcations at the fringes—an item which went under the title of inter-craft flexibility. Another proposal was the transfer of minor maintenance work from the craftsmen to process workers. A further one—the carrying out of a certain amount of slinging work by the craftsmen themselves. A points rating scheme, used for fixing wages of non-craft employees, was also abandoned because it was creating all kinds of new de-marcations among them.

A third group of proposals asked the unions to allow management greater freedom in the use of supervision. These mainly entailed that every craft group should be prepared to take administrative orders from any staff supervisor regardless of his particular craft. One proposal under this head, that union membership for first-line supervisors should be optional rather than as previously a con-dition of employment, the unions refused to accept.

The remaining proposals were modifications not so much of traditional union practices as of long-standing refinery conventions which the unions had an interest in upholding. Changes in this respect included the abolition of unproductive time allowances—walking time, washing time, set tea breaks—except where washing time was statutorily required—in exchange for a reduction in the working week from 42 or 42$\frac{1}{2}$ to 40 hours. Similarly, there was the elimination of special payments—heat money, dirt money and so on.

The unions were asked to accept the view that the increased basic rates would cover all conditions likely to be normally experienced on the refinery. There was further a drastic reduction in the number of different rates of pay, a simplification of the wage structure. Crafts-men, however, had always been on a common rate.

The second major aspect of these agreements was that they embodied a radical attack on systematic overtime. Prior to the Blue

Book, in 1959, overtime at Fawley as percentage of actual hours worked was running at a refinery-wide average among the day workers in M & C of 18 per cent and among the shift workers in Process of 15 per cent. Management pledged itself under the agreements to cut overtime down to a stated maximum of 2 per cent in M & C. No specific figure was mentioned for Process; it merely referred to a low minimum, but management hoped to cut out two-thirds of it.

The wage increase was phased in instalments. A third of it was paid immediately as an initial instalment and one-sixth of the total at six-monthly intervals over a two-year period. These phased increases were designed to correspond *pari passu* with the targets for overtime reduction so that they compensated for the dwindling overtime element in the workers' weekly pay packets. The increase had been calculated to ensure that the bulk of the workers would not suffer reductions in take-home pay. If we take the figure for craftsmen of 2s. 6d. an hour, about 2s. 0d. of this was needed to serve that purpose.

Workers were asked to accept other changes in working practices which were thought to be necessary in order to bring overtime down to the required levels. In M & C, this meant, for example, obtaining agreement to the occasional working of temporary afternoon and night shifts by day workers. In Process, it involved the creation of a new type of experienced substitute operator and a change in the system of promotion which reduced the number of moves.

It may be asked why I should separate this second outstanding feature of the Blue Book agreements from the first, when overtime itself was counted one of the sources of inefficiency in manpower utilisation on the refinery, and its reduction undoubtedly contributed to higher productivity. From that point of view, one might say it was part of the productivity package deal. There are several reasons for doing this, but the most important is that the working of persistent overtime is not something which trade unions formally approve. In principle, they deplore it. In practice, they usually tolerate it because their members want the additional income that it provides. But it is management and management alone that has the responsibility for the existence of overtime and can take the initiative in reducing it.

Apart from these strikingly original features of the agreements, the productivity package deal and elimination of systematic overtime aspects, there is another that I had better mention. All this was accompanied by a pledge of no redundancy. The proposals involved a very considerable amount of internal redeployment and had as their leading objective manpower economies, but no one was to be sacked as a result of the agreements, not even on severance pay.

Apart from some additional craftsmen who had to be taken on owing to the elimination of mates and the unions' rejection of up-grading, the labour force has slightly declined over the two years through attrition. What made it possible to effect manpower economies on a very considerable scale and yet have no redundancy was mainly two factors. First, it was possible very substantially to reduce the work previously undertaken by outside contractors and, secondly, the refinery was still expanding–new process units were coming into operation.

So much for the contents of the Blue Book and the resulting agreements. Now a few words about my own connection. I became interested just after the Blue Book had been presented to the unions and a copy was sent to me. Esso wanted an independent study made of this and asked me whether I would be willing to undertake it. They offered me very full facilities for inquiry on their side and satisfied my requests about freedom of publication. After obtaining similar assurances of co-operation from the local union officers I agreed to go ahead.

Originally, when I started to work on my book,[1] I thought of it primarily as a study in collective bargaining but I became fascinated by the processes within management that led up to the production of the Blue Book. Only recently, looking at the introduction that I had drafted a year ago, I decided to change my sub-title from 'A Case Study of Collective Bargaining' to 'A Case Study of Management and Collective Bargaining'.

My difficulty in talking to you about this subject is to know what facets of it to select. Looking at the macrocosm of industrial relations through an intensive study of its microcosm in the Fawley refinery has in fact proved a most rewarding exercise. There is hardly an industrial relations problem on the national scene that is not in some way reflected there in miniature.

To resolve this difficulty, it occurred to me that I would be speaking most directly to your interests if I simply tried to answer the question, 'What lessons has the Fawley experiment to offer the rest of British industry?' This would prevent me from getting too involved in the details of my own inquiry. In speaking to this audience, moreover, it seemed appropriate to deal with this question because I have arrived at the conclusion that Fawley offers pre-eminently lessons for management. I may have to state some of these rather dogmatically in the time at my disposal. I can only say that they are my convictions, convictions that I have acquired in the course of sifting the evidence.

The first lesson is this. *Systematic overtime is symptomatic of managerial irresponsibility.* I have chosen my words very carefully. I might have said 'industrial inefficiency' or perhaps 'managerial inefficiency' but that would not have sounded harsh enough and I want to be harsh. Nor would the lesson have been as pointed as I wish to make it.

Systematic overtime as opposed to occasional overtime is, of course, an inefficient method of work for all the reasons that I should have no need to mention. But it is far more than that. The condition of management of which it is a symptom is that of allowing things to drift, and that is precisely what the word 'irresponsibility' implies.

Perhaps the most important point about the incredibly high and sustained levels of overtime in British industry since the war (and it is a point that can be made almost regardless of the industry we are considering) is that, while there always seem to be good and sufficient reasons for increasing overtime, once this has happened, no one thinks of reasons for reducing it. Various forces come into play to provide a ratchet under the new level. Workers come to rely on it as a regular part of their incomes and cannot be deprived of it without resistance. The lower levels of supervision frequently acquire a vested interest in providing it. There are pressures from the stewards for equalisation of opportunity in its distribution. Above all, it comes to be accepted as a habit—as a way of life in industry—for which all kinds of justifications are then invented. It acquires a self-perpetuating character.

One could see all this illustrated in its growth at Fawley. The day workers in M & C had always worked plenty of overtime after the construction of the new refinery in 1951, although the level rose year by year. In Process, however, it jumped up from about 3 to 13 per cent between 1954 and 1957. There were at the time pressing reasons for this: difficulties created by granting days off in lieu instead of premium payments for public holidays, the starting up of the new Chemicals plant, the reduction of the working week from 44 to 42 hours. All good and sufficient reasons in the short run, but then it became built into the system, just as it was in M & C, and afterwards there was no easy way out. The drift of its acceptance became refinery-wide.

Now let me dwell for a few moments on my use of another word in this lesson—symptomatic. A sickness has symptoms. Why should systematic overtime be thought of as a sickness in industry? If it is accompanied by inefficiency, surely that can be eliminated by better supervision. And, from the workers' point of view, if it is not made compulsory (and it was not at Fawley) surely it offers them a choice between income and leisure and it is their affair if they prefer more income.

I do not want to appear uncharitable, but anyone satisfied with this kind of argument is either ignorant of what goes on on the shop floor in industry or else wishes to clothe the facts with intellectual camouflage. In the realms of my own direct experience, I do not know of a single case where systematic overtime is not associated with deliberate time-wasting to keep it in being. And this is futile and destructive of morale, quite apart from the additional time-wasting burden of its administration. One must take a very poor and cynical view of humanity to believe that this can be a source of human happiness, not to speak of productivity. If freedom is our standard, then the Fawley experience leaves no doubt where the balance of argument lies, for today the workers there are taking on average 40 hours to do roughly the same work that they previously did in 50 hours. They have, at no cost to themselves, or to the company, ten hours a week more which they can freely dispose of in their own time.

In proclaiming the lesson that systematic overtime is symptomatic of managerial irresponsibility, I am not thinking primarily of managements' failures in discharging their responsibilities to the company or to the consumers, though that is part of the picture. More than anything else, it is symptomatic of an irresponsible attitude towards the lives of the men or women subject to their authority.

I have heard it said that overtime is good for the workers; it keeps them quiet and prevents them from getting into mischief. Though it may not be typical, that is an abominable, patronising, authoritarian

57

sentiment. In any case, the general failure to take up the surgeon's knife and cut out this growth is at least and always symptomatic of indifference towards the squandering of human resources, which translated from economic into ethical–or 'unethical'–terms means, 'I couldn't care less what those bastards do with their time'.

One final observation on this lesson. I have tried in my book to trace the sequence of events leading up to the production of the Blue Book. The whole thing started when a keen wind of change blew across the Atlantic from Standard Oil Company (New Jersey) on the subject of manpower economies round about 1956. Detailed comparisons with overseas refineries' performance inspired the Fawley management to emulation. This led to the introduction of an American firm of consultants and various economies were effected, but it was not until one of the consultants–with a background of university studies in political science and social anthropology–produced a memorandum in November 1958, built around the notion of a 'high wage–low overtime' policy that light began to dawn on how it would be possible to pursue that part of the manpower economies object which would depend on union agreement. Once management could be persuaded to grasp this nettle, everything else began to fall into its place as a feasible programme. But the drafting by management of a feasible programme, such as found expression in the Blue Book, was one thing. The gaining of the men's and their unions' approval for it was a different matter, and that brings me to my second lesson. I hope you will find it as challenging as the first.

Here it is. *The changing of restrictive union practices is a managerial responsibility.* You see, what was rather unique about Fawley was management's departure from the general pattern of employer behaviour towards union restrictive practices in post-war Britain. That pattern may, at the risk of some over-simplification, be summarised as follows: encouraging vague but negative criticism of these practices in public, and collaborating with the unions to uphold them in private.

Fawley management accepted the responsibility to change them and thought hard and long about the methods that would have to be employed. I have heard the Fawley agreements disparaged in employer circles with the remark that Esso had to buy itself out of a bad situation–out of the inefficiencies it had allowed to accumulate.

If whoever is saying that wants to be fair, he adds, 'understandable in their case with the rapid expansion of so large a refinery in so short a time, in a country with comparatively little refining experience'. I wonder how many firms, how many managements, can put their hands on their hearts and say: 'We don't live in this greenhouse and can afford to throw stones'. Be that as it may, this type of criticism completely misses the point of the Fawley agreements. In the first place, to speak of Esso buying themselves out when what they did, far from costing them anything, showed a small profit even in immediate terms, is something of a contradiction. More important, however, it is based on a misunderstanding of the methods used by Fawley management to accomplish their objective–a misunderstanding which would be dangerously misleading for any other management wanting to profit from Esso's example.

The implication of this 'buying out' phrase is that the unions' consent was gained for changing some of their practices by offering a large increase in wage rates plus the 40-hour week. I am tempted to say in passing that it is a strange and warped mentality which suggests that there is almost something morally wrong about offering the workers a fair reward for their contribution towards higher productivity instead of expecting to get it on the cheap. If one wants institutional change, especially the modification of traditional and entrenched institutions, it is only common sense to provide a powerful inducement for its acceptance. I have no doubt that the attitudes of the men, their stewards and the union officials would not have been as co-operative if they had been offered a few trivial concessions, supported by a barrage of propaganda on their duty to the nation.

In a questionnaire that I issued to the Fawley shop stewards last year, nearly all of them listed the wage increase or the reduction in the working week, or both, as the best features of the agreements for them, and I heard the same thing from union officials. Nevertheless, whilst the inducement was important, there was very much more to the methods employed than this.

In the early stages of my inquiry, I was interviewing the man who is now Employee Relations Adviser to Esso in London for the whole Company–earlier he had been Employee Relations Superintendent at Fawley and then Assistant Refinery Manager–and he has played a leading part in all these developments. So I waited with interest upon his answer to the question that I had sent him in writing before-hand: 'What has made the production of the Blue Book possible?' His considered reply was 'The habit of discussion'. 'A number of things', he said, 'made it practicable in helping to get permission to do what was necessary, but this was the condition that made it possible'. I thought this answer distinctly odd at the time. Expecting a rather intricate analysis of causes, I was disconcerted by its extreme simplicity. Moreover, as there has been so much glib talk about human relations and democratic leadership in industry, to be frank I rather distrusted it. Only later did I perceive its truth.

Consultation, formal but to a far greater extent informal, was of the essence in preparing the minds of the trade unionists at Fawley and of their officials outside for an acceptance of the ideas on which the Blue Book was based. Here, the unusual American consultant occupied a key role.

The Blue Book was essentially a list of proposed institutional changes–changes in practices that had become institutionalised either through the rules and traditions of craft unions or more recently in established refinery procedures and conventions. These institutional changes had economic implications and they, as I have said, provided an inducement for their acceptance since both the Company and its employees could reckon on benefiting from them. But institutions–such as craftsmen having mates or various job demarcations, craft and non-craft–though upheld in the first instance by the sanctions attached to them do not exist in a cultural vacuum. At a deeper level they are perpetuated by a system of beliefs about their value or necessity, so that neither the active will to change them, nor for that matter the passive consent to their being changed, is likely to be forthcoming so long as the underlying beliefs remain unshaken. That, one might say, is what every anthropologist knows. Only we are unaccustomed to looking at ourselves, and least of all at our industrial relations, anthropologically. The consultant in this case was because of his training. He not only took it for granted that cultural change was a necessary prerequisite to institutional change; he also knew something about the methods for accomplishing it. He had to use them on management first, whose beliefs, among other things, in the inevitability of high levels of overtime, had also to be shaken.

In 1959, he was involved in regular and at times almost daily discussions with leading stewards, as also were certain members of management, in which the ideas behind the Blue Book were introduced and one by one argued about in terms of justification, long before the formal negotiations started. The same ideas were introduced in a similar fashion on to the formal consultative committees within the refinery.

True, it is impossible to give any exact assessment of the effects of such deliberate, belief-changing consultation. One cannot gauge its results except by inference. No one I have spoken to on either side denied that without this consultation, this particular kind of consultation, the negotiations would have had little chance of success. Even so, the main complaint I heard among stewards and supervisors was that they were forced to digest too much change too quickly.

However, all this is really subsidiary to my second lesson–that the changing of restrictive union practices is a responsibility of management. Whether the methods used by Fawley management were the best or not, they did set about the job. They did not try to evade their responsibility by blaming it all on the unions.

One could detail many reasons for assigning this responsibility to management but let me mention one which, in its way, is quite decisive. People as a rule will not change their beliefs in the value of institutions, of *their* institutions, if the consequence is seriously to threaten their own status or their own security. Within the workplace, only management can plan to minimise this consequence and so gain consent to change. This includes a great deal more than a no-redundancy pledge because unemployment is only the crudest threat to an individual's or a group's status and security. Some of the blunders made at Fawley, and there were some, could be traced back in my judgement to a failure to grasp all the intricacies of the familiar problem of reconciling change with security.

I must be very brief about the exposition of my third lesson. This is a pity because it is particularly appropriate to the occasion. *Management learns to manage by being forced to accept the full responsibilities of management.* That may sound trite, almost tautological, yet, taken seriously, it is probably the greatest challenge confronting British management and the most important lesson of the Fawley experiment. You will hardly expect me, as an academic, to decry what management can learn in the classroom, but formal teaching has a limited utility. Management, like trade union leadership or politics, is a profession that has mainly to be learnt by the doing, by taking decisions and facing the consequences; there is no classroom substitute for that. But what decisions?

There is the rub. The decisions which management is called upon to take in practice, and for which it is held accountable, depend on what its responsibilities are thought to be. If certain of its responsibilities, though implicit in its role and function, are disregarded or treated as of little account, nothing much is likely to be learnt about the best ways of discharging them. Worse still, a biased view is acquired of the canons of success in the job, even of the realities in the situation surrounding it.

To bring these somewhat abstract remarks down to earth, I am going to make a very sweeping assertion which nevertheless I believe broadly to be true.

The trouble with the greater part of the best of line management in British industry from top to bottom is that it does not want to accept the responsibility for the human aspects of its job, what is sometimes called, although I dislike the term, man-management. By training and inclination it prefers the greater security it experiences in dealing with the more calculable technical or commercial problems. Labour policy it is quite willing, even eager, to leave to a personnel department with the necessary expertise. A potent sign of the existence of this attitude is the widespread but erroneous belief that labour relations are, in the main, something settled with trade union officials. And if it does not work out, if the stewards turn awkward, then the unions ought to discipline them. Granted that the unions may sometimes be at fault in allowing their stewards too free a rein, especially when they become a 'union within the union' and violate agreements with impunity, it should never be forgotten that management, by its action or lack of it, is constantly influencing the stewards' behaviour. As employees of the firm, besides being lay representatives of the union, the main daily experience to which they are reacting is, as it were, management and not union determined.

A great deal has been written about the theories of line and staff structures of organisation and how personnel departments should only have advisory functions towards line management. But how much of this is really put into practice? How many members of line management at all levels are confident about their ability to decide issues of labour policy? Or, to cut a little nearer to the bone, let me rather ask, how many are *entitled* to be confident? Personnel management obtained a considerable boost during the war and immediately after because of new developments in industrial relations, from the Essential Work Orders to the vogue for joint consultation. More thought and attention to the human element was demanded, if only in coping with regulations. This was a step forward, of course, but it has to be taken much further. The danger today is that personnel departments, having had continually to explain the facts of industrial relations life to line management, tend to ossify into attitudes of extreme caution and conservatism. One cannot blame them. It is the inevitable outcome of divided responsibility. Their main responsibility is to keep the peace, so this is the side on which their judgement errs.

Apart from its direct and immediate effects on labour relations, the Fawley Blue Book has also to be viewed as an exercise in management education. As a matter of fact, long before the consultants appeared on the scene, persistent efforts had been made to interest and involve line management in labour policy. When the man whom I have previously quoted became Assistant Refinery Manager in 1956, it would not be too much to say that this was his paramount objective. From then on, as one member of the Employee Relations Department put it to me: 'We consciously, slowly at first, began to withdraw from the many executive positions we had got ourselves into, and we started to encourage the idea that the personnel functions were just as much a supervisory responsibility as ever nuts and bolts were.'

The introduction of the consultants was welcomed not least because their presence promised to create a more fluid situation. Their independent status was seen to be an important factor in facilitating changes within management. The first outstanding result of their work was a wholesale re-organisation of the supervisory structure and personnel of M & C in September 1958. The keynote of this, in which *inter alia* the former chargehands came on the staff as first-line supervisors, was clearer and shorter lines of managerial responsibility and its sharper definition at all levels. It was an essential preliminary to the Blue Book.

From that point, the events leading up to the latter's production, and later the negotiation and subsequent administration of the agreements, took the process of 'forcing' line management to be responsible much further. The effects of this experience on top management at Fawley were remarkable. It found itself spending, not a small fraction, but the greater part of its time facing up to and resolving difficult questions of labour policy. Moreover, top management increasingly became a team engaged in solving common problems, rather than a number of departmental heads conscious only of their functional differences. Some of this spirit has gone down the lines to the middle and lower levels of management, but the results here will take longer to mature.

You will have noticed that my three lessons are three variations on a single theme – the responsibilities of management. I am conscious that in confining myself to them I am leaving many questions unanswered which the Fawley experiment is likely to raise in your minds. To instance but one, collective bargaining there was based on plant agreements; what difference did this make? There were no industry agreements, no employers' association which might have hampered a separate initiative on Esso's part. As it was the company were made to feel in devious ways that they were breaking the rules of the employers' club. Furthermore, there is little doubt that the unions would have been more reluctant to co-operate if greater numbers of their members had been involved. Or that, if the union leaders had been willing, the problem of gaining the members' consent would have been all the greater on an industry scale. There are great issues involved in this question, but one cannot discuss them properly without embarking on an examination of the whole of our present national structure of collective bargaining.

I have deliberately avoided questions of this sort in order to choose lessons which to my mind are unequivocally of general application. I can assure you that when I first started on my inquiry I had no idea that it would take my thoughts in this particular direction. Uncovering the facts and trying to make sense of them forced me to realise how crucial was the notion of managerial responsibility, especially responsibility towards the managed, to an understanding of what had happened at Fawley, and of how similar advances might be brought about elsewhere. I shall not insult your intelligence by pointing out that mere mechanical imitation is dangerous because no two workplace situations are alike. That would simply betray an absence of the kind of hard thought and wrestling with problems which led up to the Blue Book. Finally, in mentioning only the lessons for management, I do not mean to imply that it has no lessons for the trade unions. It has, on how they can best improve the standards

The Fawley Experiment

of living of their members. But these are not lessons they will be able to make much use of in the absence of the indispensable managerial initiative. Fawley shows that, given that initiative intelligently conceived, it will not be taken in vain.

PRODUCTIVITY BARGAINING PROSPECTS
(1968)

Over the four years since the publication of my book on *The Fawley Productivity Agreements* productivity bargaining has enjoyed a remarkable rise in popularity. When I coined the term to convey the lessons of wider application in the striking departure from the pattern of conventional wage negotiations at Esso's oil refinery on the Southampton Water, I did not anticipate that it would pass so rapidly into common use. Is there something in Victor Hugo's romantic view of history that 'there is nothing in the world so powerful as an idea that has come into its time'?

Certainly, at first, productivity bargaining suffered the fate of every new idea challenging established beliefs: immediate reactions were invariably defensive and often hostile. What was all this nonsense about unnecessary overtime? Would employers pay for it at premium rates unless it were essential to sustain current levels of production? The 'buying out of restrictive practices' was both immoral and unwise. By rewarding past slackness and putting a price tag on union or shop-floor rules hampering efficient management, it would encourage further blackmail in the future. There would be a rush to create new restrictions which could be sold later at a good price. Moreover high increases in wage rates, even if they had a productivity counterpart and were offset by reductions in overtime earnings, would trigger off similar increases elsewhere without similar changes in working practice. Cost and price inflation, instead of being curbed, would therefore be accelerated. Not least, the spread of plant agreements, which appeared to be the typical form of most productivity bargains, would undermine the whole of our traditional structure of industrial relations by weakening trade unions and employers' associations and their joint industry agreements.

These original objections are no longer voiced as strongly. Today the advantages of productivity bargaining are more likely to be stressed than its dangers. The shift of opinion has been pronounced. The conversion of many trade unions to favourable attitudes was swift and preceded the conversion of employers' associations. The TUC brought out one of the earliest and best positive statements on the subject, but now the CBI also plans for its members an important conference on the subject in June. A year ago it was scarcely conceivable that the Engineering Employers' Federation would be asking the unions for a national agreement on 'detailed productivity criteria within which plant bargaining should be encouraged' as well as 'a comprehensive set of principles for the operation of payment by results systems . . . suitable for the conditions of industry today'. Its booklet on *Productivity Bargaining in the Engineering Industry* is almost a model for clarity of exposition and sensible practical advice. The Heavy Chemicals Productivity Agreement recently extended to the Drug and Fine Chemicals Industry, to mention one example, has demonstrated how framework agreements can be made at industry level to provide a suitable framework of control for local productivity bargains.

But why have attitudes changed, and changed so rapidly? One reason no doubt is simply that we have more experience to go on. After Fawley many productivity agreements have been negotiated in other firms and other industries without calamitous consequences, indeed usually with success and to the satisfaction of the parties. Between 1st January 1967 and 3rd May 1968 the Ministry of Labour approved 928 'productivity cases' (as it calls them) covering approximately 684,000 workers, rejecting only 90 with 39,000 workers involved. Even when we allow for the fact that very few of these cases are full-scale productivity agreements, their number indicates the extent to which productivity considerations have entered negotiations. The severity of the disease which productivity bargaining is meant to remedy–under-utilisation of labour and other resources due to existing working practices–has also been emphasised by mounting evidence on its dimensions and causes. The recent revelation in the survey conducted for the Royal Commission on Trade Unions and Employers' Associations, showing that half the managers interviewed thought that there were inefficient working practices in their plant, was given wide publicity.[2]

Yet the main reason is surely to be found in the much-maligned efforts of the Labour Government to develop an appropriate and workable productivity, prices and incomes policy. When future historians dispassionately examine the record after the Declaration of

Intent, they may point to a series of blunders but they will have, I believe, to acknowledge one major achievement. It will not be the effect of these efforts in slowing down the general rate of increase in wages and prices–although no one can know what the movement would have been in their absence–or their immediate contribution to the balance-of-payments problem. What in the long perspective could represent a 'breakthrough', and is undeniably a most significant contrast to any of the previous improvised and ill-fated forms of government intervention since the war, may be expressed in the simple proposition that restraint has been used to induce reform. This is best illustrated by the reports of the National Board for Prices and Incomes, whether on incomes or prices references, which, almost without exception, have not simply said 'no' but have proposed changes in practices and organisation that would justify a wage increase or make a price increase either justified or unnecessary.

That the Board has acted more as a reformer than as a policeman should be obvious. Equally obvious is the permanent need for an institution with powers and resources to use the critical method of enquiry to reveal hidden facts, to challenge by positive recommendations uneconomic and anti-social patterns of behaviour which tradition and inertia preserve, and to create a habit among the informed public of asking questions that were never posed with any insistence before. This method may not always have succeeded, but if there were no policies of restraint (apart from the very inadequate restraints that may or may not be imposed by the market) there would be no reformist pressures at all on any of the parties. As long as they were able to pass on wage and price increases to the ultimate consumer, they had no cause to change their ways and tread the thorny path of reform. So-called *free* collective bargaining has too often meant freedom from effective criticism; for anything you can get away with goes. The Board's activities are the beginnings of the long, slow education of the parties to an awareness that in a modern, industrial, fully-employed economy ways must be found of registering the public interest in matters of income distribution, costs and prices.

The stimulus given by incomes policy to productivity bargaining is a special case of the general proposition. The conversion of trade unions was, to say the least, aided by the first of the criteria for exceptional pay increases in the first White Paper on incomes policy:

Productivity Bargaining Prospects

'where the employees concerned, for example by accepting more exacting work or a major change in working practices, make a direct contribution towards increasing productivity in the particular firm or industry'. The Board's Report No. 36 added six guidelines or basic rules for productivity bargaining, which made it the most clearly defined element in incomes policy. It also refuted many of the misconceptions and unsubstantiated criticisms of productivity agreements by a thorough investigation of the major agreements which had been negotiated.

With the arrival of Mrs. Castle as the political head of the enlarged Department of Employment and Productivity, government policy on productivity bargaining apparently enters a new phase. Besides being approved, accommodated and controlled within an incomes policy, it is to be actively promoted by the Department. What this will mean in practice we have yet to see, but that a more vigorous approach is right in principle I have no doubt. One cannot will the end of positive government to raise our rate of economic growth, without willing among the means the encouraging of productivity bargaining by the communication of experience and suggestions, the provision of expert assistance and the like. Desirable as it is, however, to quicken the pace of reform, such a policy has its dangers and they are summed up in the word 'whitewash'. The industrial and political pressures on the First Secretary and her Department to let through or manufacture agreements which *look like* productivity agreements will be very strong. And the looser the application of the NBPI guidelines, the greater the prospect of the cynical view of productivity bargaining becoming a self-fulfilling prophecy.

To appreciate the dangers, in order to avert them, one must take up the distinction made in the Board's Report No. 36 between 'partial' and 'comprehensive' agreements. The disparaging remark, still to be heard, that there is nothing new about productivity bargaining, is true about partial agreements. Deals of this sort, when a group of workers agree to step up their effort or to revise manning standards in return for more money, are as old as collective bargaining. Comprehensive agreements on the Fawley and later improved models, on the other hand, do represent an innovation, a radical and creative break with the past. It could not be otherwise, for they are an answer to a contemporary problem which is mainly a product of post-war conditions.

I have set out the principal elements in that problem elsewhere, but in brief they are as follows:

(a) Prolonged high levels of employment have greatly enhanced the power of work groups (represented by their shop stewards) on the shop floor.

(b) In various ways managements were unprepared to cope constructively with this situation.

(c) Instead they have usually reacted by capitulating to bargaining pressures with no other objectives in mind than the immediate expediency of buying peace.

(d) One result has been, not only an upsurge in workplace bargaining, which was inevitable, but bargaining that was 'largely informal, largely autonomous and largely fragmented'.

(e) The other result has been the growth of unilateral regulations by workers to increase their bargaining power and their income and job security (whether you call them 'protective' or 'restrictive' practices depends on your point of view)'.

(f) In sum these developments have added up to a progressive loss of control over pay and work systems at the place of work, and a growing abnegation by management of its responsibility to manage.

(g) This is the root cause of labour under-utilisation (the economic consequence) and of a growing disorder in management–labour relations (the institutional consequence).

Comprehensive productivity agreements get to grips with this basic problem but, as a rule, partial productivity agreements do not. If overtime has got out of hand, reducing it must be a plant-wide, if not a company-wide, operation. If a pay structure is riddled with inequities and anomalies or a payment-by-results system has decayed and lost its incentive effect, neither can be properly reconstructed in a piecemeal fashion. If restrictive practices are to be relaxed or removed, management misjudges the needs of the situation if it produces a shopping list and sets a separate price for each of them. Above all, since at bottom the problem is one of order, equity and control throughout a plant or a company, a solution can only be found on a similar scale. Comprehensive productivity agreements tackle the problem at its roots. They are a means of diminishing the informality, autonomy and fragmentation of local bargaining, and of contracting areas of unilateral regulation by management and workers in favour of joint control by collective agreement.

To state clearly this difference between comprehensive and partial agreements, which can so easily be masked by placing them under the same umbrella of productivity bargaining, is not to denigrate partial productivity agreements or to reject them out of hand. At a time when we desperately need to make better use of our resources, that would be folly. It has to be accepted that there are firms whose managements–even with assistance–would be incapable of success-fully negotiating comprehensive agreements. There are others again where comprehensive agreements may not be required because there are no serious problems of control. The essential question is the pragmatic one of whether a partial agreement will lead to a more or a less disordered situation. Will it, for example, set off a series of chain reactions of wage claims from other groups who feel that they have in comparison been unfairly disadvantaged? Partial agreements cannot, in other words, be judged only by their immediate productiv-ity return or their immediate effect on costs. Their long-term effect on plant or company labour relations must also be taken into account. Sometimes they may truly be the best first step on the road to reform.

Returning then to possible dangers in the Government's vigorous encouragement of productivity bargaining, it must be remembered that most of the comprehensive agreements, which are still com-paratively few in number, have taken years rather than months to prepare and negotiate. The time may be reduced with increased experience, but to rush them through when they involve substantial changes in existing attitudes and institutions is to accept too many risks and to court failure. They also make very heavy demands on management and unions. One of their great long-term benefits is in fact their effect on management, by forcing it—in the words of the Board's report—to become 'better informed and better organised than before the agreements'. All this takes time yet it is the crucial assurance against the gains gradually slipping away. It is to be hoped that the DEP's Productivity Unit will not throw all its weight on the side of hastily prepared partial agreements for the sake of quick results. The consequences of sacrificing long-term strategy to short-term tactics would be just as unfortunate here as they have been in other aspects of government policy.

PAY AS AN INCENTIVE
(1968)

What do we mean when we refer to pay as an incentive? Pay in any form and whatever the method of payment, be it by time or by piece, is for most people their principal incentive to work. That is to say, if they had a sudden windfall, a big win on the pools or a legacy from a rich uncle, they would be unlikely to stay in their present jobs. Similarly, when we look at the other side of the coin and consider the sanctions at the disposal of management to maintain industrial discipline, these rest in the last resort on the severity of the ultimate penalty of dismissal, or what this entails for the individual in terms of loss of pay and prospects compared with alternative employment opportunities.

Given this overall significance of pay as the main incentive to work in market economies, there is a point in distinguishing two quite different economic functions which it may serve. In the first place a company or business enterprise has to fix such levels of pay (and other benefits) as will enable it to recruit and retain the quantity and quality of employees which it requires for its operations. This may be described as the market function of pay, for in this respect it acts, however imperfectly, as a market regulator to allocate manpower between different undertakings and occupations. With the rise of large-scale enterprise, this process of allocation and the bargaining associated with it also occurs inside the firm as well as in external labour markets. Some American labour economists have therefore introduced the useful concept of an internal labour market.[3] They have shown how a firm's internal and external labour markets are linked by certain ports of entry into particular jobs so that in deciding on its labour recruitment and manpower planning policies, it may choose to some extent between relying on its internal or external markets.

But pay has another economic function which can be seen most clearly when we look at the nature of employment contracts. A job or employment contract represents in its economic aspect a wage-work bargain. The wage side of this bargain can be made specific with

72

the help of the measuring rod of money, but the work side is within limits necessarily indeterminate. The terms of the contract can, for instance, never settle exactly the quantity or quality of effort that the individual employee is expected to supply in return for his wage. It follows then that his performance on the job may be improved if improved performance increases his remuneration above the level that the employer has a contractual obligation to provide. This may be called the managerial function of pay because here it acts as an inducement or a positive sanction deployed by management to assist it in its primary task of organising the work of others so as to provide the best and most efficient furtherance of the aims of the enterprise. In simple terms this function may be expressed as the relating of pay to performance, leaving aside for the time being the important question of what is meant by good performance.

To recognise that pay has such a managerial function, which is what people have in mind when they talk about incentive schemes, is not to deny that work behaviour may be influenced by many other motives apart from a desire to increase one's income. Although the significance of these non-pecuniary incentives should not be under-estimated, I do not believe that they can possibly serve as a substitute for pay over the greater part of industrial employment. When the work itself has comparatively little intrinsic interest for the individual (and that is true of a very large part of work in industry today) then its extrinsic rewards (and most of these can be expressed in money) must be the principal motivation for undertaking it. More-over, even if his work gives someone a fairly high degree of satis-faction, monetary rewards may still be used either to stimulate higher standards of performance or to underpin existing standards at times when interest would otherwise flag. It is ridiculous, of course, to suggest that it is degrading to work harder for more money, or that the provision of financial incentives is based on a 'low view' of human nature, when this is manifestly the driving force throughout the whole of our economic system. In any case, income for the individual not only determines his share of the material things of life but also affects his status and security as well as his access to many cultural goods and opportunities.

The next point to be noted is that in the past the managerial function of pay (as a reward for performance) has been largely, if not exclusively, associated for manual workers with piecework and payment by results. One can easily run into difficulties in trying to define the latter term. It has been taken to include production targets applied to large groups, even measured day work, in addition to direct incentives for individuals and small groups such as piecework and time-rate plus bonus. I shall be using the term in its more limited sense where the incentive payments relate to the output of individuals or small groups. They then entail as one of their essential characteristics the *possibility of variable earnings* from week to week, and as between different individuals or groups within the same undertaking.

Before looking at a few facts about the prevalence of such payment systems in this country it is worth asking why they have been confined almost entirely to manual workers on the shop floor. It has, of course, always been recognised that payment by results was inappropriate for certain types of work, but in the case of managerial employees these types of incentive were usually not required. The main positive sanction for members of management to improve their performance has been the prospect of promotion. This introduces a point of some theoretical importance. Pay structures, when they are associated with opportunities for vertical mobility, may be as much a part of an incentive system as the method of payment for work. Indeed one must regard as artificial the frequently drawn distinction between structures and methods. I am not suggesting that the prospect of increased income, and the higher status associated with it, is the only incentive for management to improve its performance. Clearly a professional man may be influenced by the codes and standards of his profession. Also the intrinsic interest of the work often increases the higher one rises in the managerial hierarchy. Even so, their career prospects are tremendously important for managers, which simply means that pay in the future as well as pay in the present can have a powerful incentive effect. The fact that the great majority of manual workers had little or no career prospects in their jobs made it important to supply as far as possible more immediate and direct incentives. It is interesting to see how the earlier picture is changing, for example, in modern process industries which offer much more of a career ladder, at least for their production workers.

But to return to the traditional types of pay incentive schemes for manual workers, piecework–I need hardly tell you–was not an invention of the Industrial Revolution. There were piecework price lists in ancient Rome, and it is said that the management principle of the incentive wage plan was first introduced by the Chaldeans in 400 B.C.[4] During the nineteenth and the first half of the twentieth centuries, however, the trend was undoubtedly towards a wider application of piecework. Partly it had its origins in sub-contracting of labour, but it was also the main method of payment in the new factory industries. Some craft unions were strongly opposed to it and insisted on time work, but they were a minority in the union world. In 1894, according to the Webbs, 49 trade unions with 573,000 members insisted on piecework, 24 with 140,000 members were willing to accept it, while only 38 with 290,000 members rejected it.[5] Later on, increasing division of labour facilitated its further introduction, and so did developments in the production engineering techniques of work measurement. During two world wars the insistant cry for more output greatly encouraged its extension. Even the first post-war Labour Government's experiment in wage restraint had the same effect. Ministers were saying that there was no objection to increased earnings accruing from payment by results since they would be offset by higher productivity. So firmly was this dogma held.

Thus the Ministry of Labour's figures on the proportion of workers covered by some form of payment by results revealed an increase in all industries from 28 to 32 per cent between 1947 and 1951–the pre-war figure being 25 per cent. Since then, judging by the most recent returns in 1961, the proportion has remained fairly stable.[6] There may have been changes in the particular type of incentive schemes in use, for the Ministry of Labour has included indirect as well as direct financial incentives, but in general we must conclude that payment by results has as yet lost little of its attraction for industry. J. R. Crossley has argued that the influence of these schemes on earnings is much greater than the proportion quoted might appear to imply. On the basis of the 1961 figures he has calculated that the earnings of as many as 73 per cent of employees in manufacturing industry could have been influenced by the operation of these systems, if one makes the extreme, but not all that improbable, assumption that 'the wages of all employees in a factory are affected in some measure if the methods are used at all'.[7]

Although these statistics give no indication of growing opposition to piecework and other direct-pay incentive schemes, there are other signs that they are now viewed with much greater doubt and scepticism than in the past. For one thing, some firms have abandoned them. But a change of attitude is being revealed less in industrial practice than in recent informed literature on the subject. An outstanding feature of almost all the studies which have been published in the 1960s is that they are highly critical of the old-style incentive systems. Personally, I have no doubt at all that the tide of opinion is gradually turning as criticism mounts.

One explanation offered for a new outlook is technological advance. It has been said that 'the demands of technology will do more to end incentive schemes than the conversion of individual managers'.[8] Changes in the technology of production are certainly an important factor in making earlier systems of payment outmoded. In capital-intensive industries the utilisation of equipment and materials may be more important factors in influencing costs than the utilisation of labour. Similarly, the rewarding of initiative and team-work, particularly in times of crisis, may have a greater significance for the firm than raising levels of individual effort. There are many relationships here which I have not the time to pursue, but which are well documented in several studies.[9] I am not convinced, however, that the conversion of individual managers is unimportant. There are too many examples to prove that their existing beliefs on the value of piecework remain a serious obstacle to change even when the case for it is overwhelming on technical grounds alone. To contribute if I can to that process of conversion, I would like to set before you the different lines of criticism to which the old payment schemes have been subjected. I can best do this by raising a series of questions.

The first question is do these schemes really reward what they were mainly intended to reward? By increased earnings they were intended to reward one thing and one thing only, increased effort. Piecework rested on the assumption that output was at least a rough-and-ready measure of the worker's input of effort. In fact, as can be seen in their present working, payment-by-results systems frequently offer four other sources of increased earnings. Earnings may be raised by improvements in the equipment when this is accompanied by no, or less than a proportionate, adjustment in time or price. They may result from improved facility on the worker's part resulting from the constant repetition of similar tasks over a long period; attempts have been made to express this relationship quantitatively in the 'learning curve' phenomenon.[10] They may occur as a result of the slackening of piecework times under bargaining pressures when times are being revised. Finally, they may come about because management finds it necessary to settle new times for jobs so that they yield initially the same level of earnings as on the old times. It may be possible in some situations to reduce the extent to which earnings are increased by factors other than increased effort. But management has always to ask what an incentive scheme is rewarding apart from effort. Where it is rewarding continuous piecemeal bargaining and a loosening of times it is, in fact, having a disincentive effect.

This leads me on to the second line of criticism. How far do these schemes in practice serve their alleged incentive function? Their basic assumptions on motivation have been queried on a number of counts. There is first the work of modern industrial sociologists, from Elton Mayo and his associates onwards, demonstrating the existence and the rationale of informal social controls operated by work groups and resulting in 'restriction of output'. The philosophy of individual, output-based incentives was not only highly individualistic in the sense of ignoring the effects of social values on the shop floor. It also assumed in F. W. Taylor's well-known words that 'what the workers want beyond anything else is high wages'. They may want high wages, but in many factory situations they are not prepared to get them at any cost, and especially not at the cost of their self-respect and the disapproval of their mates. We have also the work of Baldamus and Behrend indicating that the apparent effect of payment by results schemes may be no more than an expression of the prevalent beliefs about workers' behaviour.[11] According to their researches the higher output norms which these schemes achieve are due, not so much to the lure of more money, as to the fact that both managers and workers share a common system of beliefs that standards of effort ought to be higher on piece than on time rates.

But quite apart from these attacks coming from social scientists on the dogmatic premises of these payment systems, they are being seriously discredited by the record of experience with their actual operation in present-day circumstances. Again and again we observe what is sometimes described as their demoralisation, and at other times their degeneration. This has been expressed in the aphorism that wage incentives appear to generate their own disincentives. An

American study has summarised the four principal features of a degenerate payment by results system. These are: substantial inequities in earnings and effort as between different groups; a growing average incentive yield so that this becomes an ever larger part of the total pay packet; a declining average level of effort due to the workers taking the gains of looser standards in increased leisure as well as increased earnings; and a high proportion of 'off standard' payments and times.[12] How many managers among you can deny that one or more of these signs of degeneration are not evident in the operation of the schemes you know?

The third critical question goes back to my starting point that the purpose of any incentive pay scheme is to relate pay to performance. It is this. Should good performance be equated with high effort? There are jobs of a repetitive character where effort may be the main consideration, but there are many others in which standards of performance will depend substantially on a variety of other factors. It may be important for the pay system to reward the acquisition of knowledge and skill, or responsible behaviour in the use of discretion, or willingness to accept change, or teamwork and co-operation. Admittedly the economic value of these and other factors affecting performance will depend on the nature of the work and its technological context, but even when a system of payment is highly functional with respect to sustaining high levels of effort, it may at the same time be very dysfunctional in many other respects. In particular, as Liesl Klein has shown, one of the characteristics of an 'ideal piece-worker' is 'non-involvement in the affairs of the firm'.[13] If management are in earnest when they ask for departmental or factory-wide co-operation to achieve higher productivity, they cannot afford pay systems which disrupt it.

The three questions I have raised so far are mainly concerned with the effects of payment by results schemes on individual performance, but their wider economic and social consequences must also be considered, for the firm, for the national economy, and for our system of industrial relations. That some of these wider consequences are extremely unfortunate is hardly in doubt. They may be listed under three heads: piecework as a cause of earnings drift; piecework as a cause of inequities and anomalies in pay structures; and piecework as a cause of the fragmentation of bargaining in the workplace. Various studies have shown that the two primary factors responsible for earnings drift in this country are systematic overtime and payment by results. Earnings drift is a serious obstacle to the development of a viable incomes policy, but viewed simply within the context of a company's operations it usually represents a progressive loss of control on the part of management over labour costs, with all that that means not least for our export trade. Similarly, the growth of inequities and anomalies in pay structures, apart from being a frequent source of grievance and conflict, has a serious effect on work performance. You must all know of cases where, for example, foremen are earning substantially less than the men they supervise, or where skill differentials have been completely eroded. The fragmentation of workplace bargaining resulting from piecemeal deals over earnings with individuals or small groups within a complex enterprise is a potent source of chaos in industrial relations at the place of work. How can one produce order and consistency in the conduct of these relations when the wage system itself works in the opposite direction?

These various lines of criticism levelled against piecework and payment by results are obviously interrelated. I have sought in my analysis to distinguish them, however, to show how formidable is the mounting case against these traditional pay systems. There may well be situations where management is right in thinking that direct incentives, associated with variable individual earnings, are indispensable to sustain the levels of output which it requires. I am not an absolute opponent, a 'piecework must be abandoned' man. But if every firm were carefully to consider my four questions and then decide whether it had the best pay system for its own situation, I suspect that many would be forced to conclude that the time had come for a change. Why, then, is there not something like a stampede of firms wanting to revise their payments system? Is it simply inertia that inhibits change? To some extent this is true, no doubt, but there are two other reasons. The first is that alternative incentive pay systems to the traditional ones have their own snags and disadvantages. There is no such thing as a perfect or ideal pay system. But secondly, firms are deterred by the difficulties and the risks of changing their existing pay system, which are liable to increase the more it degenerates and the longer it has been installed. So they conclude 'better the devil we know'.

I have no time to review the advantages and disadvantages of alternative incentive pay systems to payment by results. These other systems, though not mutually incompatible, fall broadly into three classes. There is first the type of system already applying to management, which relies on the pay structure and career prospects, including possibly incremental scales. The gathering trend to place manual workers on staff status partly reflects this type of approach. Secondly, we have the category of pay systems which Tom Lupton has characterised as 'total task–total reward'[14] of which measured day work is the most popular. Thirdly, there are the enterprise-wide or large group, indirect, cost-saving based systems such as the Scanlon and Rucker varieties or even old-fashioned profit-sharing. We must also remember, however, that one further alternative to a degenerate piecework system is a regenerate one.

Whichever of these alternatives is chosen, there are, I believe, six golden rules that any management should observe in deciding on its pay system:

(1) No incentive payments system can be taken on trust. The whole of its assumptions and results must be critically examined.

(2) The system chosen should be designed to give as good a fit as possible to the total situation in which the undertaking operates.

(3) When the choice has been made the objectives of the system should be known and made explicit to all concerned.

(4) It should incorporate all the necessary controls, including firm standards of work measurement, which are required for the achievement of these objectives.

(5) It should be introduced and operated with the agreement and understanding of the workers and their representatives.

(6) Finally, it must be made the subject of periodic review (at fairly frequent intervals of probably not more than three years) to see whether it has become obsolete or is in need of repair.

You may be disappointed that I have no more to offer at the end of my talk than this list of rather general and, you may think, perfectionist injunctions. Even if I had time to discuss each of them in detail, I could not tell you which is the best of the various payment systems. They cannot be ranked in any *a priori* order of merit. Nor can anyone tell you what is the best system for your firm without making a detailed analysis of the facts, and then his judgement will be liable to error, in fact to almost certain failure to anticipate some unforeseen risks. The introduction of any new payment system must be a leap in the dark, or rather, given careful preparation, into the twilight. All I would claim is that, if my golden rules were adopted by many managements who ignore them today, they would be far from satisfied with their existing pay policies and practices.

INDUSTRIAL RELATIONS: WHAT IS WRONG WITH THE SYSTEM?
(1965)

THE NEGLECT OF THEORY

How to achieve evolutionary change at a revolutionary pace is one possible description of the most pressing pre-occupation of our time. The spectre which now haunts almost every country in the world is the fear of being left behind. It hovers, however, mainly over the closely inter-locking realms of science, technology and economics, where advances in knowledge and its application demonstrably add to national power and material progress. Certainly in Britain, when we speak about the need for change, drastic modernisation of our political and social institutions is less readily contemplated. Here tradition continues to hold sway and has an easy conquest over reason; to say that any institution has 'stood the test of time' still remains its best defence.

Our industrial relations institutions are no exception. In the two decades that have passed since the war left its imprint upon them, few innovations–and no major ones–have occurred on the national scene. Adopting a longer perspective, their underlying principles, if not their precise patterns, were largely settled in the nineteenth century. Yet, until a few years ago, the dominant attitude in this country towards our 'voluntary system', as we like to call it, was one of smug complacency. It was believed to be a model of maturity, which other countries envied and would do well to emulate, could they but muster the same spirit of tolerance to make it work.

While it would be rash to suggest that this attitude has completely disappeared, there are many signs of its having been badly shaken. Whether trade union structure is under debate, or the organisation of employers' associations, or the prospect of an incomes policy, or the frequency of unofficial strikes, or the relaxing of restrictive practices, or the failure of joint consultation to realise the earlier hopes that were placed in it, no one is any longer disputing that

83

pressing and largely unresolved problems abound. More than that, there is a widespread uneasiness that they are not being resolved because our system of industrial relations, praised in the past for its adaptability, is suffering from an excessive institutional rigidity. The actual texture of relations in industry is being continually transformed along with their technological and economic background, yet they remain pressed uncomfortably into the mould of institutions which though outmoded are strongly resistant to reform.

That the machinery creaks and groans, that new strains and stresses should become more and more manifest is hardly surprising. We are inclined nevertheless to look at each case of breakdown in isolation from the rest, and to think of it in terms of temporary repair rather than of radical reconstruction. The pragmatic approach to industrial relations, so deeply rooted in our society, inhibits a comprehensive causal analysis of the growing dissatisfaction with our traditional system as a whole. Such an analysis can only be undertaken when its leading features have been understood. But prior to that the very notion of a system of industrial relations raises difficult points of definition which cannot be ignored. On the face of things there is little that appears to be systematic about our arrangements, and one of the tritest observations that can be made about them is that they do not conform to any standard pattern.

A multitude of trade unions and employers' associations–apart from individual firms and public authorities–take part in collective bargaining, each with its own peculiarities. The collective agreements they sign display the same variety in contents and coverage. These in turn are supplemented by a wide range of unrecorded customs and practices that often differ from one locality to another within the same industry. Even the law relating to industrial relations, which one would expect to be a force for uniformity, reveals a baffling complexity. Finally, it is not enough to look at those institutions which have evolved outside the firm mainly for the purpose of regulating labour markets. Industrial relations within reveal still greater contrasts.

In what sense are we entitled then to refer to all these diverse arrangements as constituting a national system? Is some kind of unity to be found in such diversity? The notion of a system is, of course, a theoretical abstraction. We are quite accustomed, however, to describing economic and political systems in terms of the fundamental principles underlying the manifold detail of their operation. It is merely a new thought for most people that industrial relations can be treated in a similar fashion. The reason for its novelty lies in the way the subject has been studied in the past.

> To date the study of industrial relations has had little theoretical content. At its origins and frequently at its best, it has been largely historical and descriptive. A number of studies have used the analysis of economics particularly in treating wages and related questions, and other studies, particularly of factory departments, have borrowed the apparatus of anthropology and sociology. Although industrial relations aspires to be a discipline (it) . . . has lacked any central analytical content. It has been a crossroads where a number of disciplines have met—history, economics, government, sociology, psychology, and law.[1]

This is not the place to embark on a lengthy exposition of the case for treating industrial relations as an intellectual discipline in its own right. Even if the subject is regarded as no more than a field of study to be cultivated with the well-tried methods of other disciplines, its development must depend on the mutual support of theory and research. At its simplest, theory is needed to pose the right questions and research to provide the right answers, granted that a constant interplay has to take place between the two. An indiscriminate accumulation of facts leads not to conclusions but to confusions. Some framework of theoretical analysis, however rudimentary and provisional, is always needed to order one's inquiry and to arrive at general propositions.

The drawback of relying on the theory of any one of the several disciplines that have impinged on industrial relations is that it was never intended to offer an integrated view of the whole complex of institutions in this field. Theoretically speaking, these disciplines tear the subject apart by concentrating attention on some of its aspects to the exclusion or comparative neglect of others. And a partial view of anything, accurate as it may be within its limits, must of necessity be a distorted one. Hence the significance of the notion of a system of industrial relations which expresses the subject's inherent unity.

But to make any sense of the notion the first question to be answered is: system of what? Economics deals with a system of markets, politics with a system of government. What is the substance of a system of industrial relations? Nothing could be more revealing of the past neglect of the subject's theory than one simple fact. Not until recently has it been explicitly stated that a system of industrial relations is a system of rules.[2] These rules appear in different guises: in legislation and in statutory orders; in trade union regulations; in collective agreements and in arbitration awards; in social conventions; in managerial decisions; and in accepted 'custom and practice'. This list is by no means exhaustive, but 'rules' is the only generic description that can be given to these various instruments of regulation. In other words, the subject deals with certain regulated or institutionalised relationships in industry. Personal, or in the language of sociology 'unstructured', relationships have their importance for management and workers, but they lie outside the scope of a system of industrial relations.

Given this starting point, the next step is to distinguish which rules or which regulated relationships are to be included. Unfortunately the subject has inherited a misleading title. Not all the relationships associated with the organisation of industry are relevant. No one takes it to include, for instance, the cartel agreements among firms, or their trade associations, or the relations which they have with their customers or the community at large. The only aspect of business enterprise with which industrial relations is concerned is the employment aspect; the relations between the enterprise and its employees and among those employees themselves. One way of identifying these relationships is to place them in their legal setting. They are all either expressed in or arise out of contracts of employment (or service), which represent, in common speech, jobs. The study of industrial relations may therefore be described as a study of the institutions of job regulation.

ANALYSIS OF JOB REGULATION

The rules in question, like all rules, are of two kinds. They are either *procedural* or *substantive*. We can observe this distinction in the clauses of collective agreements, which are mainly composed of a body of rules. The procedural clauses of these agreements deal with such matters as the methods to be used and the stages to be followed in the settlement of disputes, or perhaps the facilities and standing to be accorded to representatives of parties to the agreement. Their substantive clauses, on the other hand, refer to rates of wages and working hours or to other job terms and conditions in the segment of employment covered by agreement. The first kind of rules regulate the behaviour of parties to the collective agreements – trade unions and employers or their associations, and those who act on their behalf; whereas the second kind regulate the behaviour of employees and employers as parties to individual contracts of employment. In short, it is the substantive rules of collective bargaining that regulate jobs. Since, however, the procedural rules of collective bargaining regulate the making, interpretation and enforcement of its substantive rules, they provide this particular institution of job regulation with its form and constitution.

To take this distinction a little further, one of the effects of rules is to establish rights and obligations, which together define status. Generally, the procedural rules of industrial relations can be said to settle the status of any of the parties participating in job regulation, whether this be through collective bargaining or by other methods. Similarly, the substantive rules of industrial relations, by attaching various rights and obligations to jobs, settle their status, regardless normally of the individuals who occupy them.[3] They fix, as we say, 'a rate for the job', but, of course, many other standard terms and conditions of employment as well.

These two different kinds of rules regulate different sets of relationships. Those regulated by procedural rules have sometimes been called *collective relations*, since they involve representative organisations. Collective relations are not confined, however, to trade unions and employers' associations. The state and society participate in them; so do managements and work groups. What such collective relations have in common is their not being an end in themselves; they are constituted as a means of regulating the basic relationships in industry in which employees are placed by virtue of their jobs.

What is the nature of those relationships covered by the substantive rules of industrial relations? They are partly but not wholly economic in character. In its economic aspect the contract of employment represents a transaction in a labour market, a bargain between a buyer and seller of labour. At its simplest the employer agrees to pay the employee so many pounds in wages for so many hours of work, but, as we know, the transaction is usually much more complicated than this. Payment may be made by results, instead of by time, or there may be a mixture of the two. Apart from fixing the normal working week, the contract may have something to say about over-time and holidays and many other matters relating either to remuneration or to the work that is to be undertaken in exchange for it. Whatever its precise terms, and whether they are expressly stated or implied, the contract is always, in its economic substance as distinct from its legal form, a wage–work bargain.

Bargaining, however, is only one of the two characteristic processes of every market, including the labour market.[4] The other is competition, and both may be made the subject of regulation. While the rules directly regulating bargaining settle standard prices for labour, those regulating competition restrict the demand for it or the supply. The latter, for example, may circumscribe the employer's discretion as to whom he may employ by limiting the number of learners or apprentices, or by distinguishing between men's and women's work, or by imposing union membership requirements, and so on. These *market relations* between employers and employees include opportunities to enter into contracts in addition to the terms on which they are concluded.

But once there is a contract the employee on the job enters another set of relationships. He has agreed to obey certain instructions with respect to his work, to submit to some kind of discipline. If he is a supervisor or occupies some higher post in management, he may also be entitled to give instructions to others, but only within the limits set by a superior level of authority until the summit of the managerial hierarchy is reached. The complexity of these relationships depends on the scale and technology of the enterprise, but every business enterprise has, in Peter Drucker's words, 'an internal order based on authority and subordination, that is, on power relationships'.[5] In the broadest sense of the word these relationships are political, not economic. We may refer to them as *managerial relations* because they arise out of the organisation of management, which has the task of governing the enterprise in order to further its objectives.

The rules regulating managerial relations in effect regulate the work behaviour of employees. But we now recognise that their behaviour on the job is not only controlled by management. This formal organisation of a business enterprise is supplemented and complemented by an informal organisation created by the employees themselves (managerial as well as non-managerial) to meet their own social needs at work. The basic unit of this organisation is the work group and its most familiar, though by no means universal, expression on the shop floor is regulation of output.[6]

The important point about this third set of relationships is not so much their informality, which is incidental, but their purpose. Whatever form they take, they are always maintained by employees to serve their own ends rather than the ends of the enterprise.[7] For this reason they have been called *human relations*, although the term is open to considerable misunderstanding. They are not unstructured personal relations, but organised group relations, and thus essentially social in character; the equivalent within the enterprise of voluntary associations in society at large.

To sum up with another phrase of Drucker's, a business enterprise has 'a triple personality'; it is at once an economic, a political and a social institution. In the first of these personalities it produces and distributes incomes by operating within a nexus of factor and product markets. In the second it embodies a system of government in which managers collectively exercise authority over the managed, but are also themselves involved in an intricate pattern of political relationships. Its third personality is revealed in the 'plant community'[8] which evolves from below out of face-to-face relations based on shared interests, sentiments, beliefs and values among various groups of employees.[9]

His job therefore places every employee in each of these three sets of relationships either with the enterprise (as a corporate entity) or with his fellow employees. They may all be regulated by the substantive rules of industrial relations. So too—and this fourth category must not be left out of account—may his relationship to the physical environment in which he works, such rules being designed in the main to protect his safety, health and welfare.

Having surveyed the various types of relationship covered by the subject, we may return to the notion of a system of industrial relations. More precisely, there is not a single system, but a complex of systems within systems. Every business enterprise is itself a social system of production and distribution. It has a structured pattern of relationships which have a permanence and a distinct identity, irrespective of the individual personalities involved. Some of the institutions of job regulation are an integral part of this system; they are, as it were, the domestic industrial relations of the enterprise. A code of disciplinary works' rules, a factory wage structure, an internal procedure for joint consultation or for dealing with grievances, are possible examples. There are other institutions, however, that clearly belong to the external environment in which the enterprise is placed. These limit the freedom of the enterprise and its members in their own rule-making activities. The provisions of protective labour legislation, the rules of trade unions or employers' associations, the regulative contents of the agreements between them, fall into this category. This suggests a distinction between what may be called *internal* and *external* job regulation.

The essence of this distinction, which is of profound analytical importance, does not lie in whether the rules are peculiar to one business enterprise or have a wider coverage. The decisive question is whether they can be changed without the consent of an external authority; whether they are settled autonomously by the enterprise and its members. Rules embodied in works agreements with trade unions, for example, cannot be included under internal regulation. A trade union is an external organisation with respect to a business enterprise. It is not part of its social system, but a separate social system, though the memberships of the two overlap.

Shop stewards, or other union representatives who are also employees of a business enterprise, usually straddle both systems. This, in itself, is a very illuminating aspect of their role. As spokesmen of work groups in the enterprise, they may participate in the making of internal rules either separately or jointly with management. As representatives of their union they have a responsibility for enforcing its rules or the agreements that it has entered into with employers. Only rules which stewards are able to make or amend on behalf of their constituents without seeking the approval of external union authorities can be counted as belonging to systems of internal job regulation.

The significance of the distinction between external and internal job regulation is, perhaps, best appreciated when we compare the different reasons for their growth. Historically, the leading theme in the evolution of external job regulation has been the social need of employees, especially manual workers, for protection against the devastating and degrading effects of unregulated labour markets. With the rise of *laissez-faire* capitalism destroying or weakening the statutory or customary defences of trades, and creating new classes of manufacturing operatives with little or no protection at all, new external rules which would qualify the freedom of employers were required to fix minimum or standard rates of pay, to limit working hours, and to reduce the worst physical hazards of industrial employment. The main driving force in building up these restraints on employers naturally came from the employees' own organisations, their trade unions.[10] Nevertheless employers were also interested in curbing 'cut-throat' wage competition among themselves; and the state increasingly stepped in either to support private regulation or, where that was lacking, to offer some minimum of protection itself.

Trade unions, it is true, grew out of 'the customary practices and social habits of wage earners at their work long before formal organisations appeared among them'.[11] Union organisation often served to strengthen or to reinforce processes of regulation that were never completely eliminated. Internal job regulation, however, as practised by work groups or shop clubs, was never a sufficient answer to the market forces that threatened the workers' livelihood and status. These forces could in the nature of things only be controlled externally, so external regulation became the unions' main concern. Moreover, with labour and product markets expanding as a result of improvements in transport and communication, the coverage of the rules of external regulation had similarly to be extended if they were to offer effective protection. Accordingly the structures of trade unions and of collective bargaining were progressively adapted to make this possible.

But it was not only the effects of unbridled competition in labour markets which furthered the development of external job regulation. Society was interested in keeping conflict between unions and employers within reasonable bounds, and so were the parties themselves. While substantive rules were applied to market relations, procedural rules were made to govern collective relations with a view to facilitating the peaceful settlement of disputes. In both respects there was a need for order which could only be met by the acceptance of rules. Later, to the extent that other than market relations also became issues of group conflict–treatment on the job for example–some external rules of a substantive character appeared within the system to regulate managements as well as markets.

The development of systems of internal job regulation, in contrast, has been pushed forward by different forces to answer different needs. Here the principal drive has come from managements seeking to bring the work behaviour of employees under greater control. As might be expected, the factors that have contributed to the production of elaborate and complex systems of rules within business enterprises (in order to regulate work directly or through the rewards attached to it) are associated with the changing character of those enterprises. If any one factor had to be selected as being of decisive importance it would be their size, but this cannot be separated from several others. With increases in the scale of organisation came the separation of management from the ownership of capital and the change from a personal to a bureaucratic type of administration. This demanded an impersonal rationality and equality of treatment in the running of business that had to be expressed in the application of rules. The fragmentation of work into many separate operations, the specialisation of knowledge and skill required for industrial purposes, the consequent problems of co-ordination, by complicating the managerial function also made an augmented body of rules the only alternative to chaos. At the same time in the realm of ideas, the movement for 'scientific management', started by Frederick Winslow Taylor, resulted in new techniques intended to submit work to greater technical regulation and measurement, often allied with new incentive wage systems.

This did not mean, as has already been shown, that the rules made by management necessarily replaced those made by the employees themselves. The same forces that were promoting a greater regulation of managerial relations were having a similar effect on human relations, if only because the informal organisation of an enterprise is, to a large extent, a response to its formal organisation. A simple example to illustrate the point would be the introduction of an incentive wage system by management, based on rules which relate pay to work measurement. In so far as this results in a spread of earnings which the workers consider to be unfair, they are induced to construct further rules of their own to regulate what individuals are entitled to earn.

These brief references to large and intricate historical processes may suffice to indicate why external should not be confused with internal job regulation. In practice, of course, the borderline between the two may sometimes be very difficult to determine. It is a moving frontier with rules passing out of the one realm into the other. Furthermore, the *de facto* autonomy of a business enterprise and its employees in their rule-making activities may not be identical with the scope of their autonomy *de jure*. The distinction is ultimately one between systems. Invariably, when we speak about national systems of industrial relations, it is the procedural and substantive rules of external job regulation that we have in mind. In any country, enterprise systems of internal job regulation evolve or are constituted within the broad limits which its particular national system sets. Obviously, the more permissive the national system, the greater the freedom of management and workers in each enterprise to follow their own preferences in regulating any of the relationships in which they are involved.

Not that national systems of external regulation are necessarily homogeneous. Their procedural and substantive rules are likely to vary from industry to industry or from place to place. In so far as these rules are derived from collective bargaining, the diverse technological, market, power and cultural contexts of the separate bargaining units are bound to produce many contrasts in their contents. And even where external rules are to be found in legislation and statutory orders, it does not follow that they are national and all-embracing in their application; they may be restricted to particular industries or categories of employees. What is it, then, that knits all the rules of external regulation together into a systematic whole? Why is there an identifiable national system?

The answer is no different for industrial relations than for economics, or politics, or the law. There are national systems of each because the nation itself is an entity. The unity in this diversity is to be found in certain underlying principles, expressing value judgements, which are broadly accepted throughout the nation. The general legal framework of external job regulation is one manifestation of such principles, but so is the administrative role of government and the attitudes which the representative organisations in industry adopt in their dealings with each other and with the government. Without some elements of a common ideology or a number of 'shared under-standings'[12] the system would lose its coherence and stability. Once serious conflict arises at this level, the system must change or be disrupted by it.

Our own national system of industrial relations appears to be anything but systematic. It was never deliberately planned; nor has theory had any noticeable influence on its design. Instead it has emerged in a piecemeal and seemingly haphazard fashion over a century of history, with much of its past still reflected in the present. As a system one should nevertheless be able to describe it as a unity. This may be done in terms of certain normative principles that have governed its working throughout. What are those principles?

PRINCIPLES OF OUR TRADITIONAL SYSTEM

The first leading principle is one that our traditional system shares with many other national systems of advanced industrial countries which are pluralistic societies. *A priority is accorded to collective bargaining over other methods of external job regulation.* Despite its somewhat misleading title, which we owe to the Webbs, collective bargaining is essentially a rule-making process. It could more appropriately be called joint regulation; since its distinctive feature is that trade unions and employers or their associations act as joint authors of rules made to regulate employment contracts and, incidentally, their own relations. They may sometimes use third-party assistance in the form of conciliation, mediation, arbitration and public inquiry, but it serves only as an auxiliary aid to reach their own agreements, for whose contents and observance they are equally responsible.

Theoretically one can distinguish five other methods of external job regulation, according to the parties participating in the authorship of its substantive rules. Trade unions may engage in it unilaterally by binding their members to observe working rules which the 'other side' has had no say in making. Employers' associations may similarly impose regulations on the firms that belong to them. There is also a form of tripartite regulation, of which our Wages Councils are an example, in which three parties are involved: independents or public representatives as well as unions and employers. The fourth and fifth alternative methods to collective bargaining are state and social regulation–the one by statute or common law and the other by custom and convention. In these methods industrial associations do not carry any direct responsibility for the rules.[13] State regulation, in this sense, is not synonymous with legal regulation, which is a broader concept; collective agreements, for example, may be legally enforced. The methods are classified not by the nature of the sanctions available for the enforcement of the rules, but by the parties actually responsible for their authorship. In practice the methods easily shade into each other at the margins: definitions always produce their frontier disputes.

In Britain, as elsewhere, the origins of collective bargaining are to be found in other methods of job regulation; it did not rise like a phoenix out of the ashes of individual bargaining. Where it did not evolve out of internal job regulation, it usually came to be preferred to social regulation or to unilateral regulation by unions or employers. Social regulation was far too inflexible to suit a dynamic industrial society, and the two types of unilateral regulation had other disadvantages. They frequently led to conflict which they could not resolve, or lacked effectiveness without some support from the 'other side'. Unilateral regulation by unions still retains a marginal significance in our system, but it is mainly undertaken in defence of craft practices such as job demarcation.[14] Moreover, the tacit acceptance of these rules by employers over a long period makes them difficult to distinguish from the terms of unwritten collective agreements. State and tripartite regulation, on the other hand, have been employed principally to cover those areas of employment where organisation was inadequate to sustain voluntary collective bargaining. That they are regarded as inferior substitutes is best shown by two facts: they only establish minimum standards which can be improved upon by negotiated agreements; and they normally include built-in safeguards against their replacing such agreements.[15]

Where the British differs from most national systems displaying a similar preference for collective bargaining can be expressed in a simple factual statement, whose explanation leads to the formulation of the second leading principle. It has provided little work for lawyers. We take it so much for granted that industrial disputes will hardly ever find their way into the Courts, or that collective agreements need not be drafted with the precision demanded of legal documents, that we rarely give a thought to the reasons for our easy avoidance of litigation. There are two complementary halves to the explanation. Collective bargaining has been made the subject of little legal regulation, but it has also been afforded little legal support. And, by and large, the second condition has been readily accepted in order not to prejudice the first. It has been realised that greater legal support would most certainly bring greater legal regulation in its train.

There are various possibilities of legally supporting collective

bargaining, depending on the three conditions that have to be fulfilled for this method of external job regulation to exist as a viable
institution. First, the parties must attain a sufficient degree of
organisation.[16] Second, they must be ready to enter into agreements
with each other – a condition known as 'mutual recognition'. Third,
their agreements must generally be observed by those to whom they
apply. Sanctions are required to uphold each of these conditions.
Consequently, where private sanctions are lacking or not strong
enough for the purpose, the state can promote the growth of collective
bargaining by making legal sanctions available to replace or to
reinforce them.

One need not go outside the British Commonwealth to find
examples of countries where one or more of these conditions have
been enforced by law.[17] British law, by comparison, has occupied a
position of neutrality on the first and second of the conditions. In
the legal sense neither union membership nor union recognition is
compulsory in any circumstances. The standing of collective agreements is a more complicated question. In general they are assumed
to have no force in law, though rejection of legal support for their
observance has not been treated as a matter of principle. Occasionally it has been made available under special legislation, when the
parties wanted it and their case was strong enough.[18] Furthermore,
we now retain compulsory arbitration under permanent legislation
to make some of the terms of voluntary agreements binding on
employers who were not a party to them, but only in a selective and
temporary fashion.[19]

Our deep-seated reluctance to turn to the law for aid in maintaining
an institution rated so highly as to be looked upon virtually as a
social necessity is only explicable in terms of fear or dislike of other
possible consequences. To some extent at least, legal regulation of
collective bargaining is an inescapable outcome of its legal support.
Once collective agreements, for example, obtain the force of law,
disputes over their application or interpretation acquire a legal
character and can be referred to the courts. Hence the special
institution of Labour Courts in many countries where they have this
standing. Moreover, once the state has permanently accepted the
responsibility for upholding any of the above conditions, it is difficult
to resist its intervention to safeguard any public interest that the
bargaining parties are thought to be infringing. Their autonomy

is that much less secure. Thus the normative principle which under-pins the broad policy of legal non-intervention is really a preference for autonomy in collective bargaining, a principle best formulated by introducing a distinction between the two types of procedural rules that may govern its working.

The procedure of collective bargaining may, in fact, be regulated either by the rules which the parties make themselves or by rules that they are forced to observe by the state under statute or common law. The terms conventionally used to describe this distinction are 'voluntary' and 'compulsory'.[20] We distinguish between voluntary and compulsory arbitration, for example, according to whether the use of this method in settling a dispute lies wholly within the joint discretion of the parties or may be decided by the government, possibly at the request of one of the parties, but in any case without their mutual consent. *The British system of industrial relations has traditionally accorded a priority to voluntary over compulsory procedural rules for collective bargaining.*

This principle, which the main Whitley Report euphemistically described as 'industrial self-government', has also been referred to, more critically, as 'collective *laissez-faire*'. It is firmly rooted not only in the law relating to the government's powers in settling disputes, but also in the daily administration of the Ministry of Labour. It has as its corollary the minimisation of third-party intervention–of any kind–in the conduct of collective bargaining. In the words of the Ministry's *Industrial Relations Handbook*:

> It has been continuous policy for many years to encourage the two sides of industry to make agreements and to settle their differences for themselves, and no action . . . is normally taken by the Minister or his officials unless any negotiating machinery suitable for dealing with disputes has been fully used and has failed to effect a settlement. The overriding principle is that where there is a procedure drawn up by an industry for dealing with disputes, that procedure should be followed. Even where there is no agreed procedure of this kind it is desirable that the parties themselves should make an endeavour to reach a settle-ment. In either case some evidence of the use of procedure or of an attempt to reach agreement must generally be forthcoming before the Ministry will accede to a formal request for its assistance.[21]

Every country has in the last resort to protect its economy against large-scale disruption. It could be argued, then, that the absence for so long of more than minor legal restrictions on the right to strike and to lock-out[22]–other than during the years when temporary wartime orders were in force–has only been socially tolerable because the voluntary restrictions were reasonably effective. There is, of course, a certain amount of law appertaining to the actual conduct of industrial warfare, on picketing and intimidation, but no legal limits have been set to the extent of aggressive action on both sides. Nor are there in Britain, as in some countries, any enforced 'cooling off' periods. The harmful effects of settling industrial disputes by a trial of strength have been kept within acceptable bounds because written or unwritten procedural rules made adequate provision for their peaceful settlement and were generally observed.

This takes us to the third leading principle of the British system which, though equally unique, is not as easily recognised as the second. Again it can be formulated by stating a priority in the choice of rules. *The parties to collective bargaining in this country have generally preferred to build their relations more on their procedural than on their substantive rules.*

> Compare the way collective bargaining is organised in a large section of the British economy with the methods used elsewhere. Here all the emphasis is on institutions such as joint industrial councils and the like, on the machinery, its constitution, above all its procedure. The substantive rules about wages, hours and other conditions are not, as they are in many foreign countries, built up as a series of systematically arranged written contracts between employers and unions. They appear as occasional decisions emanating from permanent boards on which both sides are represented and sometimes they are informal understandings, 'trade practices' never reduced to writing. A very firm procedural framework for a very flexible corpus of substantive rules, rather than a code laid down for a fixed time–such is the institutional aspect of much collective bargaining in this country.[23]

At the risk of over-simplification, collective bargaining can be said to have two contrasting national modes of evolution, depending upon how the crucial condition of mutual recognition between the parties is fulfilled. Recognition may be based in the first instance on nothing more than participation in an agreed procedure for settling certain disputes between them and those whom they represent. When they begin to charter their relations in this way some substantive rules regulating wages and other conditions of employment are likely to be observed already; perhaps as custom, perhaps unilaterally determined by unions or employers. When disputes arise these rules may need to be revised or amplified and to be made the subject of formal written agreements. The alternative is to base recognition from the start on a specific code of substantive rules. But this has to be interpreted, enforced and from time to time altered, so it becomes expedient to regulate these processes by some kind of procedural agreement. As mature collective bargaining requires the making of both procedural and substantive rules, it might not seem to matter whether the first or the second mode of evolution was followed. Nevertheless the difference in emphasis is quite decisive. It reveals a preference that persists and has far-reaching consequences for the conduct of collective bargaining.

The reason for this is obvious enough when one considers the difference in the function of procedural and substantive rules. Procedural rules are intended to regulate conflict between the parties to collective bargaining. When their importance is emphasised a premium is being placed on industrial peace and less regard is being paid to the terms on which it may be obtained. Substantive rules settle the rights and obligations attached to jobs. Stressing their importance suggests that the main object is to achieve a precise regulation of employment contracts so as to avoid discrimination or uncertainty, even at the cost of increasing the risks of conflict. A comparison of the histories of collective bargaining in Great Britain and the United States, which illustrate the two different modes of its evolution, brings out the social influences which have caused the parties broadly to adopt different preferences in these countries.

Many features of collective bargaining in the British system are causally related to this third principle. The prevalence of 'open-ended' agreements, which run for no stated period and are only revised when either side presses for a revision, is one example.[24] The readiness to leave undisturbed a wide range of accepted but uncodified working practices is another. Most important, perhaps, is our lack of concern for the distinction between conflicts of interest and conflicts of right,[25] which is fundamental in European labour law, or between negotiation and grievance procedure as in the United States. So long as the agreed disputes procedure is followed through its various stages, we are not particularly interested in whether new substantive rules are being made or old ones applied; the main thing is to find an acceptable and, if possible, a durable compromise by means of direct negotiation between representatives of the two sides.

Its Structure and Values

The three normative principles of our traditional system have been stated. Together, for the best part of a century, they have made a particular type of collective bargaining–one that is subject to little legal intervention and tends to lean heavily on its procedural rules– the centrepiece and most characteristic feature of the system. But the principles alone have endured. In many other respects, of course, the system has been far from static. Apart from the increasing area of employment covered by collective bargaining and the extension of its subject matter, there have been important changes in structure. Foremost among these has been the displacement of district by national or industry-wide negotiations, a trend already existing but greatly accelerated by the First World War and taken further by the Second. One would have to delve deeply into history for an exhaustive examination of the causes of this structural trend, but it can be shown that the principles of the system favoured it.

In the first place it should be noted that the creation of national procedures for the settlement of disputes almost invariably preceded the conclusion of national agreements on substantive matters such as wages. The former, however, were welcomed by the parties in order to preserve their bargaining autonomy and to minimise outside intervention in their disputes. At the same time lack of legal support for their agreements forced them to rely on mutual accommodation and assistance to prevent their own extremists from wrecking their joint institutions. When the only sanctions available to ensure the observance of collective agreements were those that trade unions and employers' associations could bring to bear on their members, each side acquired a vested interest in the comprehensiveness and strength of the other's organisation.

Thus a condition best described as *industrial autonomy* has been the practical outcome of the system's evolution. Power to negotiate passed progressively from the branches and districts to the national headquarters of trade unions or their industrial federations, with national employers' associations gaining a corresponding authority. This placed both sides in a stronger position to prevent their freedom being impaired either by the state or by their own central organisations. Fundamental to the argument of this essay, however, is the thesis that the principles of any national system of industrial

100

relations – and therefore their institutional consequences – are derived from the values by which the nation judges and legitimises the system's working and results. The main values supporting the principles of our traditional system have been those of economic freedom and industrial peace.

The moral defence of the voluntary character of our system has always been conducted in the name of freedom. In spite of some mutual inconsistencies, its basic elements of freedom of contract, freedom of association, freedom to strike (and to lock out) and, above all, *free* collective bargaining, have been the ultimate rationale for rejecting outside, notably government, intervention in industrial relations. Trade unions may only have flourished at the expense of extreme versions of *laissez faire*, but they sought for workers a collective freedom that was not at variance with the prevailing ethos. If individuals should be free to pursue their own economic interests as they thought best, it followed that they should also be free to combine when they thought that combination would best advance their interests. Employers in responding to union pressures claimed the same freedom, and both sides joined forces in preserving their autonomy from encroachment. But in this they were not swimming against the general tide of political and social opinion. Governments were extremely reluctant – in times of peace – to accept any responsibility for fixing wages, and the public did not urge them to.

Freedom alone, however, could lead to a battle of interests that might threaten the stability of the system. The second value that justified its results was peace, which was taken to be the measure of good industrial relations. The general public asked little more of the relations between unions and employers than that they should be unobtrusive; that the machinery of collective bargaining, like any other machinery, should function with a minimum of friction. What the machinery turned out by way of end product – the actual contents of collective agreements – was of no concern to anyone but the actual negotiators and their constituents. Consequently the government's role was largely confined to that of peacemaker, which naturally included the fostering of voluntary arrangements. That it should also act as pacemaker was categorically rejected on all sides. Its job was to hold the ring, to see that the rules of the contest were respected, but otherwise to leave the contestants to fight, or rather to argue, it out.

Industrial Relations: What is Wrong?

In the one really prolonged period of severe strife in British industrial relations from 1910 to 1926–though it was interrupted by the special circumstances of the war years–criticism of the system did develop to the point of producing a great ferment of new ideas for its reconstruction. By then, however, its institutional freedoms were sufficiently well entrenched to withstand being seriously called into question. Even so, it is arguable that radical changes might not have been avoided but for the aftermath of the 1926 national strike, when for several decades the working days that we lost on stoppages were among the lowest for any free industrial country in the world.

There is no doubt that from the standpoint of industrial peace, our traditional system could claim to have outstanding merits. Compared with many other national systems it yielded two great practical advantages that endeared it as much to the unions and the employers as to the general public. They may be described as the advantages of flexibility and responsibility. As the rules regulating their relations, whether procedural or substantive, had not to be drawn up with the rigour and exactitude of legislation, the parties could leave themselves much greater freedom to adjust the application of the rules to the circumstances of individual cases, guided by the intentions rather than by the letter of their agreements. Equally, since they both made and enforced the rules with little or no outside intervention, the responsibility for the outcome was clearly theirs, and theirs alone. By permitting flexibility and encouraging responsibility the system favoured the peaceful settlement of industrial disputes. It induced a greater readiness to compromise and to stand by whatever compromise was reached.

Peace, it is true, though the main aim that the system was expected to serve, was not the only one. Society acknowledged some obligations to prevent the worst forms of exploitation of labour. Increasingly, as a more generous view was taken of what a nation owed to all its citizens, the state intruded more into industrial relations. Protective labour legislation was progressively improved. The Trade Boards, later to become Wages Councils, fixed a statutory floor to the wages of a growing number of workers. But this setting of legal minimum standards always remained marginal to the system as a whole. The state held back from forcing the pace in voluntary negotiations and from doing anything that would prejudice their autonomy. It merely

102

made good deficiencies left by the uneven spread of collective bargaining.

Why, then, are we less certain today than we were in the immediate post-war years about the virtues of this system? What has happened to make us change our mind that it had no serious faults, at least none that would not be corrected in the course of time? For one thing, it no longer seems to work as smoothly; friction is much more apparent. Although the number of working days lost on stoppages remains remarkably low,[26] over recent years there has been a mounting wave of what used to be known as 'industrial unrest'. Politicians blame rival parties for the malaise, and unions and employers accuse each other of failing to move with the times. But these are symptoms rather than causes, and the present tensions in industrial relations have deeper causes than is commonly supposed. The very principles of the system are being challenged, not out of a passing perversity, but because new values are current in our society. They have upset our established priorities yet meet with resistance from the structural inertia of existing institutions. Other standards besides economic freedom and industrial peace are being applied, but no consensus has been reached on them or on the institutional changes they require.

Even the growing controversy and confusion over the legal framework of industrial relations following the House of Lords judgements on *Rookes* v. *Barnard* and *Stratford Ltd.* v. *Lindley* are at bottom no more than a further symptom of other and more profound challenges to our traditional system. To their analysis we now must turn. Briefly, the system has been challenged from above and from below: from above by governments acting in response to practical economic difficulties and strong public pressures; and from below in the workplace by the rise of shop stewards and an upsurge of bargaining outside the scope of national regulation. In both respects something of the order that once prevailed has been disturbed by a growing chaos.

CHALLENGES FROM ABOVE AND BELOW

The departure of post-war governments, Labour and Conservative alike, from the confines of their earlier role in our industrial relations system has been largely associated with their efforts to restrain the pace of the upward movement of wages. Long before the need for a national incomes policy was fully and openly acknowledged–from Stafford Cripps' experiment with voluntary restraint to Selwyn Lloyd's pay pause–successive Chancellors have tried to influence the outcome of collective bargaining in ways previously regarded as taboo.[27] This record of nearly two decades of unprecedented government intervention in wage determination is, however, a sorry story of one temporary and temporising expedient succeeding another. Some measures proved wholly abortive; others had a passing success in slowing down wage increases but only at the cost of indiscriminate damage either to the national economy or to industrial relations. Above all, what has been lacking is any continuity in the development of policy and its means of execution.

Two questions may be asked about this post-war challenge from above to the accepted principles of our system. What has produced it? Why has it taken so long to induce a constructive response? To answer both it is necessary to say something more about the nature of the challenge itself.

It is still sometimes viewed in simple terms of how to avoid inflation in conditions of full employment. Governments have been forced to act, so it is said, because they owe it to the consumer to keep prices down. If this were indeed the only aim and justification for a national wages or incomes policy there would be little point in pursuing the notion any further. Although Britain may still be searching for the substance–as opposed to the pretence–of such a policy, other countries in Europe, notably Holland and Sweden, have had one; and it has not enabled them to prevent prices from rising for any length of time. Prices and wages may not have risen quite as fast in countries with some permanent national controls over incomes as in those without them, but price stability has not been achieved. It could hardly be otherwise. Individual countries are in no position to stabilise their own wage and price levels regardless of movements elsewhere, even if they thought it wise to do so. Nothing short of an unattainable international system of price and wage control could combine full employment and price stability in perpetuity.

We come nearer to the truth of the matter and cut through the layers of cant under which it is submerged, once we recognise that impending balance-of-payments difficulties have been the principal factor in pushing governments into action over wages. Whatever theoretical arguments may be advanced on behalf of a national incomes policy, the practical considerations that have forced it into the foreground of public attention have usually sprung from this source. Labour costs in export industries–rather than earnings in general or still less wage rates as such–have been the nub of the problem, and the main objective of government intervention has been to keep them competitive in relation to costs and prices abroad.

Alternative measures to an incomes policy which would not infringe the autonomy of the parties to collective bargaining were always available, of course, to cope with crises in the balance of payments. Both devaluation and import controls have been used to secure relief, but these at best are short-term remedies and invite retaliatory action by other governments which negates their effect. For a period the deflation of internal demand was strongly advocated on the grounds that, among other things, it would stiffen employers' resistance to wage demands and, by producing a 'little more' unemployment, diminish the unions' zeal in pressing them. This remedy was tried in 1956–8 and again in 1961–2, only to be rejected as being 'worse than the disease'.[28] Economic growth, which it hampered, was seen to be a major aim of economic policy. When added to the earlier trinity of full employment, price stability and free collective bargaining, it further complicated their reconciliation.

Painfully and slowly, by trial and an abundance of error, we are learning to accept the necessity of a national incomes policy. This implies no more, however, than a realisation that wages and other incomes must be brought within the scope of central control and national planning. It leaves open what should be the ends and means of policy and therefore such questions as which decisions have to be taken centrally and which can best be left as before to negotiation industry by industry. Yet as soon as the level of incomes is acknowledged to be an appropriate subject for government planning–as much, say, as the level of employment–governments can no longer, as they have in the past, throw off the responsibility for many questions relating to them.

Since wages cannot fairly be dealt with in isolation from other incomes, a national wages policy naturally broadens out into a national incomes policy; comparisons between the movements of all incomes are placed on the public agenda. Similarly, the general movement of wages cannot be controlled without questions of wage structure being raised on a national scale, if only because the control can be destroyed by pressures generated by unfair discrimination and indefensible relationships among the various rates. Nor can the relationship of earnings to rates be ignored or, for that matter, the relationship of earnings to labour costs. The logic of 'in for a penny, in for a pound' has an inescapable relevance once any decisions about wages are transferred from the market place or the negotiating table to the sphere of public policy.[29] Anticipation of this consequence has been responsible for much of the prolonged resistance to a national incomes policy.

Thus the challenge from above is, at bottom, rooted in a reluctantly acknowledged yet proven social need for national planning. This is not to deny that full employment has been the precipitating factor in creating it. By enhancing the bargaining power not only of trade unions but also of work groups within the firm, and by making it easier for employers to pass on rising costs to the consumer, it inaugurated the wage-price spiral. But it has been the effect of the spiral, especially on the balance of payments, which has invalidated the earlier assumptions on which the government's limited role in industrial relations was based. The balance of payments happens to be an aspect of the nation's economy where failure to plan has serious and unpalatable results for everyone. Difficulties in its adjustment could not be brushed aside by governments, whether their political ideology favoured the planning of the growth and distribution of incomes or not. The dogma boldly proclaimed as late as 1948, in the White Paper *Statement on Personal Incomes, Costs and Prices*, that it is 'not desirable for the Government to interfere directly with the income of individuals otherwise than by taxation' has now worn very thin indeed.

The formation of the National Economic Development Council was the first sensible move in the right direction because it located the new role of government towards incomes in its proper setting. For no incomes policy can be viable unless it is agreed among the three main parties concerned with its terms and execution. It cannot be imposed by a government alone, or by a government supported only by the employers or only by the unions. Nor can it be reasonably designed or find acceptance unless it is related to the whole of economic planning, since none of the parties can be expected to restrict the free pursuit of their own interests in ignorance of how the benefits will be shared. The change in terminology from 'wage restraint' to the 'planned growth of wages' which made it possible for a majority of trade unions to lend their support to a resolution favouring an incomes policy at the 1963 Labour Party Conference was no mere juggling with words; it shifted the emphasis away from a negative and discriminatory policy which the unions had good reasons to oppose. And now at last, with the signing of the *Joint Statement of Intent on Productivity, Prices and Incomes*, the foundations of tripartite agreement have been laid on which a stable structure of policy could be erected.

The proposition that the challenge from above has been an imperfect expression of a social need for national planning in a field where collective *laissez faire* was previously the rule, takes us well on the way to answering the two questions raised regarding it. The challenge has asserted itself with increasing force over the post-war years as the need for planning has become more and more apparent. In the last few years, with an awakened awareness of Britain's economic stagnation, we have also begun to grasp that government initiative in industrial relations is required on a much wider front than wages. The Contracts of Employment Act may have been only a small breach with tradition, but it was an important breach none the less. In it, however inadequately, the government implicitly acknowledged a planning responsibility to facilitate changes in the pattern of employment by reducing the insecurity which causes them to be opposed. The setting up of the Manpower Research Unit by the Ministry of Labour and the provisions of the Industrial Training Act pointed in the same direction. With these cautious and tentative steps, the old policy of leaving the two sides of industry to work out their own solutions to every problem, which often meant no solution at all, was gradually being abandoned.

One has only to contemplate the prospect opened up by automation and the introduction of other forms of advanced technology to realise how drastically the government's role in industrial relations will have eventually to be recast. Application of foresight being the essence of planning, the more disruptive of settled relationships technical innovation becomes, the more important it is to predict its social consequences in order to counter the less desirable. This cannot be done without some central direction to provide information and to settle priorities. Moreover, it is not only a question of anticipating the social consequences of rapid technological change, but also of making it possible by minimising social resistances to it. Nor should it be forgotten that a major contribution to a high rate of economic growth could come from diminishing our present massive under-utilisation of labour, which is a product of a range of employment practices in urgent need of reform. Voluntary action by unions and employers to deal with these problems may be preferable to sweeping legislative or administrative intervention by the state, but the time has passed when this preference will serve as an excuse for doing nothing, or too little and too late.

If, then, the challenge from above is no passing aberration but something firmly embedded in the circumstances of the second half of the twentieth century, why is it taking so long to arouse a constructive response? The short answer is that the values upon which our whole system of industrial relations has been erected obstruct such a response.[30] The challenge calls for general agreement on a transformed role of government which would qualify the autonomy of the parties to collective bargaining; and their absolute freedom has been treated as sacred. As long as this continued, government, employers and unions were each at liberty to protest their innocence and place the blame on the others for the lack of a national incomes policy and for the other shortcomings in industrial relations, because the basis for an agreed sharing of responsibility had not been found. 'Passing the buck' was a game that all could play because the system favoured it. This has been the most noticeable and regrettable contrast between Britain and a country like Sweden, where democratic planning may be far from perfect but has steadily, if pragmatically, advanced over several decades.

Before we go on to consider more precisely what kind of changes in our system are required to meet the challenge from above, we must look at the other great post-war challenge which has surged up from below with the growth of workplace bargaining. There is, of course, nothing new about collective bargaining in the workplace between management and shop stewards or other workers' representatives. Apart from its eruption into prominence in two world wars, a certain amount has always gone on, particularly over piecework prices and working conditions. But our system worked on the assumption that it was subsidiary to the bargaining conducted between full-time union officials and employers, whether on a local or a national basis.

108

Challenges from Above and Below

The assumption owed much to two decades of mass unemployment between the wars, which greatly weakened organisation in the workplace and forced trade unionists to concentrate their attention on holding the common defence line provided by a 'national rate'. This response to a particular set of circumstances came to be seen as a permanent and necessary feature of the system, to which trade unions and employers alike adapted themselves and their thinking. What stands out about the workplace bargaining of recent years is first that it has developed on a much greater scale than ever before, except under the special conditions of war. But it has also been a spontaneous development with its own independent momentum, so that it lies largely outside the control of trade unions and employers' associations. Far from being subservient to the system of external job regulation, it appears rather to threaten its stability. In other words it has assumed a form which is not so much an extension of the system as a challenge to it.

In this connection it is worth recalling that for some time after the war joint consultation, not collective bargaining, was expected to be the principal form for the future organisation of workplace relations. Even today there are firms where a consultative committee supplies the only recognised official machinery for them. Many procedural agreements, too, formally provide only for the taking up of individual grievances and complaints within the firm; that they may have a group or collective character is disregarded. Such facts may be cited as evidence of a lack of realistic anticipation of the challenge from below. When we turn to its most visible, statistical manifestations, these are principally unofficial strikes and earnings drift. Both reveal a weakening of the regulative effect of industry agreements. Both reflect what is fundamental to the challenge from below, the transference of authority that has occurred in the unions from full-time officials to lay workplace representatives.

Literally, unofficial strikes are strikes which trade unions have not officially sanctioned and which they therefore need not support. Usually it would be compromising for the unions to sanction them, however, because they are unconstitutional in the sense that they violate the industry's agreed procedural rules. That is why, if numerous, they represent a challenge to the procedure, a sign of its inadequacy, a weakening of its regulative effect. But we know that unofficial strikes are extremely eneven in their incidence as between industries

109

and within the same industry. Despite the notorious trouble spots, in many firms the rise of the challenge from below has not been accompanied by strikes.

Earnings drift is therefore a better indication of how widespread that challenge is. Drift is measured by comparing the percentage changes in average earnings and in official wage rates. So, to be exact, it is earnings gap – the resultant difference between the two – that measures the relative significance of workplace as opposed to industry bargaining in settling the contents of the workers' pay packets. Rough estimates have been made of the gap between nationally negotiated rates and earnings (excluding overtime payments) in manufacturing industries, and it rose from 19 per cent in 1948 to 26 per cent in 1959.[31] Over the same period average weekly overtime worked by men increased from about 2 to 4 hours, and by 1963 it was more than 5.[32] Together these figures give a measure of the extent of the growing failure in the arrangements for *regulating* actual wages *and* actual hours at industry level.

Admittedly, many national agreements are only intended to fix minimum rather than standard rates and it can be argued that the normal working week was always subject to overtime. But compared with before the war, when minimum were often near to maximum rates and average did not markedly diverge from normal working hours, the quantitative significance of independent workplace bargaining is now of an entirely different order and has completely changed the role of shop stewards or their equivalent. Where they had a part to play in our traditional type of collective bargaining, it was largely one of watchdog whose function was to see that union rules, collective agreements and customary practices were observed. Today they are negotiators in their own right and a substantial part of the workers' pay packets depends on their collective efforts and leadership. Moreover, in such matters as overtime, it is they who uphold the principle of 'fair shares' and are involved in the detailed administration of its allocation. Their greater authority over union members is derived from their representing the members' interests on important issues which full-time officials have little or no say in settling.

Not that earnings drift is the only foundation of the stewards' authority. One has only to study some of the issues that have led to (mainly unofficial) strikes to see that workplace disputes are not always about money. Referring to the Ministry of Labour's long-standing classification of reported disputes according to the stated issues in dispute, Professor Turner has remarked:

> In the twenty years of high employment from 1940 the proportion of strikes about 'wage-questions *other than* demands for increases', and (particularly) about 'working arrangements, rules and discipline' rose remarkably: from one-third of all stoppages to three-quarters. Now a close look at disputes so classified suggests that their increase mainly involves three types of demand. First, for what some have called an 'Effort Bargain'–that is, for the amount of work to be done for a given wage to be as explicitly negotiable as is the wage itself. Secondly, for changes in working arrangements, methods, and the use of labour to be also subject to agreement–or to agreed rules. And thirdly, they concern the treatment of individuals or groups by managers and supervisors. One *could* say that these disputes all involve attempts to submit managerial discretion and authority to agreed–or failing that, customary –rules: alternatively, that they reflect an implicit pressure for more democracy and individual rights in industry. But on this trend, the last two or three years have superimposed another: a sharp rise in the frequency of unofficial strikes against dismissals and–at last– for wage increases. So far, in effect, from reducing the frequency of unofficial disputes, recent unemployment and economic stagnation have increased it by outraging *now*-established expectations–expectations of security and an automatic annual increase in income, such as salaried employees commonly enjoy.[33]

These interesting observations are suggestive of the more fundamental causes of the challenge from below. Here again, as with the challenge from above, one must guard against the error of thinking that full or high employment is more than the starting point of an explanation. True, it was the change in the state of the labour market which helped to produce, or at least greatly to increase, earnings drift. Shortage of labour, we know, has caused employers to compete for it by paying wages higher than the national rates in many and devious ways, or by offering other pecuniary inducements such as fringe benefits that are not provided for in such agreements. Nevertheless, research undertaken on earnings drift in this and other countries suggests that it is not explicable simply as a market phenomenon. Its causes are far more complex.

It is certainly related, however, to another consequence of full employment: the transformation of power relations within the workplace. On the one hand, management finds that the negative sanctions which it had customarily employed to uphold its authority

111

are weakened; the strength of the ultimate penalty of the sack has diminished to the extent that workers can more easily find alternative employment. Management is much more dependent now on consent and voluntary co-operation, which entails the use of stronger positive sanctions or rewards. On the other hand, shop stewards have less fear of victimisation, and work groups can assert their collective will on a management which is decidedly more vulnerable to pressure when order books are full. One of the notable features of workplace relations in recent years, not revealed by strike figures, has been the increasing use of 'cut price' industrial action such as overtime bans, working to rule or going slow.

Clearly the challenge from below did not and could not develop against the earlier background of mass unemployment. But that is not to say that it can be attributed wholly to the direct and indirect effects of labour shortage. As Turner points out, up to a certain point an increase in unemployment now, instead of reducing the challenge, may augment it; because it is based in the last resort on a rising level of expectations among workers as to what industry owes them and they are entitled to obtain. These are partly expectations in regard to income including stability of earnings: they look forward to a continually rising standard of living and have entered into various commitments as a result. But equally they have new expectations as producers about the conditions of their working life. They are no longer willing, for example, to suffer individual or collective dismissal at the discretion of management or to accept its orders in a spirit of blind obedience. In many ways they are claiming a greater influence on managerial decisions, particularly in matters that affect their own welfare and status.

These changes in expectations reflect changes in the workers' opportunities to demand from management greater consideration for their interests, but together expectations and opportunities add up to a growth of democracy in the workplace. Democracy has many definitions but, in so far as it implies management by consent rather than by coercion, the challenge from below is a demand for it on the shop floor. This does not mean that every demand the workers care to make is reasonable and should be satisfied. There are other interests to be weighed in the balance and, in any case, conflicts of interests to be resolved among the workers themselves. The task of co-ordinating all the various demands that are made upon a business enterprise necessarily falls upon management. This is a responsibility which it cannot abrogate.

From the foregoing analysis of the challenge from below, it follows that, like the challenge from above, it will persist until it has been duly provided for by our system of industrial relations. But what does this imply? The crux of the problem again is one of agreement and the sharing of responsibility. In general, management and stewards have not yet come to terms with each other on the same durable basis that has been found for employer–union relations at higher levels, where the rights and obligations of the parties are reasonably well defined and respected, and where this full mutual acceptance is accompanied by subtle understandings of relative bargaining strengths and bargaining needs. New skills have to be learned in the workplace, just as they had to be learned for collective bargaining at the national level. Not having found this *modus vivendi*, the parties frequently engage in constant guerrilla warfare, each stealing what advantages their immediate position warrants. Bargaining and conflict can no more be avoided here than at any other level of industrial relations. They can, however, be contained within the bounds of agreed institutions which facilitate more rational settlements, provided always that the necessary skills are acquired for operating them.

THE SHAPE OF THE FUTURE

What then is wrong with our present system of industrial relations? Plainly it mirrors too much of the past and too little of the future, but having examined the two major challenges it now faces we can be more explicit than that. The system has to be reconstructed to accommodate more planning from above and more democracy from below. The silent revolution initiated by the transition from mass unemployment to full employment has forced us to consider new values for judging the system's methods and results. These in turn have placed new demands at both ends of the scale upon the organisations and institutions that comprise the system. As yet, however, no consensus has been reached on its future shape. Until this is settled in principle, neither the will nor the opportunity to get to grips with the manifold, detailed problems of reconstruction will be forthcoming.

Industrial Relations: What is Wrong?

One of the great difficulties in finding such a consensus is that of reconciling planning and democracy. Industrial relations are caught up in the same dilemma that confronts so many aspects of our economic, political and social life; the dilemma that is endemic to modern society. Only the extremists on either side deny that a reconciliation of the two is possible, but how is it to be accomplished? The freedoms that belong to democracy present themselves as obstacles to successful planning. The rationality implicit in planning appears to be an enemy of the sectional pressures unleashed by democracy. Many of the proposals advanced for reforming our system have failed to keep the dialectic character of the overriding problem in view.

When reconstruction of the system is approached mainly from the standpoint of national planning, it is taken to be axiomatic that trade unions and employers' associations must reassert control over their members' behaviour in the workplace. How can a national incomes policy work–it is asked–with a substantial amount of earnings drift? If the gap between earnings and rates continues to widen, it will undermine any agreement that may be reached on the general movement of wages, not least because some workers gain more from drift than others. This line of argument points to the proposal that industry agreements should be made more comprehensive in the subjects that they cover and more specific and stringent in their regulative content. As the dangers of evasion might then be greater, trade unions and employers' associations would need to arm themselves with stronger sanctions to discipline their members into compliance. The fact that members are unlikely to yield them such powers voluntarily leads further to the suggestion that the agreements should be made legally binding to ensure their strict observance.

Proposals based on such a theme have many variations, but they are all directed towards achieving greater centralisation of control in the system to restore order and to advance economic planning. Their Achilles heel is that they disregard the bargaining power that now exists on the shop floor. There may be a strong case for trade unions to exert more influence over their stewards' behaviour or for employers' associations to take more responsibility for the actions of their affiliated firms. It is quite unrealistic, however, to believe that independent workplace bargaining can be eliminated by external regulation. Even totalitarian systems have had to tolerate a certain

114

amount,[34] while in the United States the prevalence of remarkably comprehensive and legally enforceable plant agreements has not prevented the growth of 'fractional bargaining' between management and stewards, whose results are often at variance with the terms of those agreements.[35]

From the opposite point of view it has also been proposed that the whole apparatus of industry bargaining is now outmoded and should be dismantled or greatly reduced in its significance. Workplace bargaining is said to be in closer touch with the economic realities of the situation. It more accurately reflects the state of the local labour market and also permits the linking of increases in earnings with increases in productivity and so is conducive to reducing labour costs. Moreover, once attention is directed away from national negotiations–so the argument continues–there will be a better chance of codifying workplace relations in written agreements signed with the unions. Instead of dishonest evasions of standard rates and conditions, which have to be masked by the cloak of informality, we would then have clearly defined rights and obligations. In this event not only would order be restored; the whole system would become much more democratic. The rank-and-file union member would have a real say in determining the terms of the agreement under which he worked, compared with the present remoteness of formal union negotiations from the shop floor.

The advocates of a radical decentralisation of collective bargaining have a strong case when it is argued solely from the standpoint of industrial democracy, but once the need for national planning is considered their position becomes untenable. They defend it by claiming that the 'cost-push' element in inflation would disappear, or at least cease to be a source of anxiety, if wages were regulated solely by works or local agreements. The experience of the United States in periods of low unemployment does not support them. There, in spite of the predominance of plant bargaining, 'key bargains' have set the pace of wage movements throughout industries by comparisons which have been described as 'coercive'.[36] Nor does the experience of our own engineering industry, in which industry agreements are among the weakest in their regulation of earnings, suggest that unrestrained plant bargaining is an answer to inflation. It does not curb the force of comparisons in generating uncontrollable pressures for wage increases. On the contrary they are afforded greater play than in industries with better ordered wage structures. The truth is that the dismantling of industry agreements would make an unacceptable degree of state control the only alternative to the abandonment of any attempt at planning the growth of incomes.

Nothing less than a fully developed three-tier system of industrial relations promises to meet the challenges from above and below. We need a top tier of central or truly national negotiations above industry level and another bottom tier below for supplementary and compatible workplace negotiations. This is the first and most fundamental thing to be said about the shape of the future. In elaborating the point, what was said ten years ago about collective bargaining in the country still applies:

> As a method of wage determination the present weakness of collective bargaining lies mainly in its competitive, sectional character, in the difficulty the parties have in taking a broad enough view of the consequences of their bargains. As a method for introducing the rule of law and democratic participation into industrial relations its present weakness is due rather to its being conducted on too large a scale. Are we then faced with an irreconcilable conflict of purposes? There is a way out of this dilemma providing the voluntary system can escape from some of its present institutional rigidities. It has, in fact, to become more flexible so that agreements are concluded with a coverage appropriate to their contents. One of the clues to the future of collective bargaining is surely to be found in making a clear distinction among the appropriate levels of its regulative influence. In this as in many other aspects of economic organisation, we have to decide what is the concern of society as a whole, what should be settled on an industrial scale, and what is the affair of the employees in a single enterprise or a smaller group within it.[37]

It would be throwing out the baby with the bath water to reject our present structure of industry agreements because they fail to offer a complete answer to the demands of our time. Apart from the fact that trade unions and employers' associations would not contemplate abandoning them and only an all-powerful state could prevent their being negotiated, they still have many useful functions to fulfil. The question is how those functions are to be combined with both more centralisation and more decentralisation of the rule-making processes of industrial relations. How can two further tiers be added to what has officially become largely a one-tier system?

Naturally this depends on changes in the organisation on both sides of industry. The central bodies have to gain more authority and influence, and at the same time the relations between their affiliates and their members at the place of work need to be strengthened. The integration of the system has largely to proceed through this structure of representative organisations. But organisational change must be preceded by clarification of the purposes it is meant to serve. As a nation we are unlikely to advance in the right direction until we have a clearer idea about the future shape of national planning on the one hand and of workplace relations on the other.

At present we stand only on the threshold of economic and social planning in the field of industrial relations. The main impetus for embarking on it has come, generally, from a recognition of the importance of steady economic growth, and, specifically, from the work of the National Economic Development Council in setting targets in a growth programme. Thus economic rather than social objectives have been placed in the foreground, but they are so interdependent that we shall have to advance on both fronts, or there will be no advance at all. Similarly the two main subjects which have planning implications for industrial relations, incomes and manpower, are so closely connected that they have to be considered together. The crucial questions at this stage all turn on the type of planning which is feasible for this country in the near future, both as a technical and as a political proposition.

In the first place it should be realised that the breakthrough into planning hinges less on the government being granted extended powers than on its using existing powers more purposively. There has been no lack of government intervention in industrial relations in recent years, but it has failed by being erratic and short-sighted. It has expressed 'not neutrality but incompetence' because there has not been enough 'looking ahead' and use of powers with some 'sense of design'.[38] Insufficient knowledge partly accounts for these defects. The methods of forecasting economic trends have to be improved and supplemented by much more intensive research into the significant areas of change. Forecasting, however, is not simply an intellectual exercise; it must rest on policy assumptions. Agreement on policy which has a reasonable chance of being put into effect and therefore creates a climate of certainty and confidence is the ultimate *sine qua non* of successful planning.

This is not just a matter of the government having a mandate or a substantial body of public support for engaging in incomes and manpower planning. It has always been self-evident that any planning affecting industrial relations would not work unless it evoked the active co-operation of the overwhelming majority of trade unions and employers' associations. No government can hope to go it alone for long against the concerted opposition of either side of industry. Nor is there any prospect of a central planning authority, however it may be constituted, compelling individual unions and employers to fall into line with its decisions. Even when it includes responsible representatives of their central bodies, these possess no powers to force affiliated organisations to obey their instructions, and it would be unrealistic to anticipate their formal powers being substantially increased.

In these circumstances industrial relations planning must perforce be 'indicative', in the sense that it must rely on guidance rather than on direction. Guidance, however, can mean many things. In its 'soft' form of vague and pious exhortation with no sanctions to support it, it is little more than a face-saving gesture. Appeals for an undefined restraint we have had in plenty and their futility demands no further demonstration. An incomes policy to be effective in its application to wages and salaries must offer 'hard' guidance by being made explicit in rules formulated in a master agreement to which the government and the representatives of unions and employers subscribe.

The attainment of tripartite agreement on national policy that offers specific guidance of this kind presupposes, however, that it has to be bargained as well as discussed. Compromise is the essence of agreement at this level as much as in ordinary collective bargaining. While the representatives of unions and employers can be expected to take the facts and the consequences of the country's economic situation into account when they are fully and impartially presented, it is unreasonable to demand of them that they cease to act as advocates of the sectional interests of their constituents. The idea, for example, that economic arithmetic can yield some 'objective' formula for increases in wages or other incomes, thereby placing the content of policy beyond the bounds of argument, is a fiction that deceives no one who does not want to be deceived. Conflicts of interests over the division of the national product are inescapable; and in national, no less than industrial, negotiations union and employer representatives will naturally seek to get the best bargain they can for their own side. Moreover, as has previously been argued, even if it were possible to calculate the amount of a non-inflationary wage increase, domestic price stability cannot be the sole or even the overriding aim in incomes and manpower planning; there are several others with which it has to be reconciled including that of industrial peace.

The foremost aim, in fact, must be to reach agreement on guiding national rules which stand a good chance of being observed throughout industry because they are accepted as a fair and reasonable compromise for the time being. Probably some breaches will not be avoided. Provided they are not too serious or too extensive they are unlikely to undermine general observance. For it is not the case that these national rules will have no sanctions to support them. Once there is genuine agreement at the centre among all the three principal parties to industrial relations, they share a common commitment and responsibility for upholding the provisions of the policy to which they have agreed. This brings powerful social sanctions into play to uphold the rules; sanctions that are lacking in the absence of such agreement. In a system of industrial relations which has managed to depend so largely and for so long on social, rather than legal, sanctions for the observance of its rules, there is no reason to conclude that they will be less effective in the future than the past, or less applicable at national than industrial level. Besides, it is open to the government to use the range of economic sanctions at its command to support an agreed policy, apart from the pressure which it may put on prices to prevent undue increases in conflict with the policy. Finally, the central organisations on both sides of industry, though lacking powers of direction, have authority and influence over their members' behaviour which the very development of planning cannot but help to strengthen.

It appears that the aroused national awareness of the importance of achieving a steady and high rate of economic growth can most easily lay the foundations for this type of planning. By itself, however, acceptance of this aim will not suffice to settle all the policy questions arising. Speaking as the U.K. employers' delegate at the 1964 International Labour Conference, Sir George Pollock said:

> In origin, organisations of both employers and workers in the industrialised countries tended to be defensive. The unions were defending their members against social injustice and the employers were thinking in

terms of defending their position against the growing power of the unions. Today I believe that both are adopting a much less defensive and much more progressive and forward looking attitude. It is this new spirit of seeking *what we should do* in the light of *what we can do* which ... ought to condition our thinking in the I.L.O. for the years to come.[39]

This view of the future can only be understood as a plea for planning, since it stresses the deliberate determination of priorities. These involve choices for which economic growth is an inadequate guide.

As far as incomes policy is concerned, planning has to encompass more than the growth of wages. A choice has to be made among the alternative benefits that can be distributed among employees as the result of a particular rate of growth. It calls for decisions on what should be done in the light of what can be done. Are they to take the form of higher wages, or a shorter working week, or longer holidays, or better fringe benefits? A uniform national answer may not be desirable or practical, but central guidance on emphasis and trend cannot be avoided. Hours and holiday movements in particular tend to become fairly universal.

A similar problem arises in connection with wage differentials. To be acceptable, a national wages policy has to be considered fair, not only in relation to the movement of other incomes, but also as regards rates and earnings comparisons. No one seriously expects a precise measure of abstract justice, or that the results of history can be wiped out overnight. But income comparisons are continually being made and all the evidence points to their being the strongest force for instability in collective wage determination. In some, notably public, industries it has been found that within broad limits agreement can be found on standards of 'fair comparison' and that with their help wage differentials can be ordered. The refining and greater application of these processes, together with the settling of overall priorities in comparative wage movements among major groups, is a necessary part of incomes planning.

Enough, perhaps, has been said about the future shape of national planning to show in general how its grafting on to our existing system of industrial relations would be likely to affect industry-wide bargaining and other relations between employers and unions at this level. Planning would certainly not reduce their significance; if anything it would enhance it. The practical autonomy of the parties would not remain unqualified, it is true, whatever might be their position in law, otherwise planning would be an empty pretence. In making and revising their own agreements and in co-operating in other ways, they would be committed to the master agreements reached centrally on incomes and manpower policy; and they would be subject to various social and economic pressures to respect them. But as these agreements can only establish broad principles and priorities, as well as quantitative guidance on movements of wages and labour, their translation into appropriate and acceptable decisions industry by industry would still be indispensable. Collective bargaining would continue at this level, only it would be conducted within stated limits and with a knowledge of its national consequences. It would, so to speak, become more responsible and rational.

Planning, however, is very much more than the imposition of restraints. One of the main effects of an incomes policy on industry-wide bargaining is that it would give the parties more scope to address themselves to the long-term and constructive aspects of their relationships. Preoccupation with the amount of the next wage claim as soon as one settlement has been made, often following prolonged negotiations, has frequently crowded out attempts to deal with any other questions. Moreover, uncertainty about the future has inhibited agreement on them because of fears as to the balance of gains and losses in a few years' time.

But what of the future shape of workplace relations? How far should they retain their autonomy? And can that be made compatible with a superstructure of national planning and industry agreements? To answer these questions we must look at industrial relations at the place of work from their procedural and substantive angles.

The actual procedure followed in the settlement of disputes within individual firms or establishments is subject to little effective external regulation in this country. There is most of it in public industries, where employer and industry are one and national agreements produce more standardisation than in private industry. Otherwise the principal effect of an industry's procedural rules is to impose a peace obligation on the parties to workplace relations until the external procedure for conciliation, and possibly arbitration, has been exhausted. Though some industry agreements, as in engineering, mention the steps to be followed in internal disputes procedure, the parties are usually free to vary them according to their own preferences. So in practice we have a wide variety of different procedures, most of which are largely informal and the product of circumstances rather than of deliberate design.

There is much to be said in favour of this high degree of procedural autonomy in workplace relations. One of the most important tests of a good disputes procedure is whether it works to the mutual satisfaction of the parties; and they alone are the best judges of that. When so many factors peculiar to each firm or establishment, including personality factors, influence relations at this level, attempts to impose a standard pattern throughout an industry are bound to be artificial and cramping. The source of the malady lies elsewhere: too little thought has been given by managements to the *realistic* design of their relations with workers' representatives. This has been due in part to a mistaken belief, inherited from the past, that it is possible to find external solutions to internal problems. We see this illustrated in the frequent appeals made to unions to discipline their stewards when they are causing trouble The assumption is made that the existing external agreements with the unions supply an adequate code of agreed rules for the regulation of internal relations, and that all would be well if only the unions would insist on their members observing them, especially the peace obligation.

The fallacy in this belief is immediately apparent once it is recognised that the experience to which stewards and union members are reacting in the workplace is shaped, not by the unions, but by managements, by their decisions or lack of them. Management is apt to advance no proposals of its own for improving wages and working conditions, but merely to react to union pressures. It concedes nothing of substance until coerced by threats or a show of force, and then capitulates. When the lesson is made so clear that only coercion pays off, it becomes the very height of absurdity to ask the unions to prevent their members from acting on it. Unions cannot relieve managements of the responsibility for avoiding stoppages by providing alternative and more attractive methods of settling conflict at the place of work.

We must return, however, to our diagnosis of the challenge from below in order to appreciate the true contemporary dimensions of this responsibility. The challenge was traced back to a growth of democracy in the workplace. Managements have now to contend with demands from the shop floor for a say in matters which they have considered it to be their unfettered prerogative to decide. Ostrich-like they may, and often do, continue to proclaim their 'right to manage', meaning by this that their authority must not be questioned or opposed. For a time they may succeed in deceiving themselves into thinking that this right is unimpaired. In reality a situation prevails which R. H. Tawney once tellingly described as 'autocracy tempered by insurgence'. They dare not act in certain ways for fear of the resistance that would be aroused. What is worse, they probably have little or no knowledge of what they can or cannot do without incurring intractable opposition. So long as they avoid change, however, or change that seriously impinges on the workers' welfare, the web of fiction in which they have ensnared themselves can be given the semblance of truth. For it is change that highlights the need for consent, and consent means a sharing of authority expressed in the compromises necessary for operative decisions.

Managements cannot be prevented by law or collective agreements from indulging in self-deception. But the responsibility does fall squarely on them to see that workplace relations are governed by agreed procedural rules to facilitate the peaceful resolution of conflict. Many firms, no doubt, would claim that they have such rules, even where they have not been set down on paper. One has to inquire into actual relations on the shop floor to test the validity of this claim; to see how far two sets of procedural rules–the formal rules of management and the informal rules of shop stewards and work groups–diverge from each other. This is not apparent to the casual observer. A works or consultative committee, in which the unions participate, appears to be functioning with some success, and he takes it for granted that this is a joint institution. Yet it may be an institution imposed by management which stewards find it expedient to use as a platform, while following their own, officially unrecognised, courses of action to get results on issues of greatest moment to their members. The acid test of genuine procedural agreement is the extent to which the rights and obligations of the parties are known and accepted by all concerned, a condition that is not incompatible with avoiding the rigidities of excessive formality.

Internal workplace relations are no different in this respect from external employer–union relations. Uncertainty and insecurity of status are the enemies of stability and co-operation in both. In other respects, however, there are significant differences. Officials of trade unions and employers' associations meet occasionally, perhaps at regular intervals, to confer and to negotiate. Members of management and stewards have to live with each other from day to day as participants in the same working community. Their collective relationships are at once more continuous, more intimate and more intricate. Moreover, while for most purposes it is possible to view labour markets as having only two sides–buyers and sellers–this over-simplification is inapplicable to relations at the place of work, which are always many-sided. They involve a multiplicity of work groups, each with its differentiated interests even when they belong to a single union. Inside the plant, management–whether it admits this or not–is constantly engaged in a *multilateral* bargaining process.

Here the analytical theory of industrial relations comes to our aid in grasping the full scope of the problem. Systems of internal job regulation, it was suggested, have been developed to meet different purposes from those of external job regulation. While the latter have been principally concerned with regulating labour markets, the former have been directed towards regulating the work behaviour of employees. But systems of internal regulation comprise both the formal and informal organisation of the enterprise, the one corresponding with managerial and the other with human relation as these terms have been defined.[40] Because they serve distinct and sometimes conflicting ends these two types of organisation can never be fused into one, but they can become more closely integrated to the extent that their separate ends are made to overlap and complement each other.

In the past the typical state of the two types of organisation has been one of 'conjunction' rather than of 'co-operation'. They have existed side by side with their separate rules and, as it were, their separated spheres of interest. This is the situation, for instance, where workers uphold entrenched working practices of their own which management dislikes but does not challenge, whilst management insists on the observance of disciplinary rules which the workers do not approve but know they must obey to retain their employment. Peace may be maintained by both sides observing an undeclared non-aggression pact, but war soon breaks out when they trespass too far on each other's territory. No natural or social law makes a prolongation of this state of 'conjunction' inevitable. The possibility of 'co-operation' follows from the factual interdependence between the aims of a business enterprise, which management *qua* management has to advance, and the aims of its employees as persons. As Neil Chamberlain has pointed out: 'each party is dependent on the other, and can—as a matter of fact—achieve its objectives more effectively if it wins the support of the other. This means that when one party is seeking a change the better to secure some objective, it is more likely to succeed in its design if it anticipates what objections may be raised by the other party, *on whose co-operation in the matter depends the degree of its own success.* For such objections raise issues of divergent interest, and unless these are resolved it will prove impossible to define an area of common interest in which co-operation can be established. In order to win that co-operation, the initiating party may have to make concessions –greater perhaps than it considers "fair" or "just" and despite the fact that such concessions may be unnecessary as a matter of formal authority. They are made simply because, on their granting, co-operation is forthcoming which produces a greater advantage to the initiating party than would have been possible without them.'[41]

The key to the future of workplace relations in their procedural aspect lies in finding a realistic basis for co-operation on these lines. This entails more than formal agreement on an internal disputes procedure, more indeed than any code of rules can by itself provide. It presupposes a change of attitudes. For the 'real barrier to an agreement on divergent interests which would make co-operation possible . . . is a fear of co-operation itself'.[42] Managements fear loss of their authority; unions fear a lessening of their function and appeal; and employees fear increased insecurity resulting from improved efficiency. Given good will, none of these fears need to materialise but only the force of successful example is likely to overcome them. 'Co-operation will spread, if at all, by voluntary adoption being pioneered by those unions and firms that see in it a means of benefiting themselves. The vital factor here will be the willingness to take risks for potential gain by members of management, unions and employees who have confidence in their own powers of dealing with others, coupled with an intelligence and skill in inventing administrative machinery.'[43]

The substantive aspect of the future of workplace relations has its counterpart to the procedural. Earnings drift is not something that

125

we can ever hope to eliminate; nor is it to be condemned out of hand. Bargaining between managements and stewards is more likely to increase than to diminish. Progressive firms are devoting much more attention, for example, to devising better factory wage structures, and rightly so. These have to be based on other considerations than are appropriate to the settling of national rates for the purpose of regulating labour markets. And, wages apart, there are many issues of divergent interest leading to conflict in the workplace that are quite unsuited to uniform treatment throughout an industry. Indeed many of the 'new' subjects for collective bargaining, such as dismissals, discipline and promotion, are precisely those that are often best decided according to local circumstances and preferences.

The distinction between the purposes of external and internal job regulation is the clue to resolving the apparent dilemma arising out of the rival claims of planning and democracy. In some respects earnings drift is patently a threat to the success of incomes and manpower planning and the industrial regulation of labour markets. When employers engage in competitive bids for labour by offering veiled wage increases and fictitious overtime, they are undeniably undermining the purposes of external regulation. Yet they need the freedom to relate remuneration to changes in effort and in working practices if they are to raise labour productivity. It is not possible to obtain consent for change and agreement on the substantive rules regulating work behaviour unless inducements are offered. Only in the workplace can the regulation of work and of wages be made the subject of mutual adjustments to produce a 'productivity bargain',[44] which is the substantive equivalent of the procedural type of union–management co-operation already described.

An answer is offered once this distinction is grasped. Put in the simplest possible terms there is 'bad' and 'good' earnings drift. The first has little economic and no social justification: the second has both in good measure. Quite aside from the requirements of national planning, it is understandable that trade unions and employers' associations cannot regard with equanimity workplace bargaining that is subject virtually to no external control. Yet they should not and indeed cannot try to force it into a strait-jacket. Fortunately the choice is not between complete control and none; there is a golden mean in the form of permissive and enabling agreements at industry level.[45] These, while permitting wages to diverge from national rates, would stipulate the conditions under which this would be sanctioned.

We can begin to discern, at least in outline, the shape of a three-tier system of industrial relations which would meet the post-war challenges from above and below. In essence the whole of the problem of reconstruction can be reduced to two basic imperatives. The first is the need to find the possible terms of agreement among the interested parties at each level: national, industrial and workplace. Agreement cannot be imposed on them; it has to be bargained. At national and works level institutions have to be evolved which will reproduce the same kind of conflict-resolving co-operation and sharing in responsibility that has been built up steadily in the past at industry level. The second requirement is a clarification of the appropriate functions of job regulation at these three levels. We have to agree on a differentiation between those rules that are a necessary adjunct of national planning, those that should apply at the industry level and those which are best left to be settled at the workplace; according to the purposes for which regulation is required in each case.

No one can prescribe exactly how the existing institutions should be adapted in the light of these imperatives. What is wanted more than anything else at this stage is a general sense of the direction in which to travel, rather than a detailed route. But the view of the future presented here does preclude the false trails and misleading short cuts that are being suggested. Many of these turn on changes in the law. The growing disorder in our present system and the conservative attitudes of unions and employers have not unnaturally stirred up an interest in legislation as a means of speedy and drastic reform. Those who think trade unions are too powerful want to place legal restrictions on the right to strike or to ban 'restrictive practices'. Those who think them too weak would like to see the law assisting them in increasing their membership and in securing recognition from employers. Other proposals advanced include the legal enforcement of collective agreements and compulsory works councils.

The point is missed that it is not the so-called voluntary character of the British system which is the source of its present malaise. Rather does this remain its strength. Certainly we are not compelled to abandon our long-standing preference for avoiding the rigidities and complications of legal solutions to industrial problems. Neither the challenge from above nor the challenge from below calls for such an answer. On the contrary we can be sure that changes in the law will not produce the kind of co-operation and consensus that the reconstruction of the system demands. That is not to say that the law can remain as neutral or as marginal an influence as in the past. The positive planning role that the government and the central organisations on both sides of industry have now to fill has its legislative consequences. This raises many questions that cannot properly be examined here, but these consequences are most likely to be found in the setting of new national minimum standards to ensure that the pace of voluntary action is both forced and under-pinned.[46]

One final observation must be added. Nothing has been said here about the changes required in the organisation and activities of trade unions and employers' associations, although clearly the reconstruction of our system of industrial relations cannot be accomplished without them. This omission has two defences. The first rests on the essay's leading thesis. The necessary changes will only be brought about when the new values implicit in the demands for national planning and workplace democracy are fully worked out and accepted as a basis for the system's reconstruction. Structural inertia has been overcome before, but not until the necessity for change and the direction it must take have been perceived with clarity and conviction. The second defence is also one of the most important practical conclusions to be derived from the diagnosis of the challenges to our system. The primary responsibility for changing it rests on the government and on managements. Only the government can create a viable system of national planning. Only managements can introduce well-ordered and co-operative systems of workplace relations. Trade unions and employers' associations are most likely to put their own houses in order when they have to respond to bold but enlightened initiatives from above and below.

THE INTERNAL SOCIAL
RESPONSIBILITIES OF INDUSTRY
(1966)

INTRODUCTION

Is it a good thing for industry to bother about its social responsibilities? For a long time it ignored them and found a rationale for this neglect in the 'dismal science' of economics. When, after the work of Elton Mayo and his colleagues, these intellectual defences were breached and 'the end of economic man' had been proclaimed, industry became increasingly concerned with questions of morality and with its obligations towards its employees and the community. A few years ago the inevitable reaction to this trend set in, when the influential *Harvard Business Review* published an article on the dangers of business attempting anything other than to maximise its profits. 'In the end,' wrote its author, 'business has only two responsibilities, to obey the elementary canons of everyday face-to-face civility and to seek material gain.' When companies interested themselves too much in their social responsibilities they were liable to transform 'an important and desirable economic functional group into an all-knowing, all-doing, all-wise father on whom thousands became directly dependent for cradle-to-grave ministration. This is the kind of monolithic influence the corporation will eventually have after it becomes so occupied with its social burden, with employee welfare and the body politic.'[1]

This attack cannot be brushed aside as being merely an exuberant expression of a belief in 'free enterprise' which is part of American folklore. The dangers to which it refers are real. Theories have been developed which taken to their logical conclusion raise totalitarian claims on behalf of the business corporation: either alone or in conjunction with the trade union, it is expected to provide the worker with his 'society', one that will satisfy all his basic social interests outside the family.[2] At a practical level, too, it is alarming in the extreme to see big business using the immense funds at its disposal

129

to propagate for commercial motives its views on what is right personal or social behaviour. When this is accompanied by deliberately strengthened material ties of dependence which encourage uncritical acceptance of these views, even by political manipulation masquerading under the guise of high ideals, the prospect is more repulsive than the brutal but open forms of economic exploitation we have known in the past.

One can readily agree that 'the business of business is business; economic business to create economic values and to minimise economic costs'.[3] Industry is made up of associations with economic ends–not political, social or cultural ones. Regardless of differences in their legal form or underlying reality, all business enterprises are constituted chiefly for the purpose of distributing incomes by producing marketable goods or services. They have therefore to survive tests of economic viability whether these are imposed by the markets in which they operate or, in the case of public enterprise, partly by the state. Similarly, the work which people perform in industry is undertaken primarily for its material rewards, not for its own intrinsic interest; to enable them to earn their living or, if they are fortunate, to accumulate wealth.

This has to be stated clearly if we are to see industry's social responsibilities in their proper perspective. To recognise that industry has such responsibilities does not imply that it should be run as a charity or to serve some social cause. Its social responsibilities arise, in fact, out of its choice of means rather than its choice of ends. Every society, even during the heyday of *laissez-faire* capitalism, has always set some social, and by implication moral, limits to the means that might be employed in the pursuit of economic values. Apart from excluding the use of violence, dishonesty and fraud were invariably penalised to greater or lesser extent. Today, moreover, there are few societies without some protective labour legislation to fix minimum standards, especially for the employment of women and children, or which do not seek to curb manifest public nuisances such as the pollution of rivers or other industrial hazards to safety and to health.

To act responsibility, however, means to take into account the consequences of one's action for others as well as for oneself–*all* the reasonably foreseeable consequences. Whether a nation in its law takes a broad or a narrow view of what it regards as anti-social activities on the part of industry, we can be sure that the mere observance of its legal obligations is never a sufficient acknowledgement by industry of its social responsibilities; often the things most worth doing no law can demand, still less effectively enforce. The full scope of these responsibilities is only revealed by the facts of the situation. These show in what ways the means employed in the pursuit of economic values have other than economic results, how they affect the whole of the life of man besides his material welfare.

One way in which the decisions of a business enterprise are seen to have social as well as economic consequences is in their effect on the local and national communities of which it forms an integral part. A local community, we know, has sometimes been destroyed by the closing down of an uneconomic enterprise. The location chosen for the site of a new factory may, if it is large enough, have all kinds of national, as well as local, implications for housing, education, and other social services, even, in some countries, for 'race relations'. Illustrations need not be multiplied of what is widely recognised today: that industry has some social responsibilities because its decisions have manifest social consequences.

It is worth remarking that growth in the scale of industrial associations has probably been the most important single factor in forcing this obvious, but long-neglected, conclusion upon the public mind and into the political arena. When a small business goes bankrupt, no one is likely to be deeply disturbed apart, possibly, from the owners. When a large corporation, which may otherwise be flourishing, loses a contract and dismisses thousands of workers, this is likely to stir up a storm of protest and may have serious repercussions for the government. The attention paid by large firms to their public reputation and their public relations activities reflects their awareness of the social consequences of their decisions, though not necessarily an adequate acceptance of the attendant responsibilities.

Granted that industry in spite of its economic ends has, for the reasons stated, certain social responsibilities, it is possible to separate them into two broad categories. For want of a better description we might call them external and internal. Industry's external social responsibilities are those which it should meet towards society at large, including of course the consumers of its products. Its internal social responsibilities, with which this essay is exclusively concerned, are for what it does *to* the people that it employs, a very different

131

conception incidentally from what it does *for* them. Here again, while it is clear that as a rule men seek industrial employment for its economic return, what they experience in the course of their work affects them in many other ways. Though only part of a man may be used in industry–with increasing subdivision of labour often a very small part–all of him comes to work and, since personality is indivisible, his experience there cannot but fail to diminish or to enlarge him as a person. This applies both to the content of his particular job and to the character of the social relations in which it involves him. As long as paid employment remains a major and overriding claim on his time, each of these aspects of his work is likely to condition his attitude towards life and society.

THE WORKER AND THE FIRM

In the absence of slavery or forced labour, the relationship between the worker and the firm where he finds employment is generally thought of as being a contractual one. Certainly it has always been given some kind of contractual foundation in law. Apart from those imposed by statute, the legal rights and obligations between employers and employees have either been explicitly stated in the individual contract of employment or can be read into it as implied. The doctrine of freedom of contract assumed that they met as equals in the labour market and voluntarily entered into a bargain on the terms which work would be exchanged for wages, because it was to their mutual advantage to do so. The law for its own purposes has accommodated many fictions and this is one of them.

There is the familiar point that the resources of the employer were invariably greater than those of the individual employee, so that the latter bargained from a position of weakness–of extreme weakness in the presence of severe unemployment. No less important, however, was the fact that the very nature of the obligations accepted differed profoundly on the two sides. For an employment contract is not only an economic bargain on a par with the sale of a commodity in a product market or the payment of interest for the use of capital. In return for the price which the employer is prepared to pay for his labour, the employee surrenders control over a large part of his life. The employer 'makes a payment in money which he confidently expects to recoup and which, therefore, rarely involves any personal

132

sacrifice or deprivation'. Indeed, where 'the employer is a corporate body, such as a company . . ., no personal involvement or sacrifice arises in giving employment. The employee, on the other hand, makes a personal sacrifice of his freedom.'[4]

One can, it is true, overstate this loss of freedom in industry, although it is one of the foremost characteristics of wage labour. Craftsmen, for example, have often retained considerable freedom to decide how their work was to be performed, while having to submit to an external discipline which governed other aspects of their behaviour during working hours. In general, modern industrial sociology has drawn attention to the so-called 'informal organisation' of a business enterprise, based on the work groups which emerge as social units within the plant. In contrast to the 'formal organisation' designed by management to further the impersonal ends of the enterprise, this is created by the employees themselves to serve their own ends as persons, and consequently maintains an element of self-government in industrial employment by providing a collective defence of certain freedoms which management may be powerless to infringe.[5] There is, in fact, an inevitable lack of precision on the work, as opposed to the wage, side of the employment contract. It is within this area of discretion, which varies according to the methods of production and the type of work, that the workers' own protective institutional controls have found scope for development.

Even so, any idea that in market economies employers and employees enter into relationships on a basis of freedom and equality cannot be sustained. The progress made in overcoming the degrading effects of an unbridled competition for jobs in labour markets has been built upon its rejection. Part of the case for trade unions was the employees' need for organisation if they were to redress their position of bargaining inequality. But the growth of collective bargaining which followed did not only help them to drive a better bargain with their employers on wages and working conditions. Its great and enduring social achievement has been to create 'a secondary system of industrial citizenship parallel with and supplementary to the system of political citizenship';[6] or, in another opinion, to recreate 'a society based on status' instead of the one we have known 'based on contract'.[7] The effect of collective agreements has been to establish rights for workers in industry, rights permanently attached to jobs.

The Internal Social Responsibilities of Industry

Where voluntary organisation has proved to be inadequate to sustain collective bargaining, the state has increasingly intervened either to support it by legal sanctions or itself to regulate labour markets by fixing minimum standards of employment. The other great social change which in many highly industrialised countries has further modified the earlier relationship between the worker and the firm has been the achievement of an enduring condition of high or full employment. In free societies this has been the outcome of a rather reluctant acceptance of national planning, intended in the first place to deal with cyclical fluctuations in the economy but gradually and inevitably extending into other realms, including incomes and manpower. This has meant, especially where it is combined with fairly high degrees of trade union organisation, that the balance of power between employers and employees has been shifted very much more in the latter's favour. The trade unions have also gained a new place in society and its economic government which gives them a greater voice in the nation's affairs.

Although these developments are more marked in some countries than others and there are, in any case, vast differences in the workers' conditions and status as between the rich and the poor countries, the question arises whether in the most favourable conditions the internal social responsibilities of industry are now being adequately fulfilled. The answer one gives to this question must depend on a clearer definition of these responsibilities than has been attempted so far. Responsibility, however, is a function of power. It follows that we must first decide where power in industry lies.

THE POWER OF MANAGEMENT

Nowadays in some countries trade unions have acquired considerable power in industry and one would have to be very partisan to assert that this power is always used responsibly. They may abuse their power in two, rather different, ways. A trade union may seek to protect or to advance the interests of its members without paying any regard to the effect of its action on other workers and the rest of the community; perhaps by obstructing necessary change, perhaps by pressing for more than its fair share of wage increases. It may also employ the power of its organisation to override groups or individuals in its own ranks with genuine grievances and com-

134

plaints. If the first results from a lack of social conscience, the second could be regarded as failure in its internal democracy. The fact that trade unions serve a valuable and necessary social function is not a satisfactory reason for ignoring either of these problems, but their discussion has to be conducted against a background of the precise circumstances of the case. To generalise on this subject, even within a single country, is quite impossible. Moreover, this is a question of the social responsibilities of trade unions, not those of industry, and we should not confuse the two.

If we return, then, to the freedom which employees are paid to relinquish in industrial employment, the decisions they have to obey as a result are taken by management. The management of a business enterprise, regarded for the present as a collective entity, represents its government; on behalf of the enterprise it rules the lives of all employed in it during their working hours. The power of management resides in its function–that of deciding about the use of resources, human and material or, what commands them both, financial. This function has no necessary or unique relationship to the ownership of any of these resources. The relationship, such as it is, depends on the legal form of a particular business enterprise and generally on the rights attached to ownership by law or custom. Where management is, for example, made legally accountable to a meeting of shareholders or to the members of a co-operative society or to any other body, this does not transfer its power to them; it only provides some kind of control, of greater or lesser efficacy, over its use. The power remains with those who take decisions, though their freedom in using it is contained. The worker, too, if one likes to put it that way, continues to own his own labour, only management, again within limits, decides about its use.

The source of the power of management is not ownership as such but organisation. In this respect it resembles any other bureaucracy–be it in an army, a public authority, a government department or a trade union–whose power is related to the authority assigned to it (or which it is able to acquire in practice) within the organisation in question. Obviously the transfer of an industry or a single enterprise from private to public ownership does nothing in itself to diminish the power of its management. It may, of course, lead to a change in the managers, or in the policies that they are expected to follow. The system of accountability undoubtedly does not remain the same.

But these are all matters relating to control over the uses of power, not to its source or, what is more, to its distribution.

As all business organisations of any scale have a hierarchical structure, it is really misleading to refer to management as a corporate body. The power of a supervisor may be negligible–not infrequently less than that of a shop steward. Together the scale and the structure of the organisation settle the extent and the distribution of power within it. Regardless of forms of ownership, a combination of large-scale organisation and centralisation of decision-making will result in massive managerial power at the top. From the 'worm's-eye view' of the man on the shop floor the authority to which he is subject appears just as remote and indifferent to his welfare whether he works in private or public employment. Hence the widespread modern concern with 'communications' and 'human relations' in both sectors to overcome the difficulties in labour relations which have resulted from the growth in the size and complexity of business organisations.

So, discussion of the internal social responsibilities of industry really turns on the responsibilities of management at different levels; or rather on those which it has in managing people because of the effects of its decisions on their lives. On this, one important observation must first be made, if only because social scientists are inclined to overlook it. In some degree the problem of power confronts every individual manager, from the director down to the foreman, with a personal and moral problem. Once anyone belongs to management he invariably has some area of discretion in which his own decisions will have human and possibly, if only in a small way, social consequences. Taken to extremes 'organisation man' is a figment of the imagination because no type of organisation can wholly determine the behaviour of its members, including those with authority within it. When that has been said, however, we must proceed to the wider social aspects of the subject by considering how the several institutions of control may curb the uses and abuses of managerial power.

THE INSTITUTIONS OF CONTROL

The various social controls that are to be found over the power of management fall into four different categories: control by the market; control by countervailing power; control by the rule of law;

and control by accountability. Let us look at each of them in turn to see whether they can suffice to prevent possible abuses of managerial power.

In a free society the ultimate sanction which enforces discipline within a business enterprise is dismissal, expulsion from it and consequent loss of employment. The strength of that sanction for each employee depends on his chances of finding alternative employment, whether this employment is likely to be as rewarding, and what will be his losses, if any, in changing jobs. Consequently the state of his particular labour market, including ease and costs of mobility as well as the rate of unemployment, decides the magnitude of the power that management has over him. The market is therefore one of the social controls over managerial power. It operates to the full when an individual employee can choose among employers and freely decide for whom he prefers to work.

Control by countervailing power means no more than that management may meet with organised resistance in carrying out its decisions. Trade unions may organise that resistance in the form of strikes, or they can bring pressure to bear on employers in negotiations when the possibility of their resorting to strike action is enough to establish their bargaining power. But smaller groups of employees within the firm may also resist the decisions of management, and sometimes do so effectively, irrespective of union approval or support. An unofficial or 'wildcat' strike is an example of such resistance; but equally it may be expressed in less overt forms of organised action, such as slowing down the pace of work.

The third control is often confused with the second because to some extent it has evolved out of it. In labour relations, control by the 'rule of law' is more than control by legislation. Every instrument of regulation that compels management to respect rules in making its decisions has to be included: the provisions of collective agreements and unwritten custom and practice as much as the statutory requirements of protective labour legislation. Even the rules which management makes unilaterally regulate its use of power, though it is not a matter of indifference to workers whether they have participated in making these rules. Only then have they any assurance that their interests have been taken into account and can they feel any responsibility for seeing that the rules are observed.

Taking these three controls together, it is clear that in most of the advanced industrial countries they have been progressively strengthened during the twentieth century. Managers have usually to reckon with losing some of their workers if they become too dissatisfied with their treatment. Managers have to allow for the possibility that they will have a strike on their hands if they antagonise any group too much. Managers are now much more circumscribed in their actions by the provisions of legislation or collective agreements. Given these circumstances it would be ridiculous to pretend that workers are the helpless victims of managerial power. There are, indeed, managements who genuinely believe that the boot is on the other foot, that they are far too much in the hands of the workers they are supposed to manage.

Yet before any exaggerated claims are made on behalf of these controls, it should be pointed out that all of them are negative in their effect. That is to say, they impose certain limits on management's freedom of action, restrictions on how it may use its power. Provided, however, those restrictions are respected management can manage as it chooses. None of these controls offers the workers any share in deciding their industrial destiny; they are protective more than participative. No worker has any reason to feel any responsibility for the conduct of the enterprise that employs him by virtue of their existence; nor has he any stake in its success. If by democracy is meant not only the division of power which we have in any pluralistic society but participation of the governed in government, they do not necessarily contribute to industrial democracy.

This brings us to the fourth control on managerial power, that of accountability. It differs from the rest in not being merely negative. It is intended to do more than check abuses of power and to control instead the purposes for which power is used. It works through questions, reports and criticisms, but also in the last resort by the application of sanctions. If control by accountability is to work, those who are responsible for taking decisions must be movable, and in the last resort removable, by those to whom they are accountable. In democratic politics governments are made accountable for their actions to the legislature, but it is the people's vote at elections which gives them the opportunity of applying sanctions, of removing a government which in their judgement has failed.

One of the great criticisms advanced against the present legal position of the joint stock company is that in law its directors are accountable only to its shareholders and to none of the other interests affected by their decisions. 'The human association which, in fact, produces and distributes wealth, the association of workmen, managers, technicians and directors, is not an association recognised by the law. The association, which the law does recognise, the association of shareholders, creditors, and directors, is incapable of production or distribution, and it is not expected by the law to perform these functions.'[8] 'I foresee that one of the great tasks before us in the coming years is to modify the company system. The aim would be to see that directors were no longer regarded by the law as managing on behalf of the shareholders only, but were regarded as representatives of all vital interests. The method of appointment should be such as to secure this representation.'[9]

Strangely, in spite of such eminent comment, there is still no noticeable swell of public or political support in Britain for changing company law to extend and strengthen managerial accountability. Detailed proposals to this end have been formulated by George Goyder, who suggests reforms that would 'bring the voice of workers, customers and the community into the counsels of big business, not as of grace, but as of right'.[10] His main proposal is for a new type of limited liability company to be known as a Participating Company. It would have a General Purpose Clause in its articles specifying its social responsibilities; workers would be made members of the company and enjoy parallel rights to those of shareholders; dividends would be subject to compulsory limitation; and provision would be made for an independent social audit of its activities.

The present state of company law is indefensible either in logic or in justice. It reflects a view of property rights—that ownership of a firm's material assets gives exclusive entitlement to ultimate control of its activities—which has no relevance to the facts of the modern world. Doubt arises, not on whether the law should be reformed, but on what its reform will accomplish. Will, for instance, extending the legal accountability of management by providing for representation of workers on boards of directors really do much to alter their present status in industry? We have some experience to guide us and it does not induce optimism about the results.

The Internal Social Responsibilities of Industry

Take first the case of the nationalised industries. Though they may have many achievements to their credit, no one would seriously claim that the status of workers within them has been raised appreciably above the level of what exists in the best of private enterprise. Yet private shareholders have been excluded altogether and management of the industries has been made subject to a general public accountability instead. It has further to answer specifically to representatives of consumers and workers through consumers' councils and arrangements for joint consultation. Yet one socialist comment, characteristic of many, has been that: 'The public corporation does not appear to be satisfactorily accountable to anyone.'[11]

Notable experiments in private enterprise designed to make management formally more accountable to the managed do not appear to have yielded very different results either. In a few small firms, where there has been a full and fair sharing of the proceeds, a genuine spirit of partnership may have prevailed, but here the problem of managerial power can hardly be said to exist. The founder of the large John Lewis Partnership expressed the trinity of his objectives as the sharing of gain, the sharing of knowledge and the sharing of power. Without prejudging the results of a research project which is meant to discover what the Partnership means to the Partners,[12] it can be said that, while the first objective is substantially achieved, the second presents greater difficulties and the third remains largely an aspiration.

The Glacier Metal Company, due to the initiative of its remarkable Chairman and Managing Director, has developed representative and legislative systems in its management together with an appeals procedure, which provide for a high degree of internal accountability and control. Yet in a recent study, in which he sets out his own conclusions from all the novel and radical developments which have taken place in his company over the past twelve years or so, he has still to declare his disappointment with 'the split at the bottom of the executive system' which remains an unresolved problem. The workers 'dissociate themselves psychologically from their daily work' and become identified with aims centred elsewhere outside the workplace. They prefer to use their own representatives (shop stewards and work councillors) to take up complaints rather than supervisors. The relations between operators and supervisors are, indeed, 'of a different order' compared with those between supervisors and their next superiors in the managerial hierarchy.[13] In short, there are still 'two sides' in the company and a big gulf exists between them.

The most significant European experiment in extended accountability, if only because of its scale, is the system of codetermination in the German coal and steel industries. German company law provides for two bodies with authority at the top. There is a Supervisory Council (*Aufsichsrat*) meeting at fairly long intervals to which in the past the stockholders delegated their authority. This has very limited control functions, mainly those of authorising large capital expenditures and appointing key personnel, but with no power to determine the details of managerial policy. The real seat of managerial power is a second body, a Board of Management (*Vorstand*) appointed by it, which actually runs the concern. In coal and steel the trade unions secured, as a result of their pressure, a law which gave the workers parity of representation with the owners on the Supervisory Council, usually five a side; a so-called 'eleventh man' was chosen by the other ten under an extremely complicated procedure to hold the balance. The other main provision of the law, and one to which the unions attached great importance, was that there should be a Labour Director on the Board of Management. He is nominated by the union and workers' representatives on the Supervisory Council and legally has parity of responsibility with the Commercial and Technical Directors, the other two members of the Board.

This scheme, it was originally believed, would not only give the workers a decisive voice in management but lead to joint decision taking or codetermination. Critics said it would never work; management would be crippled by a constant series of stalemates or hair-splitting decisions. This has not happened, but for an interesting reason that was brought out in an early American study of experience in the steel industry:

. . . the decision-making process under codetermination did not, in practice, conform to the provisions of the law. 'Joint' decision making without much controversy and with few voting deadlocks was possible largely because labour and management did not, in fact, share fully in all important decisions. In order to make codetermination operative, the managerial and labour sides resorted to a form of collective bargaining under which primary spheres of interest were allocated to each group. Labour was given a preponderance of power over wages and working conditions and management, in return, retained its unilateral authority to act on most other matters. Through bargaining or 'horse trading', an accommodation was effected which satisfied the major interests of each group by *dividing* rather than by sharing decision-making powers. Labour, in practice, relinquished many of its stated rights in return for special concessions and powers in one area of company activities.[14]

It is generally accepted that codetermination has helped to improve communications between management and workers and has raised standards of personnel policy in the German coal and steel industries. But similar results have been achieved in other countries through collective bargaining and direct union pressure on management. Much can be said in favour of this great social experiment in the German context; none the less it belies its name. It has not led to joint decision taking. Nor has it radically improved the workers' status in industry. Hence its description as 'a sheep in wolf's clothing'.[15]

The lesson to be drawn from the experience of controlling managerial power by extending the formal institutions of accountability is not that these arrangements have no value. It is rather that at best their value falls far short of the ideological claims made on their behalf. They have not diminished the feeling of there being 'two sides' in industry. They have not notably strengthened the workers' desire to participate responsibly in management. Above all, they appear to leave managements behaving much as they would without such arrangements. Two reasons can be advanced in explanation. The first is that control by accountability to be effective presupposes broad agreement on the purposes which those who are entrusted with power should follow; and this is usually lacking within industry. The second is that in large-scale organisations management necessarily enjoys a high degree of autonomy, whatever arrangements may be made for its accountability.

LIMITS OF INSTITUTIONAL CONTROL

In any organisation, unless what is asked of those who are placed in positions of authority is known and agreed by those to whom they are accountable, accountability as a control breaks down. If standards for judging their performance are uncertain or in dispute, the institutions of accountability simply become another arena for the conduct of a power conflict. When this does not wreck them (as has happened on occasions) the conflict is settled either by *ad hoc* bargaining and compromise or by a division of spheres of interest. While that may be preferable to disruption, it does not mean that purposes are shared or that accountability works. In internal trade union democracy, for example, the officials may be made genuinely accountable to the members where the latter are in broad agreement on what they expect of their officials, say in presenting a wage claim. When, on the other hand, trade union leaders make pronouncements on political issues their personal views often have a much freer rein, because there is no real consensus of political opinion among the membership.

But does industry lack common purpose? It is often assumed that it has one, or that given the right conditions a common purpose could emerge. Economic conflict over the distribution of the proceeds is seen to be unavoidable but once this is settled, either by the compromises of collective bargaining or by some system of profit sharing, it is then believed that there should be co-operation among all the participants to increase what is available for sharing out. When, in practice, conflict continues, this is attributed to failures in communication, or to bad human relations, or perhaps to outside disruptive influences. Such views are not confined to enthusiasts for private enterprise. Advocates of common ownership have held them with the proviso that this is a necessary condition for industry's common purpose not to become submerged under irreconcilable conflicts of economic interest.

The fundamental error in all these theories claiming that industry has or can have some inherent common purpose is their failure to recognise the character of the human association on which it is built. Because the ends of business enterprise, whether it stands under private or public ownership, are primarily economic, the association is always based on considerations of expediency.

All economic relationships are essentially relationships of expediency, entered into for the net advantage which the parties expect to derive from them. In simple terms, people seek employment (or opportunities for investment) in industry for what they can get out of it for themselves and, of course, for their families and dependants; their purposes for associating are personal, not social. Not that the income which their work yields them, although often an overriding consideration, is their only concern. This extends to everything–including status, prospects, security and work satisfaction–which their job contributes directly or indirectly to *their* lives.

This is just as true of the members of management as it is of the men and women on the factory floor. Their 'loyalty' to the firm may appear to be greater, but it bears no resemblance to the loyalty which people display towards a social cause in which they believe. The main difference–compared with manual workers–is that the career interests of managers are much more closely identified with the success of the enterprise which employs them; and the higher they stand in the managerial hierarchy the more this is likely to be the case. That is why we frequently find 'informal organisation' among managerial employees being used to counteract the shortcomings of the 'formal organisation' of a business enterprise, whereas informal work group organisation among manual workers tends to be entirely protective and to conflict in its purposes with those of the enterprise.

It is also far too narrow a view of the sources of industrial conflict to think that it does not extend beyond the obvious clash of economic interests. At a deeper level we can always discern a clash of social values for judging managerial performance in the everyday tussles over the organisation of work. While management is rightly expected to place a premium on efficiency, the managed are particularly attached to the value of security: security of earnings and employment but also settled expectations and stable social relationships on the job itself. If there were not this clash constantly asserting itself it would be very much easier for management to introduce change. Often we find managers–and economists–dismissing workers' resistance to change as stupidly irrational. In reality it may be wholly rational from the workers' point of view; they are rationally pursuing other aims than those of management in its role of furthering the ends of the enterprise.

George Goyder acknowledges the need for a common purpose if his proposals for extending the accountability of management are to succeed. He appears, however, to believe that this problem can be solved by writing an appropriate general purpose clause into the Articles of Association of his Participating Company. There must, he says, 'be a stated purpose if industry is to unify its members in pursuit of that purpose' and 'it must be so defined as to embrace

144

and relate the several responsibilities of the company'.[16] This surely is an exaggeration of what words, even legally binding words, can achieve. Law cannot override the social realities of industry, the forces that really determine the attitudes of those employed in it. If industry lacks a common purpose, the state cannot give it one. It may, as in the totalitarian countries, suppress the free expression of conflict, but this creates no more than a pretence of common purpose.

The other serious limitation placed on control by accountability when applied to large-scale industry is the inevitable autonomy of its top management. Admittedly this autonomy is qualified. Apart from the limits placed upon management by the markets in which it has to operate, it has constantly to satisfy a variety of organised group interests if the enterprise is to remain a viable concern. Indeed, it has been argued that management's 'unique function' is the 'co-ordination of the bargains of all who compose the business'. It is confronted by a complex of groups all wanting to fulfil their aspirations through the medium of the enterprise: the many differentiated work groups on the shop floor and the functional groups within management itself, as well as the suppliers of materials and capital, the shareholders and the customers. Yet 'only one decision can be made with respect to any issue and that decision must bind all the participants in the company's operations'. Furthermore, 'each decision must be [*should be?*] consistent and compatible with all other decisions'. As distinct from a purely technical co-ordination of work, the conflicting and ever-changing demands made upon the enterprise have constantly to be reconciled anew. Management alone can assume this responsibility by engaging, as it must, in what is really a 'multilateral bargaining process'.[17]

But Neil Chamberlain, the author of this plausible view of the characteristic function of management, also points out that this does not make management 'a kind of neutral agent, manipulating bargains to achieve a workable organisation, but without any positive drives of its own'. If it 'is able to satisfy the demands which all the interested parties make . . . all residual discretion and re-sources accrue to it'. The consequent 'power of initiation and innovation', he suggests, 'must surely be the icing that gives piquancy to the cake, the lure which makes all personal sacrifice of high position somehow seem not too high a price for the end to be gained'.[18] Management has to take its decisions within limiting conditions, but it retains a sphere of freedom of choice where it is autonomous and where the values it holds will decide what uses it makes of its power. It is precisely this autonomy which permits such experiments as the John Lewis Partnership or Glacier Metals within a general framework of private enterprise relying mainly on the profit motive.

The minimal character of the control exercised by the generality of shareholders over management in the large joint stock companies has often been emphasized. When it operates at all it is usually because the shareholders are dissatisfied with their dividends. Since they are 'a constantly changing group . . . most of whom are remote and have little, if any, personal association with the day-to-day activities of the company', its 'real control . . . passes to the top flight of professional managers who are able, with little difficulty, to consolidate their power and establish themselves as a self-perpetuating ruling group'.[19] Similarly, parliamentary control over top management in the nationalised industries does little to diminish its autonomy, although the 'ruling group' may be less self-perpetuating. It is also admitted of codetermination in Germany that its general effect on the Boards of Management has been 'to strengthen their authority and to increase their entrepreneurial freedom'.[20]

Once the limits of any arrangements for managerial accountability are acknowledged it follows that they will not suffice to ensure that industry meets its social responsibilities. They may contribute something to the system of checks and balances in addition to the other methods of control, but in the last resort whether managerial power is used responsibly will depend on the values held by management and the conception of its responsibilities which they impart. It is futile in T. S. Eliot's words to dream 'of systems so perfect that no one will need to be good'. All institutional controls over the uses of power have their limits and can never offer an adequate substitute for morality, however much they may be improved.

IMPLICATIONS OF HUMAN DIGNITY

It was stated earlier that industry's social responsibilities arise in regard to its choice of means. We must now return to that proposition in order to take up the question of what values *should* govern the uses of managerial power. Whether and how they *can* govern its uses has then to be considered. In its proper pursuit of the economic ends of industry, management has to take decisions about the utilisation of material and human resources within the setting of a given but changing technology. These are decisions about means. Human resources, however, are people and they do not cease to be persons, whose dignity claims our respect, when they are selling their labour to earn a living. Industry's internal social responsibilities are all based on this simple, yet overriding, consideration.

Respect for the intrinsic worth of the human personality, or the dignity of man, is easily acknowledged in the abstract. As a principle it finds wide approval. The difficulty is to know precisely what that principle implies and when it is violated. One possible yardstick, which can be applied to industry, is the attitude adopted towards managerial paternalism. By paternalism is meant the use of power to impose values on people, for their alleged benefit, which they would not freely accept. It may be associated with a manifestly autocratic style of management, but equally with a manipulative approach to labour relations which employs more subtle techniques to control motivation. In either case it treats workers as objects, not as persons, to be cajoled where they cannot be coerced. In depriving them of opportunities to work out their own salvation by choosing the good for themselves it is an affront to their dignity. A mere bestowing of benefits can never compensate for the insult of being treated with the contempt implicit in being thought incapable of moral choice.

From this point of view there is much to be said for the main conclusion reached by Benjamin Selekman in *A Moral Philosophy for Management*, one of the best-known and most honest studies of contemporary business ethics. 'What one should expect and, indeed, demand of business, in my opinion, is justice. Management must so organise its corporate operation as to ensure justice to the various groups and individuals associated with the enterprise.'[21] Justice, like dignity, may be an abstract and elusive concept but anyone familiar with industrial relations knows that its absence, as expressed, say, in earnings inequities or in unfair treatment of a subordinate by a superior, is keenly felt and resented. When justice is disregarded in industrial organisation–as in all personal or social relations–there is little point in searching for the realisation of other values. If the victims of injustice have not the possibility of redressing their wrongs, they can only view as hypocrisy any pretensions to a higher business morality. Even so, there is more to be said about the implications for management of a respect for human dignity. That 'more' turns on the opportunities which are available to workers and all employees to participate in taking decisions that will materially affect their lives at work.

To have one's life ordered by others is in some measure an inescapable consequence of industrial employment and organised society in general. But this, as we know, can be carried to the point, not only of extinguishing freedom, but, still more seriously, of undermining the love of it. The Webbs concluded their classic study of trade unionism, *Industrial Democracy*, with the observation that 'the very fact that, in modern society, the individual necessarily loses control over his own life, makes him desire to regain collectively what has become individually impossible'.[22] It is unfortunately true that modern society has not always had this effect. Its massive and complex organisational structure tends to weaken the individual's confidence in his capacity to control his life and, consequently, his feeling of personal responsibility for shaping his social environment. If this trend is not taken to be inevitable, however, and we are concerned with what industry does to people as well as for them, it is of great significance that the necessary disciplines of industry should be combined with the fostering of freedom and responsibility within its walls.

The advocates of industrial democracy, who favour the setting up of representative institutions in the management structure of a company, have usually taken this premise as their starting point. They have rightly argued that responsible participation by the managed in management cannot be fostered unless they are given a voice in managerial decisions. The problem has been to see how managerial power could be effectively shared without management's responsibility for advancing the economic ends of the enterprise being impaired. Hugh Clegg, in his most recent essay on the subject of industrial democracy, reaches the conclusion that 'it is impossible for workers to share directly in management'.[23] This is partly due to 'the complex nature of industrial management and the demands imposed on social organisation by modern industrial techniques'. He also contends, however, that representative institutions intended to give workers a voice in policy–though not in its administration–'*by proxy*' are not 'an exercise in collective freedom'. They only provide another opening for 'pressure group democracy', such as we have already in collective bargaining. They also overlook the fact that 'many decisions which are matters of administrative detail to the firm are just those which concern the daily life of the workers most acutely'.[24] Genuine self-government on a basis of freedom and equality is only possible in modern industry, he argues, under the device of the collective contract, where certain functions of management are fully transferred to groups of workers who share their pay and work among themselves. His main ray of hope is that: 'It might turn out to be to the advantage of industrial undertakings . . . to foster self-government . . . by voluntarily limiting their own authority in personnel matters.'[25]

Must this conclusion be accepted as a realistic assessment of the facts of modern industrial life, or is it unduly pessimistic about the future of industrial democracy? Is the latter fated to find expression, if at all, only in a few entirely self-governing groups that rise up as small islands of freedom in a vast sea of necessity? It is undoubtedly true that the individual employee takes as his first, and often his sole, measure of freedom in industry what he experiences in his own job and the social relations immediately surrounding it. He is unlikely to be interested in any wider aspects of the company's activities when his views on the things that he knows best from immediate experience are treated as of little or no account. The growth of responsible participation must therefore start at the bottom; it cannot be imposed from the top. There are invariably dangers of paternalism and pretence in experiments introduced from above, which make assumptions about what the workers want without ascertaining their actual views. The economic sanctions at the disposal of any company make it possible for its top management to force an alien culture on its employees which they may outwardly accept in order to retain their employment.

We should not forget, however, that workers do not wholly relinquish their freedom when they enter industry. The indeterminacy of the work obligations in their contract of employment offers scope for the development of their own protective institutional controls which are intended to safeguard an area of collective freedom. Through the informal organisation of their work group, and probably through a more formal structure of shop and union organisation erected upon it, the workers seek recognition of *their* values and so protect, not only their wages and working conditions, but also their own dignity. Here we have in many cases an existing, solid foundation on which a growing industrial democracy could be built. The business enterprise does not have a unitary structure of authority; in some degree it is always a pluralistic society composed of groups with divergent interests and values. Whether management appreciates this or not, it is invariably confronted with the problem of reconciling the impersonal aims of the enterprise with the personal aims of its many constituent groups.

Clegg acknowledges the work group as an example of self-government in industry, but is doubtful of its future, since its informal measures of control conflict with 'the purposes . . . of management' and are 'a constant source of inefficiency and conflict'.[26] An alternative and more realistic view would be that management must come to terms with it, not by mere acceptance but by trying to bring about a greater integration of its purposes and those of the company. Although there is no inherent common purpose in industry its constituent groups are dependent on each other to achieve their own objectives, and the area of common interest and overlapping purposes can be extended as the *quality* of their relations improves. This depends, not on preaching co-operation, but on how the inevitable conflicts springing from divergent interests are resolved.

This brings us back to the values underlying the uses of managerial power, since the initiative for developing such co-operation must lie with management. Managements have not notably displayed much initiative in this social direction in the past, but nevertheless it is integral to their function and responsibilities. In political terms they represent the government of the enterprise and a government which it is very hard, when not impossible, to displace. Their high degree of autonomy places them, moreover, in a position largely to determine the quality of relations prevailing in industry. Their behaviour in this respect may be influenced by economic and technological factors, but it is not strictly circumscribed by them. They have—in the title of one of the most important post-war studies of an industry by social scientists—*Organisational Choice*. To quote that study: 'It is the goodness of fit between human work organisation and the technological requirements which ultimately determines the efficiency of the whole system.'[27] Thus, even industrial efficiency and material progress demand that managements should not be—as they have been—almost exclusively concerned with economics and technology.

Implications of Human Dignity

Neglect of human values and their attendant social responsibilities can be inexpedient as well as wrong.

Douglas McGregor in *The Human Side of Enterprise* has made explicit the nature of the alternatives that are open to management in the social relations it creates and helps to perpetuate. 'Behind every managerial decision or action,' he points out, 'are assumptions about human nature and human behaviour.'[28] To this one could add that these assumptions are, more than anything else, an expression of the values which managements hold. In his theory X he sets out the established traditional view of direction and control in industry, which at bottom relies on 'rewards, promises, incentives or threats and other coercive devices' because it assumes that no one will work without these motivators. To this he opposes his theory Y whose main assumptions are:

(1) The expenditure of physical and mental effort in work is as natural as play or rest.
(2) External control and the threat of punishment are not the only means for bringing about effort towards organisational objectives. Man will exercise self-direction and control in the service of objectives to which he is committed.
(3) Commitment to objectives is a function of the rewards associated with their achievement.
(4) The average human being learns, under proper conditions, not only to accept but to seek responsibility.
(5) The capacity to exercise a relatively high degree of imagination, ingenuity, and creativity in the solution of organisational problems is widely, not narrowly, distributed in the population.
(6) Under the conditions of modern industrial life, the intellectual potentialities of the average human being are only partially utilised.[29]

The assumptions of theory Y may not, McGregor admits, be 'finally validated', but they are 'far more consistent with existing knowledge in the social sciences' than those of theory X. Clearly the assumptions of theory Y also respect the dignity of man whereas those of theory X do not. The latter are, in fact, little more than a set of primitive dogmas about human behaviour, with no scientific foundation, which managements have blindly followed as canons of industrial efficiency. McGregor brings together a great deal of convincing evidence to show how the often unrealistic and limiting assumptions of traditional theories of management have hampered economic growth, by encouraging restriction of output and by leading to indifference and resistance among workers. Once they are abandoned in favour of less cynical and more enlightened views of human nature the whole organisation and process of management has to be completely re-examined and revised.

One is reminded of Mary Parker Follett's earlier *cri de cœur*: 'I do wish that when a principle has been worked out, say in ethics, it didn't have to be discovered all over again in psychology, in economics, in government, in business, in biology and in sociology. It's such a waste of time.'[30] That the insularity of intellectual disciplines should have such time-wasting consequences may be regrettable, but we are now in a stronger position to assert that neither the economic nor the technological requirements of modern industry demand the sacrifice of human dignity from those employed in it. Rather has the scientific study of social behaviour thrown the weight of its evidence on the other side. Whether this is acted upon depends on the prevailing philosophy of management.

What are the prospects of changing that philosophy in the direction of a greater acceptance by management of its internal social responsibilities, which would imply – on the previous argument – making the government of industry more democratic? They are surely better today in this country than they have ever been before for eminently practical reasons to be found on the workshop floor. In one way or another managements have been forced to reckon with the bargaining power that exists there in their daily dealings with shop stewards and other workers' representatives. Power is something managements cannot afford to be unrealistic about for any length of time because, if they disregard it, it is brought to their attention by stoppages of work or the application of other sanctions which disrupt production. They are, in other words, compelled to engage in *collective* bargaining with work groups within the firm as well as with unions outside it, and continual earnings drift, though it may have other causes, is the inevitable outcome. Yet how they bargain has a profound effect on social relations in the enterprise.

When they have no long-term view of the social relations they wish to create – and this on the whole has been typical – they are apt to be consistent in one respect alone. Most of the time, for the sake of immediate peace, they yield to power and only to power. Apart from placing a premium on aggressive action and militant attitudes by constantly rewarding them, the general outcome is loss of control and abnegation of management. Chaotic wage relationships, growing indiscipline, more restrictive working practices and increasing resistance to change are the familiar results. The integration of the manifold separate decisions involved in the running of a business enterprise which it is the task of management to achieve, not to speak of its necessary power of innovation, is progressively undermined.

In conditions of full employment the only viable alternative to such a disastrous policy of drift is for managements to engage in a new type of creative workplace bargaining, of which existing examples of productivity bargaining offer valuable prototypes. This does not ignore the existence of power relations in the workplace, but attempts to transform them to further the interests of the enterprise and of its employees by establishing new grounds of mutual advantage. Instead of trying to build co-operation on a chimerical common purpose, which must in the end prove futile, it seeks to bring about a reconciliation of conflicting interests and values with the help of the benefits which such a reconciliation can bestow. Such bargaining is not only creative in the sense that it contributes to higher productivity. It also serves to create new social relations in industry in which it is possible for the participants to act responsibly. Managements and workers' representatives are not called upon to abandon their own proper functions and the different responsibilities entailed, but they are placed in a position to fulfil them in ways that pay regard to the wider social consequences of their actions. Finally, bargaining of this sort represents an approach to industrial democracy which promises to have most meaning for industry's rank and file. It enables them to participate in influencing managerial decisions where they have the greatest impact on their lives and, while it may set in train events that will modify their traditional values, they are not being forced or tricked into relinquishing the principle of self-determination which protects their dignity as human beings.

COLLECTIVE BARGAINING:
PRESCRIPTION FOR CHANGE
(1967)

The Problem of Unofficial Strikes

Much of the popular criticism of our system of industrial relations has focused on the frequency of unofficial strikes. On their present scale they are certainly a nuisance and a fault in the system. Very many of them may be too shortlived and insignificant to do much damage, except perhaps to industrial discipline, but some have been costly to the nation's economy and exasperating for the general public. Moreover, their indirect effect on our export trade, by lowering our business reputation abroad, is probably greater than their direct effect. They have also damaged the good name of trade unions, who are thought to be failing in their obligations by allowing them to occur. Yet despite these unfortunate consequences the over-dramatising of this particular problem has serious dangers.

In the first place such an attitude usually expresses and supports a mistaken view of what constitute good industrial relations. The assumption is made that relations between employers and employees are likely to be co-operative and constructive when open conflict is avoided in the form of action which temporarily disrupts production. In fact peace may be preserved by constant capitulation of the one side to the other's demands, or by joint acquiescence in stagnation and the avoidance of any change that would stir up resistance. Peace at this price, apart from obstructing economic growth and social advance, merely stores up trouble for the future. At best it is only one yardstick of good relations and then a very imperfect one. Employees can give vent to their dissatisfaction in many other, less open but no less costly, ways than a complete stoppage of work.

A further danger in giving the problem of unofficial strikes undue prominence is that it easily leads to the advocacy of remedies for our industrial disorders which are more concerned with suppressing

155

symptoms than removing causes. All strikes, whether unofficial or official, are–to adapt the well-known phrase–the continuation of industrial relations by other means. They are therefore symptomatic of the state of these relations, often over a long period. Nothing could be worse than a policy which succeeds in blocking safety valves and alarm signals while leaving unchanged the conditions which have built up pressures to the point of explosion.

That this objection is not just a theoretical one can be illustrated by the present popularity of proposals for the legal enforcement of procedural agreements. It is difficult to believe that anyone is interested in making all the rules in a voluntary agreed disputes procedure part of the law. Many are intended to be guidelines more than binding commitments and the parties would be quite unnecessarily deprived of their freedom to adapt their behaviour to the circumstances of the case. The real attraction of these proposals is their prospect of introducing legal penalties to deter trade unions from silently countenancing breaches of the *peace obligation* in procedural agreements and so force their hands in disciplining dissident members. Whether there is a case for such a remedy or not, it is undoubtedly one which relies wholly on the suppression of symptoms.

Lastly, too great an obsession with unofficial strikes may easily result in more important deficiencies in our industrial relations system being overlooked. The problem is not spread evenly over all industries; it is quite substantially concentrated on four–coal mining, motor vehicles, shipbuilding and port transport–and even here mainly on some establishments or localities.[1] If unofficial strikes were all that was wrong with our system, then the greater part of industry could be given a clean bill of health. In reality there are far more fundamental and universal problems to be solved. Only when these have been explored can we decide why our system is less effective than it was, at least in the more recent past, in bringing about a peaceful resolution of industrial conflict. Unofficial strikes, in short, are a limited and subsidiary problem which should not be placed in the foreground of attention.

What are the greater problems thrown up by our present system of industrial relations? In my view they fall into three categories. First, although collective bargaining is generally accepted as the best way of conducting industrial relations, it is given insufficient support by the state. Second, although our present arrangements for collective bargaining are as a rule conducive to industrial peace, they tend to sacrifice other acknowledged public interests. Third, although a good deal of collective bargaining occurs at the place of work, relations between management and shop stewards are usually unsatisfactory and not infrequently chaotic. I propose to enlarge on each of these shortcomings.

INADEQUATE GROWTH OF COLLECTIVE BARGAINING

The idea that as a nation we fail to give enough support to collective bargaining may at first appear strange and unconvincing. Apart from the many public pronouncements made in its favour, from those of the Royal Commission on Labour of 1891–4 onwards, nowadays more than three-quarters of the total number of employees in this country are covered either by collective agreements or by their statutory equivalent in Wages Regulation Orders. This is a high proportion compared with most other advanced industrial countries and it is far in excess of the proportion of employees who are union members, which barely exceeds 40 per cent. Even so, there are several reasons for viewing this achievement critically.

First, the gaps left by this coverage are very much larger among non-manual than manual workers, although the former are the rapidly growing section of the working population. More than one in two non-manual workers lack the protection of trade unions in settling their remuneration and working conditions as compared with about one in ten manual workers. But the average for non-manual workers masks an important difference: some 85 per cent of them have no union representation in manufacturing industries but the figure falls to 40 per cent in non-manufacturing.[2] The main reason for this contrast is not hard to find. Public employment is concentrated in non-manufacturing industry, and the nationalised industries as well as national and local government accept collective bargaining for all employees as a matter of public policy.[3] The great majority of non-manual workers in the private sector of the economy have no collective agreements; nor are they covered by statutory regulation.

The second critical query relates to Wages Councils (or Wages Boards in agriculture), which for some time have covered around 4 million workers. The proposals of Wages Councils, which are given legal force in Wages Regulation Orders, have so far been treated as the equivalent of collective agreements. Up to a point this is a valid assumption. From its inception in this country statutory wage regulation was devised to reproduce as far as possible a similar process and effect to voluntary negotiation. This has earned it the description of 'compulsory collective bargaining', but the parallel must not be exaggerated. The two representative sides of a Wages Council can only produce agreements for subjects on which they are legally empowered to make proposals, namely minimum remuneration and holidays. They cannot control the amount of overtime worked in the industry or consider fringe benefits or deal with productivity and its relationship to pay. Nor can they set up and operate a disputes and grievance procedure. The earlier expectation was that these statutory bodies would pave the way for, and finally be superseded by, voluntary collective bargaining arrangements. But, as the Ministry of Labour has pointed out, 'while a small number of Councils have been abolished, employers and workers alike have for the most part been content to rely on statutory machinery provided by the Government'.[4] In the event nearly one in four manual workers (one in two in the case of women) continue to depend on a most inferior form of collective bargaining.

Thirdly, it must be remembered that the growth of collective bargaining has a further dimension apart from the proportion of employees covered by collective agreements—namely the range of subjects regulated by those agreements. One of the striking contemporary features of British collective bargaining, compared say with collective bargaining in the United States, is the poverty of its subject matter, the limited range of substantive issues regulated by written and formally signed agreements. The principal subjects remain wages and working hours—and in view of the prevalence of high levels of regular overtime in many industries the regulation of the latter must be regarded as defective. Holidays with pay in the 'thirties and provisions for a guaranteed week in the 'forties have been the only new subjects introduced into the main stream of collective bargaining since the first world war. Rarely are fringe benefits or contentious issues like union security and job security, not to speak of many other working conditions, brought within the realm of formal joint regulation. Admittedly one cannot ignore 'custom and practice', which though upheld by union members is tacitly

158

accepted by employers; nor the informal understandings arrived at by individual managements and shop stewards. Their significance will be considered later, but they are not identical with the provisions of collective agreements for which trade unions and employers or their associations accept a full and unqualified responsibility.

If for these principal reasons it may be argued that collective bargaining has considerable scope for further growth, the next question to be answered is whether its growth is hampered by lack of public support. The answer turns on the conditions which must be met for collective bargaining to survive as a viable institution. 'First, the parties must attain a sufficient degree of organisation. Second, they must be ready to enter into agreements with each other—a condition known as "mutual recognition". Third, their agreements must generally be observed by those to whom they apply.'[5]

As sanctions of one kind or another are needed to uphold each of these three conditions, the growth of collective bargaining depends on whether such sanctions are available and effective for their purpose. When, for example, we refer to its voluntary growth in Britain we really mean that it has been sustained by the private sanctions of trade unions and employers' associations. Of these by far the most important has been trade union control of the strike. This sanction has served to force non-unionists to join a union, to force employers to recognise unions, and to force the recalcitrant among them to observe collective agreements.

Public, and notably legal, sanctions are an alternative or additional means to the same end. In other democratic countries as an act of public policy collective bargaining has been promoted by the legal enforcement of one or more of the above conditions. In New Zealand union membership is made compulsory by law; in the United States and Canada employers are legally compelled to recognise trade unions if their employees want unions to represent them; and in many countries collective agreements are legally enforced. Whether any of these things are desirable in Britain is an open question, for a price has to be paid for them. Direct legal support for collective bargaining invariably entails in some degree its legal regulation, and this is a consequence which most British trade unions and employers have wanted to avoid. They have preferred to supplement their own by public sanctions which would not entangle industrial relations with the law.

Broadly speaking, for many years the law in this country, if not public opinion, has occupied a position of neutrality on the first and second of the above conditions; neither obstructing nor promoting them but leaving them instead to be settled by the free play of social forces. Occasionally collective agreements have been enforced under special legislation, when the parties wanted it and their case was strong enough, but these have been the rare exceptions. Public support for collective bargaining has depended in the main on the strength of those informal social sanctions that we call the pressures of public opinion, which have sometimes, and particularly in war-time, been supplemented by the more direct pressures of government. It is probably true that these sanctions are particularly effective in Britain and we could therefore more easily dispense with their legal counterpart. The only other measures of public support for collective bargaining have been applied exclusively to the third condition of agreement observance. They are the Fair Wages Clause and the use of compulsory arbitration to enforce 'recognised terms and conditions of employment'.

The first of these measures employs the state's economic sanctions. By appearing as a clause in government contracts, or those of nationalised industries or local authorities, the economic power of the public sector as a purchaser is used to secure respect for relevant collective agreements. Similarly, where the government provides financial and other assistance to particular industries, the Fair Wages Clause has been incorporated into the legislation. Its enforcement, however, is not a matter for the ordinary courts. This is made effective in disputed cases by compulsory arbitration, which is also the means employed, under section 8 of the Terms and Conditions of Employment Act, 1959, of giving further public support to the substantive clauses of collective agreements.

The recent history of our use of compulsory arbitration for this limited purpose has some interesting lessons on its rationale. When in 1940, with the introduction of the war-time Order 1305, the unions were temporarily deprived of the sanction of the strike to force reluctant employers to respect their agreements, they had to be offered a substitute. Hence the general obligation which the Order placed on all employers to observe 'recognised terms and conditions of employment in the district' (or terms and conditions 'not less favourable'), which usually meant those fixed by the relevant collective agreements. In practice, however, the machinery provided

160

for the enforcement of this obligation was the compulsory arbitration tribunal,[6] whose awards automatically became implied terms of the individual contracts of employment of the employees concerned. Although the general obligation disappeared and the freedom to strike was restored when Order 1305 was replaced by Order 1376 in 1951, the essence of the same procedure was retained, it having proved its value as a prop to collective bargaining. And it was still retained for this one purpose, now under permanent legislation in the 1959 Act, when Order 1376 was revoked in 1958 and the use of compulsory arbitration was abandoned for the settlement of other disputes.

The attraction of compulsory arbitration as a means of offering some public support for collective bargaining was its compatibility with our voluntary system. It did not directly entail legal proceedings, nor threaten the standing of voluntary agreements. Perhaps the greatest value of this device has been that its very existence provided an inducement for employers to observe agreements or face the prospect, usually unwelcome, of being bound by a compulsory award. On the other hand the support which it gives to agreement observance is both partial and temporary. Under the 1959 Act to bring an employer into line, a trade union has to report a 'claim' for the observance of recognised terms and conditions to the Ministry of Labour and seek to obtain a compulsory award from the Industrial Court. This it must do for each employer separately regardless of the size of the firm, and if the award is favourable the next round of wage negotiations could render it obsolete.

Compared with other industrial countries then it must be conceded that, because of our attachment to the 'voluntary principle', we have been most reluctant to support by law any of the conditions on which viability of collective bargaining as an established social institution depends. Legal support has been limited to promoting the observance of collective agreements and applied only in a selective fashion by means which left their application primarily within the discretion of the bargaining parties. This is undoubtedly the crux of the explanation for the limited growth of collective bargaining in this country. Whether its further growth can be fostered by measures which do not entail the risks we have always sought to avoid is a question to be answered later.

Collective Bargaining: Prescription for Change

COLLECTIVE BARGAINING AND THE PUBLIC INTEREST

The second major shortcoming of our system of industrial relations has been progressively revealed over the post-war years: its lack of provision for bringing to light and safeguarding the public interest in the results of collective bargaining. Collective agreements are made to satisfy the interests of those who are represented in their negotiation. Although there is, of course, no preordained harmony between these sectional interests and the interests of society at large, they may nevertheless coincide, and that was generally considered to be the position in the past for the following reasons.

Once trade unions and employers' associations had been accepted as necessary and valuable institutions, despite the restrictions which they placed on the free play of markets, society displayed an interest mainly in two things so far as industrial relations were concerned. It was interested first in maintaining industrial peace and second in setting certain common minimum standards of employment. But these interests were shared by unions and employers and their own efforts to satisfy them best met society's demands. They jointly made their procedural rules to curb unnecessary strife in their relations and such voluntary disputes procedures, supplemented by public facilities for voluntary conciliation and arbitration, proved on the whole to be a most effective means of preserving peace. Similarly they agreed their substantive rules to regulate wages and working conditions and here again the public preferred voluntary to statutory regulation because it appeared to offer less of a threat to economic freedom. Thus the pursuit of collective, if not individual, self-interest was believed to accord sufficiently with the public good, as seen at the time, to rule out greater intervention by the state.

Why then should the ever-present possibility of conflict between sectional and national interests have become so much more pronounced and apparent in recent times? The answer lies partly in the impact of sustained high levels of employment on the conduct of collective bargaining, and partly in the consequent growth of new conceptions of the public stake in its results. In broad terms the effects of full employment are well known: it has created the inflationary wage–price spiral and it has brought about a serious degree of under-employment of employed labour (and of capital). Both of

162

these are highly complex phenomena, not yet fully understood, but a few leading points can be made about each of them.

Although one cannot separate the 'cost–push' from the 'demand–pull' elements in inflation, there is evidence enough to show that bargaining pressures have pushed up wages and prices in ways and to an extent which cannot wholly be explained by the prevailing state of labour and product markets. It is a matter of repeated and common observation, for example, that employers, even in highly competitive industries, offer little ultimate resistance to wage increases because they know that increased costs can be passed on to the consumer in higher prices and at the same time be used to justify an increase in profits. Their attitude is sometimes attributed to our system of industry-wide bargaining, which is said to assure individual employers that their competitors will face a similar increase in labour costs. Yet the same convention operates in industries which have no national wage agreements, not to speak of those where the regulative effect of such agreements is very weak. Moreover, there is a strong case for concluding, as the Confederation of British Industry has argued, that a general dismantling of industry-wide bargaining in favour of an enormous variety of completely unco-ordinated plant bargains would further aggravate wage inflation by giving trade unions greater scope to play off one employer against another in a whipsawing fashion.[7]

For another social convention has played a most significant part in the mechanics of inflation under full employment: that of comparability. Again we may lack a comprehensive and definitive explanation of the causes, but it is not open to doubt that comparisons as between rates and between earnings have exercised a powerful influence on wage settlements, and their force cannot be adequately accounted for either by market or by power theories of collective bargaining. The force of comparability seems in fact to be compounded of a mixture of considerations of administrative convenience (negotiators on both sides can more easily defend a settlement which is based on an already established pattern) and of its being accepted as a rough measure of social justice (why should we fall behind the rest?).

Be that as it may, as I pointed out some years ago: 'the familiar problem of the wage–price spiral under full employment is rather like a set of Chinese boxes. It contains within it the problem of the wage–wage spiral, which in turn contains the problem of the rates–earnings spiral.'[8] Both of the latter are manifestations of the force of comparability. The wage–wage spiral is most evident in national negotiations. Increases in wage rates or reductions in the standard working week obtained by strong trade unions placed in the most favourable bargaining situations set a pattern which then tends to be widely transmitted throughout the system, with Wages Councils eventually bringing into line those who are most in the rear. But the uneven incidence of earnings drift above national rates among different groups of workers itself creates strong pressures for compensatory increases in rates for the less fortunate, and these serve to throw up new comparisons leading to further wage increases. Everyone is, as it were, engaged in a self-defeating race for higher incomes. Not only do higher wages lead to higher prices, but in the race itself, while some are always in front and act as pace-makers, the relative position of the contestants stays much the same.[9]

The analogy is appropriate because at bottom the problem is one of unrestrained competition: political and social as well as economic wage competition. Employers engage in economic competition for labour in short supply by bidding up earnings above agreed rates. But trade unions are also forced to compete for success and its measure is what they can get for their members. Political wage competition has already been the theme of a number of studies of trade union wage policy; competitive bidding on wage claims among unions in rivalry for members or between factions struggling for leadership within the same union are examples of it. This is reinforced by another kind of competition for social status which influences the attitudes of union members and is the outcome of their conflicting notions of 'fair' wages. One could cite in illustration the status competition, conducted through wage claims, between the maintenance craftsmen and the production workers in steel and other process industries, but it has a wider scope. Better-paid workers seek to uphold their existing differentials and consequent status advantage over other groups and defend this as fair on grounds of custom or tradition, while the lower-paid claim preferential treatment and higher status by an egalitarian appeal to social justice.

Unless regulated by law competition of any kind can only be restrained by rules agreed among the competitors. The written and unwritten rules of collective bargaining have restrained it in limited areas, but it is left uncurbed in the above ways because here no effective rules apply. Most national agreements, explicitly or in practice, fix no more than minimum rates of pay, so there is little restraint on economic competition among employers for labour. And the sectional character of collective bargaining leaves political and social competition among trade unions and their members free play outside the many separate bargaining units. That is why the politicians' favourite remedy of exhortation has no effect. Asking the bargaining parties to take the public interest into account must be ineffective as long as the impersonal forces of the system compel them to act differently. For the same reason piecemeal intervention by the government to hold back some wage increases where its influence is greatest must break down. However great the parties' sense of social responsibility they cannot afford to lose their place in the race. Their behaviour, in other words, is not freely chosen; it is structured by the conditions in which they operate.

The general movement of incomes and prices, like the earlier booms and slumps of the trade cycle, is consequently the product of a whole series of interrelated responses of separate groups to their own immediate situation. It is a matter of chance whether the trends to which these responses aggregate bear any relationship to national economic requirements, for they are outside the scope of institutional regulation. There is further no possibility on a national scale of ordering wage relativities according to any economic or social criteria, because this again implies institutional regulation where none exists.

We have taken much longer to acknowledge the second phenomenon thrown up by free collective bargaining in the context of full employment: a growing under-employment of nominally employed resources, especially human resources. This is not surprising because it is hidden from public sight. Under-employment is not statistically recorded and, until the Royal Commission on the Press offered the public one of the first glimpses of its extent in a part of one industry, national newspapers, the problem was hardly discussed. At the time W. W. Allen's article[10] had its dramatic impact because so little had previously been written to direct public attention to the realities of the situation on the shop floor. Even now we have no idea of the national dimensions of the problem, although more evidence has accumulated about its extent in some industries and establishments.

Certain of the factors which impede a fuller utilisation of labour may have nothing to do with industrial relations. They may simply be due to bad management in its technical aspects; the result, for example, of poor production planning. Many factors, however, have a strong causal relationship and reflect the results of bargaining pressures, although in this case mainly on pay structures and working practices within establishments rather than on the contents of formal collective agreements. The nature of the relationship is still not generally appreciated. In the popular view under-employment (or overmanning) is due to the 'restrictive practices' of trade unions, practices which are believed to be the heritage of craft unionism from the nineteenth century and to have lost their social justification with the coming of full employment. This is so much less than a half-truth as to be positively misleading.

Some of the working practices in question, such as job demarcations and the employment of mates, may have had early craft origins, but they are rarely to be found in union rule books. How far they are inefficient restrictions on the use of labour depends very much on how they are applied in particular workplace situations. Nor are these practices confined to craftsmen. Over the post-war years they have tended to become much more stringent among all highly organised workers who have been able to build up strong unilateral controls on the use of their labour at the place of work. These controls are not enforced officially by trade unions, but by work groups in the workplace represented by their shop stewards. Still more important is the fact that under-employment is particularly associated with other workplace institutions which are not normally included under the heading of 'restrictive practices'. The rise of systematic overtime on a large scale in some industries and the progressive demoralisation of incentive pay systems in others, or possibly a combination of both, must be counted as among its most significant causes.

The common denominator in all these things and the real nub of the problem of under-employment (be it of labour or capital) has been a progressive loss of managerial control over pay and work, and therefore over labour costs, at plant level. When this is grasped the causal relationship to full employment comes into view. Few detailed studies have been made of workplace relations, so one is forced to generalise from personal knowledge of particular cases, but the following situation can repeatedly be observed. Ill-prepared managements have found themselves faced with a much stronger, and often a new, bargaining power on the shop floor: not the bargaining power of trade unions as such, but of work groups who have their own sanctions ranging from the instant stoppage to bans on overtime or the withdrawal of co-operation. Having no other objectives in mind than immediate peace and uninterrupted production, managements have followed the practical man's dictum: 'to concede nothing he doesn't have to, but to give if pushed'. By yielding to power and only to power they have destroyed order.

The workers for their part can hardly be blamed for advancing their interests with the means at their disposal. They have used their greater bargaining power and strengthened their own unilateral controls not only to get more money, but to enhance their income and job security and, not unnaturally, to give themselves an easier time at work. The responsibility for considering how this would affect the overall position of the enterprise was management's not theirs. And no one was there to speak for the national economy. Full employment gave workers the greater bargaining power, but it did not determine management's response. That has been determined by the state of management, a point to which I will return.

These economically damaging results of collective bargaining in the conditions of the post-war world have led to a gradual realisation that its freedom could no longer remain sacrosanct. In effect this has meant both an enlarging of the conception of the public interest in industrial relations and a recognition that, for it to be made more effective, positive action on the part of governments was required. The vulnerability of the country's balance of payments has invariably been the principal factor in forcing governments into action to restrain the growth of incomes, regrettably at the cost of economic growth, but the problems to be solved are far greater and more permanent than those of immediate expediency. In industrial relations as in other aspects of our social life they are essentially problems of reconciling planning and freedom, with the scales heavily weighted by our history in favour of freedom. More and more we see the need for planning but we draw back from introducing the restraints that are needed just as much as incentives to make it more than an idle pretence.

For the new public interests in the outcome of collective bargaining are national planning interests in incomes and manpower. In a mixed economy and a democratic society like our own, where there is private enterprise and freedom of association, it is inconceivable for the decisions which settle the formation of incomes and the supply and utilisation of manpower to be centrally controlled. They need, however, to be taken in a knowledge of their possible consequences and to be influenced, where necessary, to make them accord with the objectives and priorities which the government and society set. That is the enduring significance of our present attempts to develop a national 'productivity, prices and incomes policy', after a whole series of *ad hoc* and largely ineffective interventionist measures by governments aimed mainly at curbing the movement of wages.

COLLECTIVE BARGAINING IN THE WORKPLACE

The third major shortcoming of our system has been touched upon in dealing with the second. It is to be found in the prevailing institutions for conducting industrial relations at the place of work. Admittedly there is so much diversity of practice at this level that any generalisations about the deficiencies of existing arrangements might seem out of place. Certain propositions may be stated, however, which have such widespread validity that the notable exceptions only serve to prove the rule.

One of these, and the most fundamental, is that collective bargaining in the sense of a method for arriving in an orderly fashion at agreed rules and decisions in matters of mutual concern has yet to be accepted as a proper basis for workplace relations. The qualification is all important, for in another sense there is no lack of plant, or rather intra-plant, bargaining in this country. Bargaining on the shop floor over piecework prices and conditions of work has always gone on to some extent in some industries, but an outstanding feature of industrial relations over the post-war years has been the great upsurge of negotiations between management and shop stewards over pay and a wider range of subjects. The result as regards pay can be seen in earnings drift, which, however uneven in its incidence, is a universal phenomenon. The growing gap between officially negotiated union rates and actual earnings may be partly the result of unilateral decisions by employers to offer higher wages in bidding for labour in short supply, but much of it is the outcome of the bargaining pressures previously described as weakening managerial control over pay and work within industrial establishments.

168

Collective Bargaining in the Workplace

Three things can be said about most of this intra-plant bargaining which in conjunction reveal the problems it has raised and clearly distinguish it from collective bargaining as joint regulation. It is largely informal, largely fragmented and largely autonomous.

Formal plant agreements, signed on behalf of unions by their full-time officials, have been mainly confined to non-federated firms in this country.[11] In other firms, while there may in fact be some jointly agreed or tacitly accepted rules regulating relations between management and workers, they usually remain uncodified or, if they appear in writing at all, in the minutes of meetings or perhaps in a statement of company policy. The Ministry of Labour's survey of redundancy policies and agreements in existence at the end of 1962 showed, for example, that only eighteen out of a total of 371 policies in private firms had been embodied in signed agreements. Yet 45 per cent of them had been settled after consultation with employee representatives, and it would be a fair assumption in present conditions that the object of such consultation had been to gain the workers' consent.[12]

Fragmentation of plant bargaining means simply that it is conducted in such a way that different groups in the works get different concessions at different times. To select one example from many, in the summer of 1966 more than 14,000 of Standard-Triumph's 15,000 workers at five factories in Coventry, Birmingham and Liverpool were idle because of a stoppage over the piecework rates of sixty machinists at the Coventry plant.[13] We find this typical result of fragmented bargaining repeated again and again, especially in the context of piecework. Sometimes fragmentation may be due to union divisions and rivalries within the plant, but that is not its basic cause. After all, such conflicts are held in check at industry level by several unions being party to the same agreement. Within the plant, however, in the absence of any common and comprehensive system of negotiation, an inadequately ordered pay structure encourages separate work groups to press their own advantage and exploit its anomalies and inequities.

Much of this bargaining is also autonomous in that neither trade unions nor employers' associations have any real control over it. Frequently they have very little knowledge of it either, unless it leads to a stoppage of work. Some industries have agreements fixing standard national rates. These limit the scope of plant bargaining so far as wages are concerned but they do not suppress it altogether; overtime, for example, may gain an exaggerated importance by providing the one flexible element in local pay structures. On the trade union side the workers come to attach more importance to the negotiations of their stewards with management than to the negotiations of their full-time officials with employers' associations. As in any case the officials are often dependent on the stewards for maintaining membership, they would find it difficult to discipline them. The sanctions of employers' associations over their affiliated firms, on the other hand, are usually weaker than those of a trade union over its members. And neither side is staffed adequately to keep in touch with, let alone influence in detail, the bargaining that is going on from day to day on the shop floor.

Most industries, it is true, have procedural agreements which bring trade unions and employers' associations into the settlement of disputes which cannot be satisfactorily resolved within the firm. These might be regarded as limiting the autonomy of plant bargaining, even where the substantive agreements at national or district level do not. In fact employers' associations have a strong tradition against interference in the domestic affairs of their affiliated firms. Moreover, such procedural limits, where effective, are only operative in the small minority of cases when relations within the plant have broken down and there is a threatened or actual stoppage; and, as the number of unofficial strikes reveals, they have been weakened even in these cases. Nor is this surprising or to be attributed to the perversity or political motives of shop stewards. Where workplace disputes take place over issues on which the parties have no agreed rules to guide them, an external procedure is bound to be distrusted by the workers as not offering a satisfactory means of dispute settlement. They know the employers collectively will be most apprehensive about setting precedents which could be cited in other firms.

These three pronounced characteristics of the greater part of plant bargaining in this country have been treated separately but they have a common cause. Because of our long-standing reliance on national (and earlier district) agreements to settle the main terms of employment and to provide disputes procedures, plant bargaining has developed, not as a deliberate policy, but haphazardly and as a result of the pressures of the moment. It has been forced upon employers and unions, at first largely against their will, by the logic of the

170

prevailing industrial situation. Hence its autonomous growth and their reluctance to formalise it and integrate it into the industrial relations system. Many employers and unions may now recognise that plant bargaining in one form or another has come to stay, but they cannot exert much influence on it without far-reaching changes in their organisation.

The autonomy of workplace bargaining is a challenge to trade unions and employers' associations and an obstacle in making a national incomes policy work. Its excessive informality and fragmentation are mainly a reflection on managements. They alone are in a position to take the initiative to place it on a satisfactory foundation and to encourage the growth of more stable and co-operative relationships within the plant. I have referred to managements being ill-prepared to cope constructively with bargaining power on the shop floor. We must know how and why they have been ill-prepared. An explanation can be offered at three different levels: the training, the structure and the ideology of management.

Few managers have been prepared by their education or experience for the social aspects of their function. That managers at all levels should pay some attention to the human or personal problems of the people they were managing became one of the clichés of the post-war world. Less thought was given to what is more important, especially in large organisations: the need for them to understand the social implications of their decisions because a business enterprise, like any other organised community, has a social structure which influences the behaviour of its members. Labour relations have therefore been conducted in almost complete ignorance of the social sciences and frequently on the basis of the most primitive dogmas about the determinants of behaviour. In these circumstances the reactions of workers and their representatives could hardly appear other than unpredictable, and the natural desire of those who have been trained as technicians to fight shy of labour relations has been fortified by the apparently baffling nature of the behaviour they observed.

This in turn has encouraged the separation of personnel management from management in general, a structural factor which has also inhibited managerial initiative. In itself, of course, the growth of personnel management, which was accelerated during and after the war, was a welcome sign that industry was giving more weight to personnel problems. But the principal role of the personnel manager in industrial relations was usually taken to be that of the peace-maker; the man who sorted out disputes when they were threatened and knew how to get along with the unions and to anticipate their demands and the settlements they would accept. Rarely was he given a place in the formulation of policy or in forward planning because it was not thought necessary to define objectives and look ahead in industrial relations. This organisational split between personnel and line management was 'too artificial not to lead to serious difficulty in practice on both sides'.[14] Above all, it permitted line management to take a too limited view of its responsibilities and this reduced its effectiveness in its relations with shop stewards and work groups.

The neglect of these questions of training and structure can be traced back to the prevailing ideology of management which rejected any division or sharing of authority within the firm.[15] In theory it was held that there should be no collective bargaining with shop stewards, but only joint consultation with workers' representatives, who having expressed their opinions must leave management to decide. The history of joint consultation over the post-war years shows how unrealistic were the assumptions on which it was based. Though necessary, it could not serve as a substitute for negotiation on issues in which workers had strong interests. Management was in practice faced with a rival authority on the shop floor and had to come to terms with it and negotiate settlements. It could continue to pretend, however, that this was a temporary aberration which on no account should obtain the seal of approval in formal agreements lest certain of its highly valued prerogatives should be lost for all time.

This mixture of realism and pretence, of being forced to yield to bargaining power on the shop floor while denying it any legitimacy, is the most fundamental cause of the weakening of managerial control and the growing anarchy in workplace relations. The paradox, whose truth managements have found it so difficult to accept, is that they can only regain control by sharing it. Co-operation in the workplace cannot be fostered by propaganda and exhortation, by preaching its benefits. Nor does it depend primarily, though this is an important factor, on improved systems of communication, because any system of communication is auxiliary to the system of control and the former will be designed to suit the latter. Co-operation demands first and foremost the progressive fusing of two systems of unilateral control—which now exist in conjunction and frequently in conflict with each other—into a common system of joint control based on agreed objectives. Such agreement can only be reached through compromise.

The practical implications of this conclusion will be considered later. It is now appropriate to return to the problem of unofficial strikes. One thing is certain about the vast majority of them: they are a phenomenon to be explained in the prevailing context of work-place relations. In the absence of agreed rules to regulate these relations it is to be expected that contentious issues will be settled by a trial of strength.[16] As always the only alternative to the rule of war is the rule of law, and where law cannot be imposed by tyranny it must be sustained by consent. This means in workplace relations not just the consent of trade unions but, above all, the consent of their members in the particular work community. It is therefore foolish to believe that peace can be preserved by enforcing an external law provided by national or district agreements when there is no proper agreement on the rules of internal job regulation. The solution to the problem of unofficial strikes should then be sought in the reconstruction of workplace relations and managements bear the main responsibility for finding it. They are evading this respon-sibility, as well as revealing their own lack of understanding of the nature of the problem, when they place all the blame on trade unions for failing to discipline their members or ask for the legal enforcement of the peace obligation in procedural agreements. Though the numbers of unofficial strikes might possibly be reduced by both these means, it would be at the cost of better standards of manage-ment and a permanent improvement in industrial relations.

THE VALUE OF THE VOLUNTARY PRINCIPLE

Having offered a diagnosis of the main shortcomings of our present system of industrial relations, I now turn to a discussion of the appropriate remedies. As in medicine, however, one has to avoid killing the patient in trying to cure him. Our system may have some serious faults, but it also has some outstanding merits. It would be folly to pursue reforms which place these seriously at risk.

Many of the merits of our system are all centred, I believe, on one remarkable feature which is practically unparalleled in any other country in the world. I refer to our success in preventing the conduct of industrial relations–and especially the settlement of disputes– from becoming entangled with legal process. This is no mean achievement. 'Most workers want nothing more of the law than that it should leave them alone'.[17] The fact that litigation can be both complicated and costly is not the decisive consideration, though it cannot be ignored. Other countries have met this objection, as we could do, by setting up special labour courts, whose proceedings are much more informal and involve less delay and expense for litigants than ordinary courts. What is really at stake is the social value of the 'voluntary principle' on which our system has been based.

The term has been used in this country to describe at least three separate features of industrial relations. Unless they are distinguished from each other we are unlikely to make much headway in resolving our current dilemmas. In the first place it refers to our preference for collective bargaining to state regulation as a method of settling wages and other terms and conditions of employment. Secondly, it expresses a preference for our own voluntary or non-legalistic type of collective bargaining. Thirdly, it is identified with the preference of the bargaining parties for complete autonomy in their relations. They have wanted their bargaining to be free and have accordingly rejected not only intervention by governments but any control of their bargaining activities by their own central organisations.

Of these three different features of voluntarism, as we have known it for many years, it is only the third which must now be unreservedly consigned to the rubbish bin of history. As a nation–after long hesitation and much futile searching for more palatable alternatives– we are committed to developing a national productivity, prices and incomes policy and, whatever may be its precise content, this necessarily implies placing some restraints on the freedom of collective bargainers. Their previous autonomy must be qualified where their behaviour conflicts with the agreed policy and the public interest. The only consistent case that can be argued against restraint is the one based on an outright rejection of any planning of incomes and manpower, which says in effect that the market always knows best. This, however, is to advocate a return to the nineteenth century. There may still be powerful minorities who are reactionaries in this literal meaning of the word–whether they stand at the extreme right, the extreme left or, for that matter, the centre of the political spectrum. But they are fighting a rearguard action which they will lose in the end, although they may seriously delay and hamper progress in the meantime.

The other two features of voluntarism are not open to the same objections. They may need to be reviewed, and to some extent revised, to accommodate the more active and positive role which the government has now to play in industrial relations but, in essence, they are well worth defending and indeed are likely to endure. That we should continue in general to prefer collective bargaining to state regulation of incomes and conditions of work is so self-evident that it would be pointless to spend much time on explaining why. Collective bargaining in industry is the equivalent and counterpart of democracy in politics. Its extinction would be a denial of freedom of association and representative organisation and would put an end to trade unions and employers' associations. No one in fact is seriously suggesting that.

What has to be questioned is the earlier assumption that the government should always leave the two sides of industry to settle every problem in industrial relations regardless of the time they take to find an answer or whether they find any answer at all. That assumption has already been set aside. The Redundancy Payments Act, 1965, and the Industrial Training Act, 1964, point the way to two kinds of measures which will increasingly be needed; the one kind to set new minimum standards on terms and conditions of employment, the other to set up and finance institutions which can assist in solving urgent planning problems with an industrial relations content. Such measures do not undermine collective bargaining. On the contrary they can be used to force the pace of voluntary action and to underpin its results.

A more controversial aspect of voluntarism is the second, which relates to the legal standing of collective agreements in this country— the fact that they have not as a rule been given the force of law. This should not be looked upon as a museum piece. It is a valuable gift which our special history has bequeathed to us and on which much of the health and vitality of our system depends. It accounts for our success in keeping the law out of industrial relations and preserving our own non-legalistic style of negotiation. I have summarised its twin advantages as 'permitting flexibility' and 'encouraging responsibility', which together have 'induced a greater readiness to compromise and to stand by whatever compromise was reached'.[18]

The first advantage has followed directly from the voluntary character of collective agreements. As they had not to be drawn up with the exactitude demanded of legislation, the parties could leave themselves with a good deal of freedom to adjust the application of their agreed rules to the circumstances of individual cases. They could be guided more by the spirit of their intentions than by the letter of their text. They could rely on many unwritten understandings and conventions which serve as flexible guidelines for their behaviour. Not least, since they not only made but themselves applied and enforced the rules regulating their relations, they were able continuously to adjust them to suit changing conditions.

The second advantage has sprung from the same source. Responsibility for settling difficult issues of conflict, whether over the terms of a new agreement or the application of an old one, could not easily be transferred to a third party. While arbitration is occasionally used to resolve deadlocks in negotiation it has never, as in some countries, become a habit-forming drug; an easy escape from the responsibilities of negotiation. Employers and unions usually recognise that it is best for them to come to terms with each other and defend the result to their constituents. Above all, in the absence of any legal props they have been forced, even in times of considerable stress and tension, to accept a common responsibility for safeguarding the viability and continuity of their collective bargaining relationship against extremists on either side. This factor in itself has been a force for order, an ever-present restraint on the potentially disruptive effects of passion and polemic.

We have enjoyed these benefits for so long that we take them for granted. We have come to assume that they are inherent in the process of collective bargaining, but we should not overlook the following facts. For some forty years, with very few exceptions, we have had no prolonged and large-scale stoppages of work. As a result, in terms of working days lost in proportion to workers employed, our record still compares favourably with many other highly industrialised countries, and is certainly decidedly better than that of the United States.[19] Over much of the time this record has been sustained with hardly any legal restrictions on the freedom to strike and to lock out, even in the form of enforced 'cooling off' periods. Keeping the peace has been wholly a voluntary undertaking; a responsibility discharged, admittedly in their own interests, by the representative organisations on both sides of industry. The safeguards have been provided, however, less by the wording of the parties' agreed procedural rules than by the implicit understandings governing their actual behaviour, which are rarely if ever articulated. These understandings may now be strongly reinforced by tradition in many industries, but they could be destroyed overnight if the conditions in which they are rooted were drastically changed by clumsy legal intervention.

But the case for preserving as much as we can of this aspect of voluntarism does not rest solely on grounds of social expediency. It finds its strongest defence in the very character of the human and social problems which industry creates; and the more dynamic and advanced industry becomes the stronger the defence. The fact that industrial activity changes day by day, that technology and markets are constantly in flux, means that it cannot be directed with a sensitive regard for the manifold and diverse interests of those involved by a régime of strict external law and outside regulation. Fixed codes of rights and obligations, rigid notions of justice and equity, are not applicable to industrial relations. Every modification of a process may produce a redistribution of tasks and rewards and so provide occasion for deciding whether the terms offered are reasonable and fair. Since we have no objective or socially agreed yardsticks to settle these questions they are best decided–within such limits as the public interest may impose–to the satisfaction of those who are most directly and intimately affected. This can only be done by representatives of their own choosing, who know the facts of the case and the feelings of the people for whom they speak. Such democratic considerations are a substantial part of the case for preferring collective bargaining to state regulation, but they are equally powerful arguments for our own non-legalistic style of collective bargaining and for not settling industrial disputes in the courts.

We should not regard voluntarism then as if it were a single absolute principle. We should take it apart in order to analyse and appraise its constituent elements in the light of contemporary needs. We have every reason to find ways of reforming our industrial relations system that will extend and strengthen collective bargaining and, at the same time, preserve our own flexible and responsible type of bargaining. Neither of these things should be confused with the outmoded assertion that collective bargaining must be free, which implies that sectional advantage should never be subordinated to the common good.

TRIBUNAL FOR RECOGNITION AND PROCEDURAL DISPUTES

It has been shown that one of the principal shortcomings of our present system is its failure to give collective bargaining enough support. Collective bargaining demands union recognition, i.e. a readiness on the part of employers to conclude collective agreements with a representative trade union or unions. As things stand, if a union is denied recognition by an employer, the strike is its only available sanction. It has, in other words, to organise a stoppage of work in order to prove that it has enough support among the employees whom it is seeking to represent and so is a force with which the employer must come to terms. It cannot turn to arbitration under s.8. of the Terms and Conditions of Employment Act, 1959, because the Industrial Court has refused to make an award even to extend collective agreed clauses on union recognition.[20] Occasionally recognition disputes have been dealt with by Courts of Inquiry, but this device is used far too sparingly for it to be an appropriate method for settling the general run of recognition disputes.[21]

There are two strong objections against leaving recognition disputes to be settled by strikes. The first is the familiar one that for the community this is an unnecessarily costly way of deciding a question of this sort, which turns to a considerable extent on finding out the facts of the situation – how representative is the union and so on. But it is also particularly unfair to those groups of employees, notably among white-collar workers, who do not easily resort to industrial action or else have not the cohesion or resources to sustain it. There may be a good case in any free society for retaining an ultimate freedom to strike or to lock out on any disputed issue in industry. There is no case at all for not providing a suitable peaceful procedure as an alternative in order to minimise the likelihood of these sanctions being employed.

Furthermore, the British Government has ratified the ILO Convention 98 which in Article 4 includes an obligation on governments 'to encourage and promote the full development and utilisation of machinery for voluntary negotiation between employers or employers' organisations and workers' organisations, with a view to the regulation of terms and conditions of employment by means of collective agreements'. True, no more is said about the fulfilment of this obligation than that 'Measures appropriate to national conditions shall be taken, where necessary ...' But have we in any sense honoured the spirit of this international obligation, or indeed any of the other obligations in this Convention such as those set out in Articles 1 to 3, which include protection of workers against acts of anti-union discrimination?[22] The Government in adopting the Convention in 1951 qualified its acceptance with the proviso 'that the negotiation and application of collective agreements, and the establishment of disputes procedures, were essentially matters for settlement by the parties concerned and not by the Government'.[23] This was tantamount to saying that they did not intend to do anything about it.

What is needed if the institution of collective bargaining is to be given more practical support is a permanent public authority empowered to hear recognition disputes and to make recommendations for their settlement. Although one does not wish at this time to multiply the separate pieces of machinery for public intervention in industrial relations, I would favour the creation of a special Tribunal for this purpose rather than extending the powers of the existing Industrial Court.[24] One important reason is that a body dealing with disputes of this character would not be acting as an arbitrator but more like a permanent Court of Inquiry. It could not possibly rely, for example, only on the parties' submissions for evidence. It would probably have to employ its own investigating officers to discover relevant facts, such as the degree of support for the union and whether other unions were involved. It should certainly be empowered to arrange a secret ballot, if this was thought to be desirable, although equally it should not be compelled to do so. Contrary to the usual practice in arbitration, it would also be necessary for such a Tribunal to give reasons for its decisions and ensure that they were reasonably consistent with each other. It would in fact have gradually to evolve a set of working principles.

The arguments for having a special Tribunal are further strengthened when one considers whether it should deal only with recognition disputes. Another type which it would be appropriate to bring within the same procedure are jurisdictional disputes. These are not the same as demarcation disputes though the two are sometimes confused. A demarcation dispute is over the allocation of work by an employer which becomes an inter-union conflict when members of different unions are in competition for the same job territory. A jurisdictional dispute, on the other hand, is one where two (or more) rival unions are in conflict over their claims to represent the same group of workers. The employer may be willing to recognise either union so in this sense it is not an ordinary recognition dispute, but as the unions are virtually competing for recognition the two types of dispute are closely related. The TUC Disputes Committee is one existing 'court of appeal' for the settlement of jurisdictional disputes and some industrial federations of unions have a procedure to deal with them when they arise among their affiliates. These existing means, however, are far from adequate. There would appear to be no objection to their being supplemented by an alternative appeal to a public authority, the more so since employers and, of course, the public have an interest in their speedy settlement.

It is arguable in fact that the Tribunal should be empowered to hear any disputes arising out of procedural as opposed to substantive issues in the organised relations between employers and employees. There may, for example, be questions relating to charges of unfair practice on the part of employers or trade unions or over the status, security or facilities to be accorded to representatives of either side, including various types of 'closed shop' disputes. At present no satisfactory public provision is made for the peaceful settlement of such issues. Questions relating to the revision of existing disputes procedures are on a somewhat different footing. As a rule it would not be advisable for the Tribunal to assume the responsibility for designing the whole of a disputes procedure for an industry. This is too fundamental an aspect of the relations between the parties for any outside body to determine. But the process of reform of an outmoded or inadequate procedure might be assisted and speeded up if there was a possibility of referring particular issues for enquiry and an impartial recommendation, at the request of one of the parties or the government.

One consideration which would favour the Tribunal having all procedural questions included in its terms of reference arises out of a possible objection to reliance on such a device for extending union recognition and collective bargaining. A trade union with no real capacity for strike action might secure recognition through the Tribunal only to find that the employer was unwilling to negotiate on a basis of parity or 'in good faith'. What redress would it have? Should it have recourse to compulsory arbitration?[25] This would be one solution, but there is an alternative which would not require the general reintroduction of a measure like the Industrial Disputes Order. A model worth bearing in mind is the Civil Service arbitration agreement which may be regarded as the foundation of collective bargaining for the staff associations. This transforms into negotiation what would otherwise merely be consultation by placing the unions on an equal footing with the government in access to the Civil Service Arbitration Tribunal. If a union entitled to recognition could secure a similar binding commitment from the employer to abide by arbitration in the last resort, its negotiating position would be secure. This would be a sensible ruling for the special Tribunal to give in these circumstances. In making a recommendation on recognition it would in any event have to state the subjects on which the employer was expected to bargain. In doubtful cases the working of the agreement could be made subject to further review by the Tribunal after a stated period to see whether its recommendations were being fully observed.

For all the above reasons it would be best to set up a new permanent authority, in addition to the Industrial Court and the National Board for Prices and Incomes, to which any procedural disputes over union recognition and collective bargaining might be referred. Although such disputes would usually be reported unilaterally, their reference to the Tribunal should lie within the discretion of the Ministry of Labour, which would first seek to resolve them by conciliation in the usual fashion. Once a dispute had been referred to the Tribunal for settlement, however, it would be advisable to impose a restriction on strikes and lockouts, possibly on any form of aggressive action, until it had published its recommendations. The provision in the Industrial Disputes Order, which merely allowed the Ministry to stay the proceedings in the event of a stoppage or a 'substantial breach of an agreement' would be too weak. Financial penalties would have to be imposed to deter either side from frustrating the purpose of the reference.

Should the findings of the Tribunal be made compulsory? The

traditional device in this country for enforcing awards under compulsory arbitration, by making them automatically implied terms of the individual contracts of employment, would be inapplicable to most procedural disputes. It would be possible, however, to amend the Fair Wages Clause Resolution of the House of Commons to make observance of the recommendations of the Tribunal a compulsory condition in government contracts. This proposal is open to the objection that the Tribunal might wish to regard many of its recommendations as advisory rather than mandatory, much as the recommendations of a Court of Inquiry provide a fresh basis for negotiation and settlement between the parties and give them an opportunity to adapt them to their own preferences. In procedural questions, which are likely to affect their relations for a long time to come, there is much to be said for not enforcing them without giving the parties a chance to reconsider their position. As in any case it is likely that clear rulings by an authoritative body would carry a great deal of weight, the question of formal sanctions might be left in abeyance until some experience had been gained with the operation of the Tribunal on the same voluntary basis with respect to its recommendations as the National Board for Prices and Incomes.

It would not be in keeping with the British approach to industrial relations to specify in detail the terms of reference of the new Tribunal in the legislation which created it. Although they would have to be extended, some of the main guidelines for its operation could be taken from the relevant International Labour Conventions, especially Nos. 87 and 98. Otherwise, apart from defining its organisation, the nature of the disputes which might be referred to it, and the powers it would require, the development of policy would best be entrusted to the good sense of the Tribunal itself so that it has the freedom to look at each case on its merits, while building up from experience a set of working principles. One illustration of the advisability of giving it a fairly free hand would be the difficult question it would often have to settle in cases of union recognition – the scale of the appropriate bargaining unit. There are so many considerations which could influence a recommendation on this subject in a country where bargaining units have largely emerged through the free play of social forces, that any attempt to reduce them to a set of standard formulas would probably do more harm than good.

LEGISLATION TO STRENGTHEN COLLECTIVE BARGAINING

A further weakness in collective bargaining was previously related to the role of Wages Councils. The earlier expectation that they (or the Trade Boards which preceded them) would be a transitional phenomenon leading to the setting up of voluntary collective bargaining arrangements has not been fulfilled. The unsatisfactory nature of the present situation has been stated, but how should it be changed? A crucial reason 'why the number of Councils abolished has remained so small' has been mentioned by the Ministry of Labour: 'In many industries neither employers nor workers want to lose the services of the wages inspectorate in enforcing wage rates.'[26] This is not necessarily due to laziness or indifference but depends on the structure of the industries concerned. Wherever there are a large number of small units in an industry, even when as in baking much of its production is concentrated in a few large firms, to police the agreement *throughout* the industry by voluntary action becomes an impossible or impracticable venture, short of compulsory organisation on both sides. Even then collusion to evade the agreement in small units would be difficult to detect.

To deal with this situation the Ministry proposes that the Minister might be 'empowered to continue for a limited period to use the inspectorate, after the abolition of Council, for the enforcement of the statutory rates last negotiated between the two sides of the industry concerned prior to abolition'. Once it had strengthened its voluntary machinery with this temporary prop then any further problems of enforcement after the transitional period could be met, the Ministry suggests, by using the Industrial Court under s.8 of the Terms and Conditions of Employment Act, 1959.[27] This proposal does not go far enough. The problem of enforcement is a permanent one as long as the structure of the industry remains unchanged. Using the provisions of the 1959 Act is an inadequate solution in an industry with many small employers because it is necessary for the union to bring every single non-federated employer separately before the Industrial Court and the award applies only to the existing wage agreement. As soon as it was revised it might be necessary to bring each employer before the Court again.

A more straightforward and effective solution would be to introduce permissive legislation which allowed the Minister of Labour to enforce certain substantive clauses in collective agreements throughout an industry on joint application of both sides after public enquiry into the justification for this course. The same sanctions could then be applied to ensure the observance of these clauses as for Wages Regulation Orders, including the use of the Wages Council Inspectorate. Most industries would doubtless prefer to continue with voluntary agreements, but those whose organisation is good enough to negotiate them, yet too weak to make all the relevant employers and employees observe them, would then be able to conduct collective bargaining outside the limiting framework of the Wages Council system. The farce of having independent members whose only function is to 'rubber stamp' previously negotiated agreements, which now characterises the operation of some Wages Councils, would be ended.

An alternative proposal would be to extend the existing powers of Wages Councils, beyond the fixing of minimum remuneration and of holidays and holiday remuneration, to all the normal subjects of collective bargaining, including the setting up of a grievance procedure for the industry and the making of agreements relating productivity to pay. Some extension of the powers of Wages Councils is probably desirable, but if this were combined with permissive legislation for the enforcement of substantive agreements there would be a much better chance of replacing many Councils by voluntary arrangements where the parties were free to negotiate on any subjects they chose. One of the great drawbacks of Wages Councils is that they tend to encourage lethargy in recruitment and organisational activity among the unions and employers who rely on them. The organisations on both sides are, as it were, 'established' by the Wages Council and enjoy limited negotiating rights regardless of whether they make any efforts to extend their membership or to keep in touch with the views of those whom they represent.[28] To increase the powers of the Councils without providing a stronger incentive for their abolition would result in reinforcing this unsatisfactory state of affairs.

The strong objections which can be raised against a general legal enforcement of procedural agreements would not apply to a selective use of legal support for substantive agreements. Even in this country the latter device represents no new departure in principle. It was employed to save collective bargaining from collapse in cotton weaving in 1934 and earlier still in coal mining in 1912 to give miners a legal claim to the minimum rates fixed by joint district boards. And the post-war Dock Labour Scheme of 1946 provides yet a further example where negotiated agreements have been given the force of law.[29] None of these cases have threatened the substance of the voluntary principle, whereas the legal enforcement of procedural agreements would completely change the character of collective bargaining and force the actual conduct of negotiations and the process of dispute settlement into a restrictive legal form.

The third major weakness of collective bargaining in this country has been shown to be the comparative poverty of its subject matter, so far as the formal agreements between employers and unions are concerned. These do not regulate issues which ought to be brought within the realm of joint regulation in present-day circumstances. The solution to this problem lies partly in the development of more formal plant agreements, a question to be examined later. At the level of national or industry-wide negotiations, however, there are some subjects which should be dealt with by collective agreements and frequently are not. It is here that a judicious use of the method of state regulation might contribute further public support to collective bargaining without threatening its voluntary character. An example of how this may be achieved was given by the Baking Industry (Hours of Work) Act, 1954, which restricted and regulated night work in the industry. The Act made it possible for the Minister to exempt bakeries from its provisions where they were covered by suitable voluntary agreements. When the Fourth Exemption Order was issued in 1959 the smaller bakeries were brought into line with the rest so that now any baker who wishes to do so can operate under conditions settled by collective agreements rather than those imposed by the Act. Legislation was, however, an important means of stimulating the negotiation of agreements and retains its importance as a spur to their observance.

The essence of the method then is to use state regulation to set minimum conditions, while allowing the parties to opt out of legal enforcement when and where they negotiate agreements with not less favourable terms. It would appear to have immediate application to a question which the Ministry of Labour is actively considering, with the help of a committee of the National Joint Advisory Council— the provision of better safeguards against the arbitrary dismissal of workers. Without pre-judging in detail a matter of such legal complexity as the type of additional protection which is required, we may assume that it will have to include, first, some definition of invalid reasons for dismissal and, second, an impartial appeals procedure which will enable workers to seek redress against dismissal without just cause. Given legislation to set minimum standards on these lines, it would probably be expedient to apply it by making use of the same tribunals which have to deal with disputes under the Redundancy Payments Act. But some industries and firms already have disciplinary codes and procedures for appeals against dismissal, and many others might be encouraged to devise them. To support such voluntary action it would therefore be desirable to write into the legislation a 'contracting out' clause. Subject to approval by the Ministry and a general proviso to the effect that the purpose of the legislation was being satisfied, industries or firms should be allowed to apply their own agreements with trade unions instead of being governed by the legislation.

The same method could be used to tackle another problem which is now causing serious concern – the working in many industries of excessive and unnecessary overtime. The case for reducing overtime is now widely accepted, but how is this aim to be accomplished? With the spread of productivity bargaining some individual managements are taking the initiative to bring hours more closely into line with the standard working week fixed by collective agreements, but they are the few exceptions. A quicker and more universal solution to the problem is required on economic and social grounds. It can only be provided by the legal regulation of maximum working hours, such as we already have under the Factories Act for women and young persons but not for adult males. In some industries the overtime worked by men is limited either by union rule or by collective agreement but these restrictions, where they exist, are not very effective. Nothing short of legislation seems likely to force the pace in overtime reduction.

If it is accepted that there is now a good case for following the example of many other countries and fixing maximum hours of work for all employees by law, then clearly this should be a phased reduction to avoid disruptive effects and must include some provision to offset any substantial loss in earnings. It would have in any case to be combined with an arrangement for special permits to sanction overtime limits where the pressure of work in a factory genuinely demanded it, such as already operates for women and young persons under the Factories Act. But here again legislation could serve mainly as a spur to and an underpinning of voluntary action.

From the two different instances cited – protection against arbitrary dismissal and the reduction of unnecessary overtime – it will be seen how the Government could increasingly adopt a more positive role in the field of industrial relations without prejudicing the future of collective bargaining. Indeed it can combine this with giving voluntary agreements stronger support. It is a mistake to regard state regulation and collective bargaining as incompatible alternatives. One method of regulation may be used to strengthen the other as long as voluntary agreements continue in general to take precedence over statutory orders as instruments of job regulation.

THE FUTURE OF INCOMES POLICY

The same fundamental problem of how to reconcile the present responsibilities of government with the merits of voluntarism is raised in remedying the second major shortcoming of our industrial relations system – its lack of provision for safeguarding acknowledged public interests. Considerable progress has been made over the last few years in setting up or strengthening institutional machinery for exerting some national influence on the behaviour of the parties to collective bargaining. The National Economic Development Council and the separate Economic Development Committees for particular industries, the Industrial Training Boards and the Ministry of Labour's Manpower Research Unit, not least the National Board for Prices and Incomes, are all from this point of view valuable innovations. The fusion of the several central employers' federations into the CBI and the TUC's newly acquired powers to screen its affiliated unions' wage claims must also be counted important advances in a similar direction, which only a short time ago were thought impracticable. Yet so far their total impact on the actual conduct of collective bargaining has been slight. Quick results were not perhaps to be expected, but there is more to it than that. We are far from sure whether the existing means will suffice. The question persists whether greater powers of compulsion will have to be introduced.

187

Partly because its voluntary incomes policy had so little effect the Government was forced to impose a wages and prices standstill and a period of 'severe restraint' with the help of reserve statutory powers. No one would have anticipated these events and one of the difficulties of saying anything about the future of incomes and man-power planning in this country is to know what effects the amended Prices and Incomes Act will have. When the temporary restrictions in Part IV of the Act have been lifted, will the early warning and delaying system (supported possibly by the sanctions provided in Part II of the Act) and a strengthened National Board be able to control the flood which so often follows a freeze? In one way or another social attitudes will surely be altered by so drastic an experience which everyone has shared. But how they will be changed one cannot predict although that may be the decisive factor in settling the immediate fate of our incomes policy.

To avoid speculation about the future let me return to the earlier diagnosis of the problem of incomes policy and consider how far we have gone towards solving them. Leaving aside the more technical aspects of manpower planning,[30] they fall into three main groups. First, there is the need to formulate agreed national rules, which have not existed in the past, to guide the behaviour of the parties to collective bargaining. Second, we have the question of compliance – how to ensure that the rules are observed. Third, since planning does not only involve regulation and restraint, we need a strategy for reforming existing arrangements and practices which are not conducive to the achievement of the agreed aims of national policy.

With the publication of the White Paper on *Prices and Incomes Policy* (Cmnd. 2577) in April 1965 a start was made with the form-ulation of national rules to regulate the planned growth of incomes. This has been taken further by the interpretations placed upon it in the reports of the National Board on particular references.[31] The two constituent elements of incomes policy, a general norm (or norms) and criteria for exceptional increases, are clearly essential, but both have now to be re-examined in the light of subsequent experience.

The current concept of the norm describes it as 'the average rate of annual increase of money incomes per head which is consistent with stability in the general level of prices'.[32] Past practice has been to fix this at the same level as the anticipated 'average annual rate of growth in output per head'. Increases above the norm were to be justified only in exceptional circumstances and were to be balanced by lower-than-average increases to other groups. A strong argument can be mounted, however, against this use of the norm concept. As it is meant to be an average struck from a very large number of settlements, it cannot serve as a guide for individual industries, for how are they to know what 'exceptional' increases are in the making and how their own settlement is meant to adjust the balance? The norm represents the desired net outcome of their own settlement plus countless others which they know nothing about. By definition, therefore, it cannot give the guidance required. It is not surprising that the norm has come to be taken as the 'standard' settlement, on which every claimant group naturally tries to improve. Few increases of less than the norm are likely to emerge as 'balancing' items against exceptional increases. If the norm is to serve as a genuine guide, therefore, it needs to be set at a point significantly lower than the 'average rate of annual increase of money incomes per head which is consistent with stability in the general level of prices'. This could then safely be taken as the 'standard' settlement, on the assumption that exceptional increases will raise the average to a point not too much above the desired level.

It is another question, however, whether overall price stability, taken literally, is a desirable or feasible objective, as the original Declaration of Intent stated. The curbing of unnecessary price increases and, indeed, the forcing of some price reductions must be a policy objective, but some degree of inflation is probably unavoidable under full employment; and other countries, with whom we compete in world markets, are not immune. It is most important to fix a realistic norm which the great majority of unions and employers seriously intend to observe, rather than one which, though it would theoretically prevent any rise in the price level, would go disregarded in practice.

Of the White Paper's four criteria for exceptional pay increases the National Board has made most use of the first: 'where the employees concerned, for example, by accepting more exacting work or a major change in working practices, make a direct contribution towards increasing productivity'. This is understandable. In the absence of any means of enforcing its recommendations the Board had to try to make them as acceptable as possible to both sides by proposing offsetting economies for wage increases which could not be prevented. Thus the spread of productivity agreements has been stimulated by the existence of an incomes policy. As long as they are genuine and lead to a better utilisation of labour this is a development to be welcomed, despite any difficulties which may arise on account of consequential comparisons. There is, after all, no practical alternative for changing inefficient manning and working practices which lie within the workers' control. Authoritative guidance should be given on the conditions which productivity agreements are expected to fulfil, but that is a task which has now been taken in hand by the Board.[33]

The other three criteria can hardly be allowed to stand indefinitely in their existing form. The one relating to the distribution of manpower has largely been set aside by the National Board in its Report on the Pay and Conditions of Busmen.[34] If it were to be used in other than the most exceptional cases, the whole purpose of an incomes policy would be undermined. The remaining two ('wage and salary levels too low to maintain a reasonable standard of living' and 'widespread recognition that the pay of certain groups of workers has fallen seriously out of line') are both concerned with social justice, but are too indeterminate to provide practical guidelines for policy. Even if we ignore the further vague qualifications which the White Paper places on their application, what is 'a *reasonable* standard of living' or '*seriously* out of line'? Each of these criteria raises difficulties which can only be satisfactorily resolved by a further clarification of national policy.

Acceptance of an incomes policy in the trade union world has been bedevilled by the persisting contrast between the hope that it would do something to improve the position of low-paid workers and its apparent failure to make any headway in tackling this problem. Part of the difficulty lies in deciding what is meant by 'low wages'. Loose talk about the need for a 'national minimum wage' avoids the real obstacles. If a national minimum were introduced by legislation it would have to apply to rates, but there are industries (like road haulage) with low rates and high earnings because of the prevalence of very high levels of overtime. Moreover, raising minimum rates would inevitably jack up the whole of the pay structure and so increase the earnings of the better-paid workers as well. The crux of the problem, in so far as it turns on collective bargaining and not on social insurance, is really a combination of two things: the existence in many industries of unrealistically low basic rates on which has been built a superstructure of additional payments; and the fact that these payments vary greatly in amount from one worker to another with at least some earning very little more than their basic rate. As a result the spread of earnings within industries, or even occupations, is much greater than the average earnings relativities between different industries.

It follows that there are low-paid workers in almost every industry and, in comparative terms, only few low-paid industries. The relative position of these workers cannot be improved by general increases in the basic rates, which will normally increase the earnings of all workers, unless they are coupled with an agreement to reduce additional payments. Productivity agreements aimed at cutting down excessive overtime are one means to this end, but there are other possibilities. The 'minimum earnings' provisions in the three-year engineering package deal agreement were a practical approach and their results should be carefully studied to see what lessons they offer for other industries. The important point to be grasped is that the analysis of actual pay structures must be the foundation of any realistic policy for dealing with low payment. The Government, after consultation with the TUC and CBI, could give a lead by setting national minimum earnings targets to be reached possibly in a series of stages.[35] It should also supply more detailed and up-to-date information on distributions of earnings. But actual policies have to be worked out and negotiated through collective bargaining industry by industry.

The White Paper was least explicit on the role of comparability in an incomes policy. In general it said that 'comparisons with the levels or trends of incomes in other employment' were to be given 'less weight than hitherto' so that more weight could be given to the incomes norm. By introducing the 'seriously-out-of-line' criterion for exceptional pay increases, however, it suggested that they should not be ignored altogether. The National Board has been left to decide how to apply this advice in particular cases; the negotiators themselves could not possibly know what it meant. Yet one of the strongest appeals of an incomes policy to many wage and salary earners is the prospect which it offers of bringing about a fairer distribution of incomes;[36] ethical arguments are on the whole likely to be more persuasive than economic ones in gaining their consent for restraints on the play of self-interest. One can see in any factory that the greater the inequities in its pay structure the more unstable and a source of conflict it becomes. The process of reforming and ordering wage relativities on a national scale is, of course, immensely more difficult and can only be taken in hand in stages. There is as yet no social consensus on the standards to be applied and differentials sanctioned by tradition are strongly upheld by those who gain from them. Nevertheless progress can and must be made if an incomes policy is to work. It depends in the end on developing national rules to govern the uses of comparability.

The fact that comparability has been so important a factor in inflation has encouraged some people to draw the facile conclusion that its influence on wage settlements must be eliminated. This is tantamount to denying any role for social justice (beyond curing poverty) in wage settlements; for justice must involve comparison. No surer way of destroying an incomes policy could be proposed. The conclusion which should be drawn is that the use of crude, and often quite irrational and contradictory, comparisons which have served merely to spiral incomes should be progressively refined by agreement on when comparisons are relevant and fair. This can be furthered by the tools of job evaluation and the kind of techniques which have been employed by the Civil Service Pay Research Unit, but these are not substitutes for collective bargaining for their results must have the general approval of those whom the negotiators represent. The process of refining crude comparisons therefore can only proceed by clarifying and changing the concepts of fairness or equity that are already being applied.

In the present situation there are two obvious starting points, the one positive and the other negative. First, there are certain manifest inequities which everyone knows to be indefensible; they have to be corrected. Second, the use of comparison has to be excluded in those cases where in justice it cannot be held to apply; this means, for example, ruling out wage increases comparable to those gained under a productivity agreement where no productivity return is forthcoming. Granted that it would be impossible at this stage to lay down a precise national code for the use of comparability, in this partial and piecemeal fashion agreed policies and practical rules for its application could be evolved.

The Future of Incomes Policy

Turning from the formulation of national rules for collective bargaining to their enforcement, we confront the greatest dilemma of the voluntary system. Can we rely on self-discipline in industry supplemented by the pressures of public opinion for ensuring a general observance of the rules? In other words, when we emerge from the period of 'severe restraint', can a voluntary incomes policy succeed? The prospects are not encouraging. Neither the CBI nor the TUC–though they can make recommendations–have any real power to discipline their affiliated organisations when they are tempted to transgress the rules. They may be able gradually to increase their influence and authority and this is certainly to be welcomed. Their involvement in the execution as well as the formulation of policy is a necessary condition for its success. But is it a sufficient condition? I do not think it is and for one reason more than any other: at present a voluntary system cannot work out priorities for itself because there is no consensus on them. There is more to this than the refusal of some interest groups to co-operate–the 'selfish minority' in the words of the White Paper on *Prices and Incomes Standstill*[37]–although that is part of the problem. We have as yet no agreed social norms on the subject of income distribution; criteria conflict on what is fair. It follows that any given pattern of priorities will meet with resistance from some groups because it runs contrary not only to their interests but also to their values.

The most important factor in making any incomes policy work will be the policy itself. If it fails to offer clear and specific directives, self-discipline in industry cannot possibly be observed. Equally if the policy fails to command sufficient public support, it cannot be imposed. Legal enforcement of a policy which did not enjoy a large measure of social consent would be unworkable. Any sanctions must prove to be ineffective unless they are applied only in exceptional cases. The primary aim must therefore be to achieve at least as great a consensus as possible on the national rules which should govern the conduct of collective bargaining. The case for the Government having some reserve powers of compulsion is that they will be needed for the achievement of that aim. Much of the difficulty in developing a consensus is the fear that if I keep to the rules somebody else will not and so steal an advantage over me. The chances are that incomes policy will once again quickly become little more than a façade unless there is an assurance that it does not pay to be odd man out. The rules of the Highway Code are mainly observed by self-discipline because they are thought to be reasonable, but respect for them could quickly be destroyed if there were no penalties on dangerous driving.

The main burden of interpreting the national rules of incomes policy and applying them to particular cases seems likely to fall on the National Board for Prices and Incomes. It is not suggested that this body should have any compulsory powers to enforce its recommendations. Such powers have to be taken by the Government and, as the Chairman of the National Board has suggested,[38] they should be confined to certain categories of judgement and applied only after the views of the CBI and the TUC have been sought. This, as he said, 'would help to increase the influence of the CBI and the TUC; and the opinion of the CBI and TUC would underpin the use of compulsion'. The principal purpose of providing these reserve legal powers would lie not so much in their use as in their existence. They would impart a seriousness to the observance of an incomes policy, which really came into the picture for the first time with the freeze. So far as one can judge public opinion would favour such a restricted and judicious use of compulsion.[39]

But reform is just as important as restraint. Indeed they are complementary as can be seen in the reports of the National Board. One of the salient points about reform which seems to be emerging clearly out of the experience of the past year or so is that the methods of enquiry and accountability are going to be much more widely used, and with considerable effect, to influence the conduct of collective bargaining. In the past it has been largely conducted behind closed doors, with no provision for public accountability, on the basis of arguments which had only a tenuous relationship to the facts. Subjecting it to a process of rigorous enquiry, making the parties answerable for their decisions, reviewing these in the light of agreed national policy, and presenting practical recommendations on desirable reforms–all these things together represent a means of public control with a potential which should not be underestimated. Half a century ago Sidney and Beatrice Webb referred to the 'full and continuous application of the principle of measurement and publicity' as one of the main pillars in the democratic system of public control which they foresaw.[40] This principle is being applied at last to collective bargaining.

Quite apart from its continuous application by the National Board, the old method of public enquiry is acquiring a new significance in other respects. From being used mainly as a method of the last resort for mediation and dispute settlement, the device of the Court of Inquiry (or the Committee of Investigation) is developing–as we saw most dramatically in the case of the Devlin Committee on the Docks–into a means for inaugurating major reforms in an industry's industrial relations. The provision of qualified assistance to undertake the necessary research, instead of relying entirely on *ex parte* statements of 'evidence' from the sides, is an important and obvious corollary.

The objection could be raised that a multiplicity of different bodies concerned with reform must lead to conflicting and inconsistent proposals, and that it would be better if the whole of this activity came under the auspices or control of the National Board for Prices and Incomes. Such an extreme degree of centralisation is unlikely ever to be acceptable. The main function of the National Board should be to determine the implications of agreed national policy by applying it to strategically chosen references. It then falls to any third parties who are involved in settling disputes or introducing change in collective bargaining to take the policy into account, in the same way as the negotiators on both sides are expected to do. Where they disregard it, they cannot reasonably claim a special position of privilege for their awards or recommendations. The Government must have the right to refer them to the National Board for review in the same way as directly negotiated agreements. In either case, however, it is preferable for the more important claims and disputes to be referred to the Board in their early stages before positions have hardened.

THE RECONSTRUCTION OF WORKPLACE RELATIONS

The third major shortcoming of our system of industrial relations, the chaotic state of relations between managements and shop stewards, has been traced to their having been formed by drift rather than by design. Sustained full employment has greatly strengthened the bargaining power of work groups and the authority of shop stewards, but managements have responded to this situation with no clearly defined, long-term, and–above all–consistent, objectives in mind. By making *ad hoc* concessions to pressure, when resistance proved too costly, they have fostered guerrilla warfare over wages and working conditions in the workplace and encouraged aggressive shop-floor tactics by rewarding them.

To bring together what has already been said about the consequences of this growing anarchy in workplace relations, they are to be seen: in unofficial strikes and earnings drift; in under-utilisation of labour and resistance to change; in the growth of systematic overtime and the demoralisation of incentive pay schemes; in inequitable and unstable factory pay structures; in a general decline in industrial discipline; in an undermining of external regulation by industry-wide and other agreements; and in a weakening of control by trade unions and employers' associations over their members. All these consequences in turn must threaten the success of an incomes policy, which is intended to bring both the movement and structure of wages and other incomes under an increasing measure of national control. If neither are controlled within individual establishments, they cannot be controlled at industry and national levels either. Nor is it possible to do much to safeguard the public interest in offsetting pay increases by higher labour productivity if this interest is ignored in shop-floor bargaining.

The case for a radical reconstruction of workplace relations is therefore an overwhelmingly strong one on the immediate, practical grounds that their present state is causing serious damage to the national economy and to the fabric of our industrial relations system. But there is more to it than that. Social values are changing and with them the expectations of workers with regard to their rights in industry. Differences of treatment between workmen and staff and other reflections of a social class structure in industry are increasingly resented. So too are autocratic and manipulative methods of management which offend the dignity of workers as human beings. When they claim a greater measure of control over managerial decisions affecting their working life and access to knowledge which management refuses to give, they may be seeking to protect their interests but they are also expressing their legitimate concern that they should not be treated in industry as irresponsible, second-class citizens.

How then can one formulate the objectives of such reconstruction? The uniqueness of each workplace situation, even within the same industry or large company, makes the drafting of universal blueprints for reform impractical. There is, however, a common underlying problem which is universal enough to point to an overriding objective. As I have shown it is the problem of managerial control. All the unfortunate consequences of drift in workplace relations are manifestations of a weakening of control by managements over the interrelated pay and work systems in their establishments, a control which they have lost because of their refusal to share it. The objective should be a restoration of stronger control over pay structures and the organisation of work on what today is the only feasible foundation–agreement with the workers' representatives and the building up of co-operation through an extending area of joint regulation.

Joint regulation, however, presupposes agreement on its aims. To achieve it neither management nor workers' representatives have to neglect or prejudice their own proper functions and the quite different responsibilities which they entail. They have only to take an enlightened view of how their functions may best be discharged, which means in particular abandoning the deeply-entrenched belief on both sides that if one wins the other must lose. They have to learn from experience that, given good will and fair dealing, they can better advance their diverging interests by appreciating that they are divergent and yet, by compromise, can be reconciled. The practical basis of reconciliation is that both sides can gain from it, not only materially but in more civilised relations.

Admittedly it is an over-simplification to assume that there are only two sides to workplace relations. Many conflicts of interest have to be resolved within management and among the managed. These complicate the reaching of agreement on the aims of joint regulation in workplace relations, especially on the union side. The hierarchical structure of management, and the pressures for conformity which arise where promotion depends on the good opinion of one's superiors, force it to act together on behalf of a policy once this has been decided at the top. The integration of the behaviour of different work groups all with their separate interests, even where there is not the added complication of inter-union rivalry, may present far greater difficulty. But the same difficulty had to be surmounted in the development of collective bargaining between employers' associations and trade unions. Their agreements have to be made to accommodate a variety of diverse interests among employers and among employees. Once joint institutions have been created and their value is proven, sanctions are found to prevent them being torn apart and destroyed.

The parties to collective bargaining in this country have generally preferred to rely more on their procedural than on their substantive rules for ordering their relations. The same priority is likely to be observed in the evolution of better workplace relations. The procedural rules of collective bargaining serve three different functions. First, they define the bargaining unit and the structure of relationships between the bargaining parties. Second, they determine the status and facilities to be accorded to their representatives. Third, they regulate the behaviour of the parties in the settlement of disputes; the stages to be followed and the methods to be used. There must be few plants in this country which have a code of agreed procedural rules which give clear and unambiguous answers to each of these questions. If the excessive fragmentation of intra-plant bargaining is to be overcome, then ideally the bargaining unit should comprise the whole of the plant. Moreover, negotiation taking place at lower levels, in departments or with particular groups, should be subject to overall plant regulation. Similarly the rights and obligations of shop stewards, and equally of the various representatives of management, need to be known so that insecurity and uncertainty in these matters do not constantly frustrate good relations. Not least, a well-defined disputes procedure is essential which seeks to settle disputes as near as possible to their point of origin and to secure a final settlement within the plant of those disputes which have no wider implications.

That is one aspect of building up an orderly system of job regulation in the workplace. The other is agreement on its substantive rules. This raises the question of the relationship between pay and productivity, because the relationship can only be satisfactorily determined in each establishment. The wage–work bargain, which every job or contract of employment represents in the context of a labour market, is necessarily indeterminate on the work side. One can measure a fair day's wage with the yardstick of money but what constitutes a fair day's work cannot be made precise in terms of contractual obligations. Thus, whether standard or minimum wage rates are fixed, their counterpart in work cannot be specified beyond stating the hours, or, under payment by results, the output, which are expected in return. As the TUC has stated:

> The main reason why a given job content is generally assumed in national bargaining is that in almost every industry the actual nature of the work

198

done in plants around the country presents a picture of bewildering complexity. In many cases, therefore, it would be very difficult to consider changes in job content as an explicit part of national negotiations except in the most general terms. It is somewhat naïve therefore to believe that productivity considerations can in any meaningful sense and certainly in any quantifiable way be introduced explicitly into most national negotiations. It is not profitable to seek after the unattainable.[41]

The same point can be made in another way. In their economic aspect wages serve two different functions. They have a market function of allocating labour as between different undertakings and occupations. The other could be called their managerial function where by rewarding performance they serve as a positive sanction in the organisation of work. This is sometimes expressed in the proposition that labour is invariably priced twice; once to allocate it here rather than there and again to affect the intensity with which it is applied. Both of these functions are made the subject of regulation, but while the first may be regulated by those substantive rules of collective bargaining which cover national labour or product markets, the rules regulating the second cannot span more than a single managerial authority. Where work operations are highly standardised it may be possible, as in cotton textiles, to regulate payments by uniform piecework price lists, but whether this succeeds in accurately relating pay to performance is another matter.

We have here the reason why it is a mistake to think that all earnings drift, which in its conventional statistical definition compares changes in national rates with changes in actual earnings, is bad for the economy or a threat to an incomes policy. Some of it— the part of the wage which is needed to relate pay to performance— is unavoidable and advantageous. Drift in its literal meaning of uncontrolled and functionless rises in earnings has to be condemned; drift in unit labour costs is actually the real enemy to be conquered. The causes of such drift are to be found in factory pay structures and systems of payment. Although this is a large and complex subject, which cannot be treated adequately here, a few indications can be given of what is involved in their reform.

Apart from the problem of systematic overtime, which in some cases is the most significant cause of loss of control over work and pay, traditional piecework or individual (and small group) output-based systems of payment are the greatest source of drift. There is nothing new in the idea that piecework has its drawbacks. Certain objections have always been raised against it, for instance that it leads to a sacrifice of quality to quantity, but it was accepted because its advantages were thought to outweigh its disadvantages. What is new—at least what has been happening on a very much greater scale over the post-war years—is the process called degeneration or demoralisation of piecework and associated wage structures. Some of the results of this process have been described as:

(1) substantial inequities in earnings and effort. A mixture of tight and loose standards is both cause and effect in perpetuating a multitude of grievances over standards and a distorted wage structure; (2) a growing average incentive yield or bonus (so that the incentive payment becomes an ever larger part of the total wage, *A.F.*); (3) a declining average level of effort. Workers appear to take the gains of looser standards partly in increased earnings and partly in increased leisure; (4) a high proportion of 'off-standard' payments and times.[42]

But degeneration of a piecework-based pay system involves much more than a blunting of its incentive effect. The distortion of wage relativities throws up resentments among those workers who are on time rates, and, to appease their discontent, various lieu payments and supplements have to be invented. Distortion constantly breeds further distortion, instability further instability. Conflict is engendered partly by insecurity of earnings which is a potent cause of restrictions on output, and partly by the fragmentation of bargaining which encourages the exploitation of wage inequities rather than their cure. In the end the situation may get completely out of hand; neither management nor unions can control it. And for the workers themselves, while it may produce high pay, every other interest— not least their interest in security—comes to be sacrificed.

An even more fundamental objection may be raised against piecework in the context of modern industrial organisation: that it is inconsistent with any enlightened view of the employment relationship between the worker and the organisation which employs him. It invites groups of workers to set up their own stall and act as groups of marketeers within the enterprise, to use their bargaining power to sell their effort for the best price they can get without regard to the effect of their action on the organisation as a whole. Yet an enterprise is supposed to integrate the work of all its employees. When their system of payment is such as to structure their behaviour towards disintegration it is futile to preach loyalty and co-operation.

Alternative systems of payment will have to be introduced if pay is to be correctly related to performance and pay structures are to be made more equitable and consequently more stable. Not that any one system of payment is intrinsically superior to another. They must all be judged by their results and these depend on a wide range of variables in the total situation where they operate. Nevertheless, if we are to evaluate them properly we must at least recognise the variety of incentive functions which pay as a reward or positive sanction may serve. Apart from the rewarding of individual or group *effort* (its alleged function under piecework) it may reward *learning*, i.e. the acquisition of knowledge and skills, an acceptance of *responsibility*, an acceptance of *change* and, not least, the results of *co-operation*, i.e. any joint furtherance of the ends of the enterprise.

Some choice has usually to be made among these various criteria of performance, for a pay system which is functional with respect to one may be dysfunctional with respect to another; the rewarding of individual or group effort, for example, may be destructive of a larger co-operation. How that choice is made depends on the nature of the work and the technology of the enterprise. What is always demanded of management, however, is that it undertakes this kind of analysis and knows what it is trying to achieve. And if it has decided, say, that for production workers on repetitive work the rewarding of effort should have the highest priority, the disruptive dangers of piecemeal bargaining over piecework prices may still be avoided by such methods as the Premium Payment Plan of the Phillips Group of Companies.[43]

Granted that it is impossible to generalise about the best system of payment for any plant, it can said that any system should meet the following three requirements: its objectives should be known and made explicit; it should incorporate the controls (including standards of measurement) which are needed to achieve those objectives; and it should be introduced and operated with the agreement of the workers' representatives. The reasons for the first of these requirements have been stated. The other two call for further comment.

The techniques of 'scientific management'–work study, job evaluation and the like–have been increasingly applied in this country since the war to reform factory pay systems. A great extension of their application, as well as improvements in the techniques themselves, is an essential part of the reconstruction of workplace relations, because measurement, like communication, is auxiliary to control. The defining of job content and the comparison of one job with another are as necessary for the proper design of pay structures and their subsequent control as the construction of accurate standards of performance.[44] The mere application of these techniques, however, in the absence of clearly defined objectives, may be pointless or even harmful. They are only tools which like any other set of tools prove their worth in the hands of a craftsman who has a clear picture of what he is trying to create. Measurement, moreover, is only one aspect of the control over pay systems, which also depends on the organisation and attitudes of management and, not least, the authority and morale of supervision. Management must be capable of sustaining a consistent application of work standards once these have been set.

Whether managerial controls over a pay system are effective also depends in part on the third requirement–joint agreement. If shop-floor agreement is lacking, or only grudgingly given, one has to expect that workers and their representatives will try to 'buck' or 'bend' the system to their advantage; and their opportunities are legion. Managements who assume that men will work only for money, that there are no other sanctions apart from pay for influencing work behaviour, are denying themselves other possible ways of meeting their own responsibilities. One has not to take an over-optimistic view of human nature to recognise that when job performance is governed by a set of agreed rules, and when the rewards attached to performance are thought to be justly determined, there is a much greater prospect of workers feeling a sense of obligation to give a fair day's work and of shop stewards using their influence to see that this happens. Joint regulation leads to involvement and a sharing of responsibility.

By looking at the linking of pay with productivity in individual establishments and the requirements to be met in improving their pay systems, we can see both the advantages and the implications of developing an agreed code of substantive rules for the internal regulation of plant bargaining. Another and complementary view of this aspect of the reconstruction of workplace relations is illuminated when we consider the future of 'custom and practice' in industrial relations. This conventional umbrella term covers all manner of unwritten rules regulating work and employment. Some of them may be officially upheld by trade unions, but most are enforced on the shop floor by work or unions groups. Shop stewards, not full-time union officials, are the principal guardians of 'custom and practice' in British industry.

These informal rules, which management has no say in making but tacitly has to accept, range over many subjects. In earlier times they were mainly the trade practices of the craftsmen who protected their job territory from invasion by limiting entry and upholding de-marcation. Today they are the means by which many workers who are not craftsmen protect their earnings and their bargaining power, but equally their security, their status and their values. Direct regulation of output or stint, of the allocation of overtime, of man-ning scales, of work sharing, of job demarcations of all kinds are well-known examples. The effect of full employment on workplace relations is not confined to the upsurge of intra-plant *collective bargaining*; it has also resulted in a growth of *unilateral regulation* by workers on the shop floor which is expressed in employment or working practices acquiring the force of institutions.

Where such 'custom and practice' is the cause of inefficiency and under-employment of labour or capital it needs to be changed, but change must be negotiated. Workers will not abandon the protection which it offers unless they can be persuaded that their interests will be better advanced under the new arrangements than the old. This is not just a question of 'buying out' existing job rights or so-called 'restrictive practices', of providing an economic inducement for the acceptance of change by higher wage rates or other pecuniary advantages. Income and job security are crucial considerations, and new forms of security have to be substituted for the old. Unless the firm employing them offers stronger safeguards against sudden unemployment or losses in earnings, why should workers abandon any of the defences on which they have previously relied? Even then they will be taking a risk–and this makes confidence in management's integrity another prerequisite for the acceptance of change.

Such is the setting which has given productivity bargaining its special contemporary significance on the British scene. It is a method, often the only practical one, of revising unilaterally enforced 'custom and practice' by bringing it into the realm of joint regulation. To see it simply as a device for raising labour productivity–by which employers insist on an economic return for their wage concessions– is to underestimate both its long-term contribution to the reconstruction of workplace relations and the exacting demands which it places on management and unions if it is to be undertaken successfully. One can, it is true, define productivity bargaining to include any negotiations in which changes in wages are tied to changes in work. It is then taken to include effort bargaining under systems of payment by results and piecemeal bargains struck with particular groups of workers to get them to agree to some change in their existing practices. Although minor productivity deals of this sort may have their value, there is a vast difference between them and the major productivity agreements, from the Fawley example onwards, with their comprehensive 'package deal' character. If one uses the wider definition, only the latter type of productivity bargaining qualifies as a method for bringing greater order and control into workplace relations. Piecemeal productivity deals may have the reverse effect. Not only are they a soft option for management since they make no demands upon it; they are also liable to set up chain reactions by creating new inequities in pay structures.

The distinguishing, common feature of all the major, genuine productivity agreements is that they are attempts to strengthen managerial control over pay and work through joint regulation. The object may be: the restoration of control where it has been lost as in the case of overtime or incentive payments; or to bring matters, such as craft demarcation lines, which have previously been the subject of unilateral union control, under regulation by joint agreement; or to raise the existing degrees of control, for example by the introduction of new grading schemes or staggered work patterns. The contents of the package vary from case to case, but the proposed changes in employment practices form an integrated pattern and are invariably specified in written agreements. They are usually associated as well with changes in the organisation and practices of management which are necessary if it is to gain and retain the increased control it is seeking.

If productivity bargaining–in this radical and creative sense of replacing drift by design in workplace relations–is the principal method for bringing about their reconstruction, what are its implications for the structure of collective bargaining? It will be obvious from what has already been said that the reconstruction of workplace relations implies a much greater formalisation of plant bargaining in its procedural and substantive aspects. Written agreements are needed in the first place to reduce uncertainty and ambiguity in the relations between the parties. Oral understandings can be genuinely forgotten and when this happens misunderstandings and distrust may easily result. Formal agreements will also help to dispel the cloud of pretence and subterfuge which has surrounded all kinds of additional payments made within the plant. Negotiators have to be more careful about the consequences of their decisions when they can be called to account for them, and their relations are placed on a more open and honest footing. Moreover, the object is to create a more controlled situation, and specification in agreement is one important means of control.

Nor can the excessive fragmentation and autonomy of workplace bargaining be overcome without the help of plant agreements. Once plant negotiations become comprehensive and all union and work groups are party to the same agreement, it is natural to codify results in writing in order to define commitments and curb leap-frogging rivalry. Similarly, if trade unions are to take a greater responsibility for the activities of their stewards, and employers' associations for their affiliated firms, they can hardly do so unless they know what is being settled in the separate establishments.

There are, to be sure, dangers in introducing too much formality into workplace relations. Too many rules, even agreed rules, can be as much the cause of unnecessary conflict through endless disputation as too few. Collective relationships within the plant are more continuous, intimate and intricate than at higher levels of bargaining and, given good relations and mutual trust, there is much to be said for flexible understandings and agreed administrative standards that are more in the nature of guidelines than rigid rules. This applies particularly to such questions as discipline or safety. The rules which need to be made most explicit are those regulating payment systems and the measurable aspects of work and employment. Finally, the need for formalisation is a function of size. Generally speaking, the larger the establishment the more complex must be the network of rules required to order its relationships.

The strong case which can be argued for formal plant agreements is not, as is sometimes suggested, a case for dismantling our existing structure of industry agreements. We should never forget that these remain the foundation of our industrial relations system and continue to provide the main apparatus for securing order and regulation within it. Anchored as they are in our tradition of voluntarism, to weaken them would be to weaken trade unions and employers' associations on which our society relies for controlling and influencing the character of relationships in industry. We depend, for example, on industry agreements to settle certain uniform standards against which particular rates of pay or conditions of work can be assessed. We depend on them to safeguard minimum provisions for workers employed in the less prosperous or unorganised firms. We depend on them for the maintenance of voluntary procedures outside the firm for settling disputes and avoiding strikes. Not least they offer a general structure for the relations between both sides of industry for the cultivation of important 'non-negotiating' questions such as improving the methods of industrial training. Large companies may opt out of industry agreements in favour of company agreements without themselves suffering any serious disadvantages. A general collapse of the system would be disastrous.

If industry agreements are essential in most industries, what should be their relationship to plant agreements? To avert the dangers to an incomes policy of a further spread of unco-ordinated plant bargaining, industry and plant agreements have certainly to be brought into a closer and more integrated relationship with each other. It is impossible, however, in a general way to delineate the areas of responsibility at each level without regard to the conditions prevailing in particular industries. While the autonomy of workplace bargaining has to be diminished, it would be unfortunate if industry agreements–which tend to be negotiated to suit the lowest common denominator among employers–were used to stifle managerial initiatives in the reconstruction of workplace relations. We shall have to seek a pragmatic solution to this problem in each industry according to its circumstances, placing more weight on industry negotiations in some and more weight on plant or company negotiations in others.

One thing is certain: the formalisation of plant bargaining will call for a much greater involvement of full-time trade union officials in plant affairs. A close liaison between officials and senior stewards is essential if unions are to sign and accept responsibility for written plant agreements. This implies considerable changes for the majority of unions in their own staffing and organisation–for instance, more full-time officials. From employers, too, it implies a readiness, which is often lacking, to admit union officials to their plant. They cannot have it both ways. They cannot continue to prefer dealing exclusively with representatives of their own employees on alleged 'domestic' matters and insist that the unions keep their stewards under control. In general both trade unions and employers' associations have to develop a new, positive role towards workplace relations, trying to guide them constructively by advice and assistance instead of relying on an external discipline which they can no longer impose.

Apart from these necessary changes in the policies and organisation of trade unions and employers' associations, their industry agreements have also to be adjusted to accommodate and encourage formal plant agreements. In some cases industry agreements already specify limits or guidelines within which plant negotiations may take place, although they may not be strictly observed in practice. Such framework or permissive agreements need to be strengthened at industry level by formulating the subjects of plant bargaining, the principles which should govern it and, possibly, economic margins to limit its extent. An attempt to bring basic rates into closer correspondence with actual earnings would be one of the strongest spurs to their conclusion. In certain industries they would also demand a radical overhaul of the existing national negotiating machinery. In engineering, for example, a proper articulation of the relationship between industry and plant negotiations will be difficult to attain with the present large and varied coverage of its loose industry agreements.

Significantly, the idea of the framework agreement is already being applied with the spread of productivity bargaining. Genuine productivity agreements do not have to be plant agreements. Some of the major ones so far concluded, though for a single employer, have been country-wide and cover a large number of plants. The marketing agreements of Esso and the other oil companies, the ICI and British Oxygen agreements, as well as the industry-wide agreement in Electricity Supply, fall into this category. In each case it has been possible for central negotiations to introduce specific changes in working practices or to set new standards for work provided the details could be worked out locally between management and stewards to suit local circumstances. A great deal depends, of course, on how far this latter process can be supervised or influenced from the centre to prevent the results from being uneven and incomplete. In principle, at any rate, it is possible for industry-wide productivity agreements to be negotiated between employers' associations and trade unions, if only they can create the machinery to implement them in the companies and plants concerned. This is now being attempted in the electrical contracting industry and makes it an extremely important test case.

Not that employers' associations or trade unions can ever assume the responsibilities of management. The responsibility for the reconstruction of workplace relations must fall primarily on the managements of individual companies. This is especially true of large companies. If they have not the will and the ability to act as innovators, they cannot be successfully forced to do so by external pressure. The kind of reconstruction to which I have referred is in the last resort an exercise in planning. It is planning by consent applied not only to the use of manpower but to the whole social structure of the plant; the social counterpart to investment planning. One cannot expect shop stewards to behave in an orderly fashion within a disordered framework. Consistency should be the *sine qua non* of management policy in labour relations, but consistency is impossible without planning and firms cannot be compelled to plan.

Must society rely then on a gradual process of conversion? Must it wait until management at the top, in the board room, faces up to the consequences of its progressive loss of control, takes a broader view of its responsibilities and is willing to accept the inevitable risks of radical reform? Or can the reconstruction of workplace relations be accelerated? While this sort of change cannot be *imposed* externally by law or collective agreement, it can be stimulated and assisted. Some of the ways have already been mentioned, notably a greater application of the method of enquiry and of the principle of 'measurement and publicity'. This could be strengthened by reforms in company law which obliged companies over a certain size to provide much more information on which their record with regard to their employee policies could be assessed. The type of provisions made for management education and the priorities given to relevant social research are equally important. So are the facilities extended to industry by government. The Health Service for industry is at present provided by private industrial consultants whose standards vary. A public, if fee-charging, sector in this rapidly expanding and highly significant industry may be needed as a lever to raise its professional standards, which should in any case be brought under some degree of public supervision.

CONCLUSION

The various proposals advanced in this essay for the reform of our system of industrial relations are all concerned in one way or another with the future of collective bargaining. Some are intended to further its growth and enrich its content. The new tribunal to deal with recognition and procedural questions; permissive legislation for a limited legal enforcement of substantive clauses in collective agreements; and a greater use of state regulation to force the pace and underpin the results of voluntary action in such matters as protection against arbitrary dismissal and reduction of unnecessary overtime, have these ends in view. Other proposals again are directed towards a radical overhaul of the existing structure of collective bargaining to make it accord with the transformation of power relations which has already occurred on the shop floor. These include a general acceptance of the necessity for formal and comprehensive plant and company agreements; the better ordering of pay and work systems within individual establishments; and all the consequent changes in managerial attitudes and the staffing and organisation of trade unions and employers' associations. Last, but decidedly not least, come the proposals made in regard to the evolution of incomes policy at national and local levels, which have as their overriding objective the placing of collective bargaining in the only context that makes sense today – the context of planning.

Collective bargaining has been aptly described as 'the great social invention that has institutionalised industrial conflict' in much the same way 'that the electoral process and majority rule have institutionalised political conflict in a democracy'.[45] Compared with some of the naïve views still held about it – that it is, for instance, no more than a method enabling trade unions to exercise market or monopoly power – this statement expresses a profound historical truth. It also points to one of the major reasons why the collective bargaining institutions in this country are in need of reform: industrial conflict has, as it were, greatly enlarged its domain. The range of disputed issues in the employment relationship, which have to be settled by agreement and made the subject of regulation, is much wider than in the days of mass unemployment. But equally the representatives who participate in collective decisions about terms and conditions of employment have increased in number and variety. The government has entered much more prominently into the picture to uphold interests and values different from those championed by trade unions and employers; and so have managements and workers' representatives in individual plants and companies. A system therefore which, whatever its shortcomings, once served to create a framework and semblance of order no longer fulfils this social purpose adequately. Collective bargaining has to be extended and restructured if it is to continue to offer an adequate means of resolving industrial conflict.

Order and peace, however, are not the only ends of industrial relations any more than they are the only values that we pursue throughout our social system as a whole. Our history places us in least danger of neglecting the value of freedom. The latter remains a sound justification for preserving collective bargaining, and in particular our own voluntary or non-legalistic type of collective bargaining, as the centre piece of our industrial relations system. At the same time it has to be reconciled with other values and objectives given little or no weight in the past. As a nation we are now seeking rapid economic and social advance; and the dynamic technologies of this age, which can be the servants of both, are incompatible with static approaches to industrial relations. If we are to make the fullest and best use of our resources; if we are to encourage a high rate of change with a minimum of personal hardship and social dislocation; if we are to move towards greater social justice and a more responsible democracy in the politics of industry, we must adjust the old institutions of collective bargaining to the new necessities of planning.

This implies two things which come sharply into conflict with institutional inertia and traditional attitudes. First, a decided shift of emphasis in the conduct of industrial relations to the two levels where planning has progressively to evolve in interdependence and harmony, the nation and the firm. Trade unions and employers' associations can retain and even increase their importance as essential links between these two levels. Where, out of vested interest, they act as barriers to change at either they obstruct progress and thereby throw their own future in doubt. Failure to adapt their organisation and functions to this new role may well threaten voluntary collective bargaining by forcing governments to resort to an increasing use of compulsion. The larger firms and their employees will also be goaded to free themselves from what they come to regard as useless and restrictive commitments, thus reducing the chances of effective national planning.

The second implication is a change in the character, as distinct from the structure, of collective bargaining. In the context of democratic planning it is not only important that industrial conflict should be resolved by negotiation and compromise. The question of how it is resolved – whether the agreements reached meet the requirements of economic and social advance – increases in significance. This is already manifest in the questions which press hard on the parties to collective bargaining following our embarkation on the stormy, and still largely uncharted, seas of incomes policy. Unions and employers are expected to justify their settlements with arguments that are more than an exercise in public relations, and to observe a developing framework of national rules which are not directly of their own making. Neither power nor peace is any longer an *ultima ratio*. The relationship between pay and productivity has become a dominant theme, but one to be tested against the facts rather than taken on trust. Pay structures too, formed by market and bargaining pressures and the play of chance, are coming under critical examination and questions as to their fairness and rationality have to be answered. One has only to mention a few of these signs of the times to appreciate the revolutionary nature of the demands which are now being placed on all collective bargainers, most of whom learnt their trade in a very different school of experience.

COLLECTIVE BARGAINING:
A THEORETICAL ANALYSIS
(1968)

My task is to re-appraise in the light of present-day knowledge and conditions the classical theory of a trade union acting as a bargaining agent for its members. As my starting point I intend to take the Webbs' *Industrial Democracy*. This choice can be defended on several grounds. In the first place their major works, in Tawney's words, still 'stand out, amid the trivialities of their day and ours, like Roman masonry in a London suburb'. And as he added: 'The classics devoted to Trade Unionism and Local Government reveal them at their best'.[1] Furthermore they were outstanding pioneers in approaching their subject, not only in a scholarly fashion, but as empirical social scientists. They did not, as many others at the time, merely try to fit trade unions into their own social theories or ideologies. Their conclusions were derived from 'six years' investigation' during which for the United Kingdom they 'examined, inside and out, the constitution of practically every trade union organisation together with the methods and regulations which it uses to attain its ends'.[2] Quite apart, however, from the monumental and scientific character of their achievement, I have another and even more important reason for going back to the Webbs: the widespread influence which their views have had on subsequent thought throughout the world about the nature of trade unions and collective bargaining. Indeed, I propose to argue in this paper that, although these views have subsequently been challenged in certain respects, they have not been challenged radically enough; that the very term 'collective bargaining', which we owe to them, has been a persistent source of confusion in understanding and evaluating the social institution it was meant to describe.

THE CLASSICAL VIEW OF THE WEBBS

It is a familiar point that the Webbs dealt with collective bargaining as one of the several methods used by trade unions to further their basic purpose 'of maintaining or improving the conditions of their [members'] working lives.'[3] In their analytical framework it appears as an alternative to the methods of mutual insurance and legal enactment, and all three concepts were formed in order to categorise the observed activities of trade unions in nineteenth-century Britain. These were the main things–they concluded–that the unions were actually doing and little else besides, apart from their organisation-building activities. They were providing their members with various kinds of benefits. They were bargaining with employers for their members as a collectivity. They were pressing for legislation which favoured their interests. Some unions attached more importance to one method than another and the emphasis was changing over time. To account for this was one of the theoretical tasks which the Webbs set themselves in *Industrial Democracy*.[4] In dealing with collective bargaining, however, they did not consider it other than as a trade union method, since this lay outside their terms of reference. There is, for instance, hardly any consideration in the whole of the Webbs' writing of an employers' interest in collective bargaining, apart from a most intriguing footnote in their *History*.[5]

Given this self-imposed limitation, how did they view the process itself and its relationship to trade unions and their members? Avoiding a definition of collective bargaining, they suggested that it could best be 'understood by a series of examples' and offered the following comparison by way of explanation.

> In organised trades the individual workman, applying for a job, accepts or refuses the terms offered by the employer without communication with his fellow-workmen, and without any other consideration than the exigencies of his own position. For the sale of his labour he makes, with the employer, a strictly individual bargain. But if a group of workmen concert together, and send representatives to conduct the bargaining on behalf of the whole body, the position is at once changed. Instead of the employer making a series of separate contracts with isolated individuals, he meets with a collective will, and settles, in a single agreement, the principles upon which, for the time being, all workmen of a particular group, or class, or grade, will be engaged.[6]

Their first example was that of a 'shop club', confined to a single firm and requiring little formal organisation among the workmen. The latter, by combining together in bargaining with their employer, were able to rule out of consideration the 'particular exigencies' of each individual and so drive a better bargain.

If the foreman had dealt privately with each man, he might have found some in such necessity that he could have driven them to take the job practically at any price rather than be without work for even half a day. Others again, relying on exceptional strength or endurance, would have seen their way to make the standard earnings at a piecework rate upon which the average worker could not even subsist. By the method of collective bargaining the foreman is prevented from taking advantage of the competition of both these classes of men to beat down the earnings of the other workmen.[7]

By introducing further examples the Webbs showed how, with the rise of trade unions, the scope of the collective bargain was progressively enlarged 'from the workshop to the whole town, and from the town to the whole industry'. Throughout the purpose remained the same. The workmen were seeking to enhance their bargaining advantage by 'excluding from influence on the bargain, the exigencies of particular firms or particular districts, and not merely those of particular workmen in a single establishment'.[8]

In short, for the Webbs, collective bargaining was exactly what the words imply: a collective equivalent and alternative to individual bargaining. Where workmen were willing and able to combine, they preferred it to bargaining as individuals with their employer because it enabled them to secure better terms of employment by controlling competition among themselves. And the greater the scale of the bargaining unit–so it appeared–the greater their advantage. Such a view of the institution, which included this primitive theory of its growth and structure, ignored any positive interest on the part of employers. After all, employers could hardly be expected to welcome a strengthening of the bargaining position of their employees unless it brought them some compensating advantages, but this was not a question which the Webbs explored. They tended to assume that collective bargaining was something forced upon employers against their will by strikes and other union sanctions. Today, with advantage of hindsight, it is easy to appreciate the inadequacy of any theory of either the nature or the growth of collective bargaining which sees it only as a method of trade unionism and overlooks in its development the role of employers and their associations. But the Webbs' view was open at the time to a more fundamental theoretical objection. They were not comparing like with like. Although there is little hope now that the term will ever be revised, if words are given a consistent and unambiguous meaning, then collective bargaining is not collective bargaining.

Collective Bargaining: A Theoretical Analysis

Bargaining has been accurately defined as 'the process by which the antithetical interests of supply and demand, of buyer and seller, are finally adjusted' so as to end 'in the act of exchange'.[9] The individual bargain concluded between employers and employees in labour markets, which is given a legal form in employment contracts, accords with this definition. It provides for an exchange of work for wages and, in stipulating the conditions of the exchange, adjusts for the time being conflicts of interest between a buyer and seller of labour. A collective agreement, on the other hand, though it is frequently called a collective bargain and in some countries where it has legal force a collective contract, does not commit anyone to buy or sell labour. It does something quite different. It is meant to ensure that when labour is bought and sold (the specific kinds of labour referred to) its price and the other terms of the transaction will accord with the provisions of the agreement. These provisions are in fact a body of rules intended to regulate among other things the terms of employment contracts. Thus collective bargaining is itself essentially a rule-making process, and this is a feature which has no proper counterpart in individual bargaining.

Elsewhere, it is true, the Webbs showed that they were fully aware of the rule-making character of collective bargaining. They introduced the concept of the 'common rule' into the vocabulary of industrial relations and used it to define trade-union objectives. One must recall, however, the context in which they placed it. 'Notwithstanding their almost infinite variety of technical detail', they wrote, all trade union regulations 'can be reduced to two economic devices: restriction of numbers and the common rule'.[10] Here too their terminology is surely indicative of some confusion of thought. The device of restriction of numbers, under which they included such regulations as apprenticeship quotas or limitations on the employment of women, was itself applied by the imposition of common rules throughout a trade, or as much of it as a union could succed in regulating. Why they should have included under the device of the common rule only 'the more modern rules directly fixing a standard rate, a normal day, and definite conditions of sanitation and safety'[11] is puzzling, to say the least.

A clue to an explanation can be found in their term 'economic devices'. The real basis of their distinction was between the market or economic processes that trade unions were seeking to control.

216

What they were calling the device of the common rule, by fixing a minimum or uniform price for labour or settling other standard terms or conditions of employment, was in effect directly regulating *bargaining* in labour markets. The device of the restriction of numbers, on the other hand, was directly regulating *competition* by restricting the supply of labour or its demand. Because of their interdependence these two characteristic processes of every market, bargaining and competition, are not always clearly separated, but they are distinct. Competition, which entails 'the simultaneous offer of like or alternative services to the same potential purchaser' is a relationship among sellers *or* among buyers and not, as is the case with bargaining, between sellers *and* buyers. 'Competitors do not need one another – they seek to oust one another. Bargainers offer complementary not competitive services. Each stands to gain from the transaction because each wants what the other offers.'[12] True, regulation of the one process affects the other. By controlling the supply of its members' labour a trade union may be able to raise its price. Conversely regulation of the price, by preventing undercutting, restricts competition. Nevertheless the locus of application of the rules is different, and so are their economic (and other) effects as the Webbs argued at length.[13]

We have therefore to note that the theoretical model of a trade union which the Webbs erected in *Industrial Democracy* was that of a *labour cartel*.[14] While acknowledging its regulative functions, they place them on a par with those of a trading monopoly, arguing at the same time special economic justification for the workers' efforts 'to ward off . . . the evil effects of industrial competition'.[15] Indeed, in keeping with the spirit of their times, which looked on political economy as the only valid social science, they were largely concerned with undertaking an economic evaluation of the economic consequences of collective bargaining which they treated throughout as an economic institution.[16] Their unspoken assumption was that there was no inconsistency in regarding this trade union method as being both a bargaining and a regulative process. It is this assumption, so rarely questioned, which has next to be examined. The crux of the matter is whether the 'bargaining' conducted by trade unions with employers can be legitimately equated with the 'bargaining' by individual employees.

Admittedly, when a trade union negotiates a collective agreement, it presents something of a collective will to employers and the actual settlement of conflicts of interest between buyers and sellers of labour is largely, perhaps even wholly, transferred from the market place to the negotiating table where representatives act on their behalf. In this sense collective bargaining might be said to replace individual bargaining. They are not, however, complete alternatives, for they can continue to co-exist. The precise effect of the negotiation of collective agreements is to impose certain limits on the freedom of labour market bargainers, but not fully to extinguish their freedom so long as a labour market continues to function. These limits may be drawn loosely or tightly. Where they are loose, and, for example, the agreements fix no more than minimum wages, individual bargaining may still have very considerable scope. At the other extreme the limits may be set so stringently that there is little left for the bargainers, as opposed to the negotiators, to decide for themselves. Even then, however, the workers represented in negotiations remain at liberty to relinquish their existing employment and to enter into different wage–work bargains with other employers, provided that the rules in the relevant collective agreements or other instruments of regulation are observed. The agreements remain in force regardless of the union members' market activity. The very periods of notice for terminating them will almost certainly diverge from those for terminating individual employment contracts. It is more correct then to refer to collective bargaining as regulating, rather than replacing, individual bargaining.

No less important is the point that the process of negotiation bears no resemblance to the process of bargaining *as a market activity*. We may be accustomed to refer to negotiation as bargaining. We also speak about the bargaining power of the parties or the need for hard bargaining in resolving intractable disputes. But in a similar way we talk about bargaining within or among political parties or between governments and any well-organised sectional interests. Perlman defended the earlier non-partisan policies of the American Federation of Labor as 'a method of political bargaining', in his view the logical extension of collective bargaining to politics.[17] Any of these forms of 'bargaining', whether they take place in industry or politics, are in the modern idiom 'pressure-group' activities, and the resulting deals, though they may be called 'bargains', are in reality compromise settlements of power conflicts. This brings us to the second truly characteristic feature of collective bargaining, apart from its being a rule-making process, namely that it is 'a power relationship between organisations'.[18] Accordingly the process of negotiation is best described as a diplomatic use of power. It has been said of trade unions that 'their primary function is the organisation of their economic power derived from the possession and collective exercise of the will to work or abstain from working – a power exercised as truly in the negotiation of agreements as in the conduct of strikes'.[19] To equate this use of economic or any other form of power in industrial negotiations with bargaining is a far cry from its original meaning as a market activity. Between the two is all the difference between, in the broadest sense of the word, a political and an economic process.

Paradoxically one often finds the function of the strike (or the lockout) in collective bargaining cited as evidence of its bargaining character. As a strike is the collective refusal of a body of workers to continue to work on their existing terms and conditions of employment, it is – so the argument runs – the collective equivalent of an individual worker's refusal to accept a job unless the employer improves on his offer. On closer inspection, however, this analogy does not hold. The assumption behind every strike is not that the workers will seek employment elsewhere if the employer fails to meet their demands. It is the reverse: that sooner or later their present employer will be compelled to reinstate them. In the event of his being able to replace the strikers by an alternative labour supply, the strike ceases to be an effective sanction and turns into a futile gesture. A strike is therefore a temporary refusal to work in accordance with the prevailing employment contracts (or on other conditions that are not specified or implied in the contracts), combined with the firm intention, at least on the part of the great majority of the workers involved, of not terminating their contracts. And even in those cases where workers strike in spontaneous protest, without any calculation of the prospect of success, it is still the case that:

> Sooner or later, however bitter the dispute, employees must work and the employer must have them return to work. It is no answer to suggest that the individual may elect to seek another place of employment; the employee body must remain. A few defections will not change the character or problems of the body.[20]

To take this reasoning further and complete it, no useful parallels can be drawn between the market processes of bargaining and competition on the one hand, and the negotiation of agreements and the use of the strike on the other. They are different types of social behaviour demanding separate modes of analysis. A group of workers may have their bargaining position improved when the state of the labour market changes in their favour and employers are strongly competing for scarce labour. There is then no need for them to threaten to strike in order to improve their wages and working conditions. The working of the market will see to that, and, if a union negotiates for them, it will not have to put any pressure on their employer to gain concessions. Similarly, where the threat of a strike comes into play, improvements may be gained for other reasons than shortage of labour. An employer may pay above the going rate for the sake of peace because his technology, as in process industries, makes any interruption of production a very costly affair. True, the state of the labour market is one condition which helps to determine the effectiveness of the strike as a sanction, but there are many other factors which may be equally important.

POLITICAL CHARACTERISTICS AND SOCIAL ACHIEVEMENTS

To sum up my argument so far, the fundamental mistake of the Webbs—and the source of confusion inherent in the term 'collective bargaining'—lay in their assumption that one economic process was being replaced by another as individual, or so they thought, gave way to collective bargaining. They did not appreciate, as I began by saying, that they were not comparing like with with like. Negotiation is not the same process as bargaining in markets. A collective agreement is not truly a collective bargain. Trade unions do not sell the labour of their members; nor do employers' associations, unlike individual employers, buy it. And so one could continue demolishing the false analogies which have shown a surprising capacity to survive. When, however, one goes out from the alternative premise that what is known as collective bargaining is primarily a *political* institution because of the two features already mentioned—that it is a rule-making process and involves a power relationship between organisations—no logical difficulties obstruct a satisfactory definition.

In the first place to discover further defining characteristics of collective bargaining one compares it, not with individual bargaining, but with the other rule-making processes of industrial relations.

We know, for example, that similar rules to those found in collective agreements may be decided and enforced unilaterally either by trade unions or by employers and their associations. Alternatively they may appear in legislation or in statutory orders or exist as custom and derive their authority directly from society at large. Without attempting here to define the full range and possible classification of all these different methods of job regulation, it is apparent that collective bargaining is one of them and may be distinguished from the rest by the *authorship* of its rules; the fact that they are jointly determined by representatives of employers and employees who consequently share responsibility for their contents and observance.

This, of course, does not exclude them from resorting on occasions to third-party assistance, even to the point of arbitration, in arriving at their agreements, as long as their general authority for making their own rules remains unimpaired. Nor does it necessarily imply that they enjoy complete autonomy in their rule-making activities. Apart possibly from their being subject to certain legal restrictions they may, as within the context of an incomes policy, have their autonomy qualified by government policies or the decisions of their own central organisations. Finally, it should be made clear that it is joint authorship of the rules, rather than the procedures and sanctions available for their interpretation, application and enforcement, that characterises collective bargaining. The existence of provisions for the legal extension and enforcement of collective agreements does not, in the common usage of the term, transform collective bargaining into the alternative method of state regulation, which implies that the state is the author of the rules.

The last point is of considerable definitional importance and demands further elaboration. In recent times it has frequently and, in my judgement, rightly been said that the administration just as much as the making of rules is a part of collective bargaining, if only because in practice these two processes cannot be effectively separated.[21] In such a non-legalistic system as the British no one has ever bothered very much to respect the Webbs' 'vital distinction . . . between the making of a new bargain [i.e. collective agreement] and the interpretating of the terms of an existing one'.[22] The emphasis has been on following from their point of origin the agreed procedure for settling disputes regardless of their type and whether they were, in lawyers' terms, conflicts of interest or conflicts of right.

But even where, as in many countries, collective agreements have a well-defined legal status as contracts the impossibility of applying this distinction has also been stressed. One of the most strikingly succinct formulations of the reasons comes from the United States in Taylor's statement why grievance settlement 'is not simply a process of contract interpretation'. As he pointed out: 'The difficult grievances arise because the labour contract reflects only a partial or an inconclusive meeting of minds. In such cases grievance settlement becomes an integral part of agreement-making.[23]

One cannot then so define collective bargaining as to limit it to the rule-making or legislative activities of the parties. Not only is this excluded by the integration and continuity of the mixed processes of legislation and administration, but also for another reason not yet made explicit. The parties to collective bargaining negotiate procedural as well as substantive agreements in order to regulate their own relationships as distinct from the employment relationships of their constituents. These procedural rules regulate, among other things, their behaviour in settling disputes, including possibly the assistance of third parties and the use of arbitration. Admittedly collective bargaining procedure may also be regulated by rules which are not of the parties' own making without it ceasing to be collective bargaining. No government, for example, abstains entirely from some degree of legal regulation of strikes or associated behaviour (e.g. picketing). But the fact that the joint making of procedural rules is normally an integral part of collective bargaining means that everything appertaining to the resolution of conflict between the parties, including grievance settlement, must be considered as belonging to its institutions. By the same token, however, it cannot be held essential to collective bargaining that the responsibility for the enforcement of its rules – whether they are procedural or substantive – be confined to the parties who negotiate them. That the viability of collective bargaining is quite compatible with their sharing this responsibility with third parties is particularly obvious in countries where Labour Courts deal with disputes relating to the interpretation and application of collective agreements.

Having stated more fully, though still not fully enough, this modern political view of collective bargaining, which would make *joint regulation* a much more appropriate term to indicate its essential character, that view can already be employed to clear up both a minor and a major obscurity in the Webbs' analysis. As to the minor one, it has long been appreciated that in their trichotomy of trade union methods, mutual insurance was not comparable with collective bargaining and legal enactment. The provision of benefits, as the Webbs' demonstrated, furnished the early trade unions with their main positive and negative membership sanctions, but these were needed mainly to lend support to the unions' unilateral imposition of their own working rules on employers. Consequently it was the method of unilateral union regulation which stood in true comparison with collective bargaining (or joint regulation) and legal enactment (or state regulations). The Webbs showed some awareness of this objection when they suggested that 'in its economic aspect' the method of mutual insurance was 'hardly distinguishable from imperfect collective bargaining'.[24]

The major obscurity can only be touched upon briefly and concerns the origins of collective bargaining. Even the most careful reader of the Webbs might be forgiven if he concluded that, in their view, collective bargaining developed as a reaction by workmen against the disadvantages of individual bargaining. The fact that in most cases it had its origins in alternative methods of job regulation, although implicit in some of their historical references, is never explicitly stated. They refer quite extensively to unilateral regulation by trade unions and occasionally give examples of unilateral regulation by employers, but the dynamics of the transition of either of these into joint regulation is a subject they ignored. Similarly the importance (right up to the end of the nineteenth century) of social regulation by custom for the origins of collective bargaining received no attention.[25] The most plausible explanation for this neglect was their own conceptual framework of analysis, and not least the fatal concept of collective bargaining, which made questions of this sort irrelevant. In their economic evaluation of the two economic devices and the three methods of trade unions, when they were not comparing these different categories of regulation with each other, they did so with the assumed alternative of individual bargaining and unregulated labour markets or, as they put it, 'perfect competition'.

Taking the Webbs' view as representing the classical or traditional theory of the nature of collective bargaining, I have tried to show why it is misleading. It may be further challenged on different grounds. Apart from being misleading, it is inadequate: it tells us too little about the institution it claims to describe. Because the Webbs treated collective bargaining as an economic process, a position which followed logically from regarding it as a collective equivalent of individual bargaining, they tended to overlook, as others have done who followed in their footsteps, all of its non-economic aspects. This applies firstly to its overall social consequences and achievements and therefore to its evaluation; secondly, to the forces influencing the conduct of negotiations and consequently their outcome; and thirdly, to the range and types of industrial conflict which the institution may be called upon to resolve. It is interesting to see how in later work on the subject these short-comings of the traditional theory have been progressively revealed.

If a trade union were acting as a labour cartel in collective bargaining, as the Webbs' analysis implied, then the contemporary argument of some schools of economists that full employment has deprived this institution of much of its earlier justification would be persuasive. The change in the state of labour markets, with employers competing for employees more strongly than the latter are competing for jobs, undermines the case that could once be argued that union organisation was needed to redress a position of bargaining inequality. Nor can it be denied that, with growing bureaucratisation and increased power, trade unions have become less of a social movement and more closely resemble business organisations in selling a service to their members. The rise of business unionism operating in the context of a changed labour market has been cited in support of the statement that trade unions now use their monopoly power simply to secure material gains for their members which '*like the gains of any other monopoly*' are made 'at the expense of *all* other elements of society, in other words, of the general public'.[26]

Setting aside the question whether this argument can be upheld in terms of economic analysis, one thing is certain: it entirely overlooks the non-economic consequences of collective bargaining. Through this institution trade unions may participate in regulating the price of labour as a commodity, and possibly its supply, but it is a common-place that labour is more than a commodity because it cannot be isolated from the life of the labourer. For those employees on whose behalf a trade union acts in collective bargaining (who may or may not be members of the union) the effects of its action extend beyond the securing of material gains to the establishment of *rights* in indus-

224

try; the right to a defined rate of wages, the right not to have to work longer than a certain number of hours, the right to be paid for holidays, and so on. In negotiating collective agreements trade unions act in that dual capacity already suggested: as power or pressure groups certainly but also, together with employers, as private legislators.

Moreover, these wider and more enduring social consequences of collective bargaining are not limited to defining rights of employees with respect to their remuneration by regulating the price of work. The rules in collective agreements may also regulate such matters as dismissal, discipline, promotion or training, which cannot by any stretch of the imagination be included under price. What is more, because they are rules defining rights (and obligations) they are a means of preventing favouritism, nepotism, victimisation and arbitrary discrimination of any sort. Thus one great accomplishment of collective bargaining has been its promotion of the 'rule of law' in employment relations. Far from being a change in the method of marketing labour, it has to be regarded as an institution freeing labour from being too much at the mercy of the market. Any evaluation of it which disregards this accomplishment cannot be taken seriously.

There are many modern formulations of these non-economic consequences of collective bargaining. Perhaps the most famous is Slichter's opening to his first notable study of the impact of union policies on management:

> Through the institution of the state, men devise schemes of positive law, construct administrative procedures for carrying them out, and complement both statute law and administrative rule with a system of judicial review. Similarly, laboring men, through unions, formulate policies to which they give expression in the form of shop rules and practices which are embodied in agreements with employers or are accorded less formal recognition and assent by management; shop committees, grievance procedures, and other means are evolved for applying these rules and policies; and rights and duties are claimed and recognised. When labor and management deal with labor relations analytically and systematically after such a fashion, it is proper to refer to the system as 'industrial jurisprudence'.[27]

The same theme had been somewhat differently stated by Tannenbaum as the recreation for the workers of 'a society based on status' instead of the one we have known in the past 'based on contract', with collective bargaining as the 'innocent method of this great transformation'.[28] Or again by Marshall when he speaks of the trade unions' creating 'a secondary system of industrial citizenship parallel with and supplementary to the system of political citizenship'.[29]

FACTORS IN NEGOTIATION AND SOURCES OF CONFLICT

Turning from the first to the second inadequacy of the traditional view of collective bargaining, this has been revealed by a growing appreciation that, in negotiating collective agreements, the parties have many other considerations in mind apart from the conflicting interests of their constituents as buyers and sellers of labour. The Webbs had no hesitation in stating that:

> In so far as the issue is left to collective bargaining there is not even any question of principle involved. The workmen are frankly striving to get for themselves the best terms that can permanently be exacted from employers. The employers, on the other hand, are endeavouring, in accordance with business principles, to buy their labour in the cheapest market. The issue is a trial of strength between the parties. Open warfare – the stoppage of the industry – is costly and even disastrous to both sides. But though neither party desires war, there is always the alternative of fighting out the issue. The resources and tactical strength of each side must accordingly exercise a potent influence on the deliberations. The plenipotentiaries must higgle and cast about to find acceptable alternatives, seeking, like ambassadors in international conference, not to ascertain what are the facts, nor yet what is a just decision according to some ethical standard or view of social expediency, but to find a common basis which each side can bring itself to agree to, rather than go to war.[30]

Much of this description of what happens in the conduct of negotiations still holds. They are certainly directed towards finding an acceptable compromise, with each side taking into account the likely outcome of open warfare in deciding the settlement it is willing to accept. Even so, the Webbs' reference to 'the best terms that can be *permanently* exacted' already introduces an important non-economic qualification into any purely bargaining theory of collective bargaining. Professional negotiators know the dangers of pressing a temporary bargaining advantage to the full regardless of whether it can be sustained. They are, as it were, in the business together for a long time to come, and they cannot afford to add unnecessarily to

226

the strain of their joint relationship by raising exaggerated expectations in the minds of their constituents. This consideration alone gives rise to restraints on their behaviour which are alien to the market, and institutional rather than economic in origin.

But the common need to preserve the continuity of their relationship—in other words the viability of collective bargaining as an institution—is only one of the many non-economic factors that are now acknowledged to influence the conduct of negotiations between trade unions and employers.[31] No aspect of collective bargaining has been the subject of as much debate and research in recent times as this, mainly because it is part of the search for a more realistic theory of wage determination. The original terms of the Dunlop–Ross controversy over the relative weight to be given to economic and political factors have been summarised too many times to be repeated here.[32] Moreover, the subsequent variations on this theme, and the attempts to get to grips with the concept of 'bargaining power' or quantitatively to assess the effect of union organisation on wage movements and structures or to develop typologies for different behavioural styles and strategies of negotiation, now form so extensive a literature that justice could not be done to it in the space available.[33] In the context of my argument it must suffice to offer a few simple illustrations of that intricate tangle of forces which may affect the negotiation of collective agreements and the settlement of conflict in industry.

Recognition of the force of comparisons in negotiations is now common ground among all students of industrial relations. Whether or not the phrase 'orbits of coercive comparison' can be given a rigorous interpretation and a solid empirical foundation,[34] no one denies that the parties to collective bargaining, in searching for a compromise between the conflicting interests they represent, are frequently looking over their shoulders at the results of other settlements as a possible guide to their own. A whole new vocabulary has emerged to express this effect of comparisons: 'wage rounds', 'fair relativities', 'key bargains', 'pattern-setting' and 'pattern-following' settlements and the like. It is further accepted that both political and social factors are involved in accounting for their evident force. Although Ross appeared to stress mainly the significance of political factors, such as external and internal rivalries in the trade union world, he also referred to equalising tendencies in collective wage determination resulting not only from the force of organisation but also from the force of ideas (concepts of equity and justice).[35] And other writers have particularly drawn attention to the 'large issues of social status . . . involved in wage and salary scales'.[36]

Without trying to make the list of relevant factors exhaustive, it is clear that a trade union will be concerned with the impact of any settlement that it makes on its standing in comparison with other unions and with any possible repercussions on its internal unity. Considerations of this sort are likely to be prominent in the minds of actual negotiators because they are responsible for the state of their organisations; and this also applies to the officials of employers' associations. On the other hand, the attitudes of their constituents to any proposed settlement will be influenced, not only by their economic interests, but also by what they regard as 'fair' or 'reasonable' in the circumstances. This brings social, indeed cultural, factors into play especially on the workers' side. As income is an important badge of social status, failure to keep one's place in a league table of rates or earnings may generate particularly strong and resolute pressures behind a wage claim. But so may ideas about entitlement to a 'living wage' or to greater equality of treatment which can conflict with the legitimisation by custom and tradition of existing wage relativities.[37]

The truth is that we have only recently begun to embark on the vast programme of empirical research that will be required to underpin any firm judgements on the determinants of the relative importance of these different factors in different situations. One recent study which crosses the threshold between theoretical speculation and empirical inquiry distinguishes 'economic', 'political' and 'pure power' variables–the latter being 'related primarily to the ability of the union to initiate and maintain aggressive strike action and to the ability of the employer to resist such action'.[38] While advancing some conclusions on the relative importance of these three sets of environmental factors in the six collective bargaining situations analysed, it ends by emphasising 'the extraordinary complex nature of those factors that determine the outcome of any major collective bargaining negotiation'.[39] Even so, one conclusion is of special interest in the present context, namely that 'employment conditions in the labour market did not appear to have been consistently related to the relative movement of wages'.[40] But we have also to ask whether it is sufficient to concentrate on environmental factors alone. Another timely comparative study of plant union–management relations separates 'volitional' and 'environmental' influences. In dealing with the former it points out that the parties to collective bargaining 'may differ in (1) their long-run goals or motives, (2) their immediate standards, (3) their perceptions of the factual situation, (4) their expectations of the future, (5) their sympathy for and understanding of the other side, (6) their judgement of relative power and of the feasibility of gaining their objectives, and (7) their skill in bargaining and persuasion'.[41] Plainly one cannot ignore the social-psychological aspects of collective bargaining. The parties' perception of their environment could in some circumstances be more important than the environment itself, and this depends on their 'frame of reference'[42] and other influences on processes of communication.

The third inadequacy of the traditional view of collective bargaining follows closely on the heels of the second. Just as the Webbs assumed that negotiation was no more than a process of finding a bargaining accommodation between the conflicting interests of the parties, they also envisaged that the only type of conflict to be settled was economic: the conflict of interests between buyers and sellers of labour. In meeting as organised groups, however, to decide the rules that are to regulate their relationships, the parties are inevitably involved in resolving other types of conflict. Since their relationship is broadly a political one both sides are interested in the distribution of power between them as well as the distribution of income. In disputes, for example, over provisions for enforcing union membership or over changing restrictions on entry into a trade or industry, they know very well that power is at stake. It might be argued that conflicts over power, authority and influence–the substance of the politics of industry–are no more than a reflection of a more fundamental conflict of economic interests, because comparative strength will decide the sharing of proceeds in the future. Were this true it would hardly be a good reason for disregarding conflicts over power in the analysis of collective bargaining, but it is not.

There should be no need today to labour the point that the range of interests which employees may seek to advance or to protect through collective bargaining extends beyond their interests as market bargainers. In dealing with the social achievements of collective bargaining, it has already been pointed out that their interests

229

in regulating bargaining and competition are not confined to driving a better bargain and making material gains. Non-material interests in order and equity, in security and status, and generally in diminishing a degrading dependence on market forces and arbitrary treatment, are satisfied by regulation. Nor is the regulative effect of collective agreements confined to labour markets. It has increasingly been enlarged to cover managerial in addition to market relations. That is to say, collective agreements regulate the exercise of managerial authority in deploying, organising and disciplining the labour force after it has been hired. And the conflicts of interest that arise in this realm are by no means exclusively economic. It is here in fact that we see most clearly that industrial conflict may be rooted in a clash of values as well as a conflict of interests. Conflict may develop because the parties have different standards for judging managerial decisions and behaviour. The clash is pre-eminently between the values of efficiency and security.

> Even the vocabulary of the two organisations differs in ways that strikingly point up the values conflict. For example, management will regard efficiency as being a good word, a good objective, something which is conducive to the health of the organisation. To the union, efficiency usually connotes some attempted means of chiselling out of the workers something which they have earned for themselves. Security becomes in the union vocabulary, the desirable counterpart. But this very word, in reverse, usually chills management.[43]

To ignore these far more intractable sources of industrial conflict – for it is easier to compromise on interests than on values – is to take a very superficial view of the nature of collective bargaining.

CHAMBERLAIN'S THREE THEORIES

Given the many deficiencies in the traditional view of collective bargaining, it is to be expected that any modern treatment of this subject would aim at being far more comprehensive. The outstanding attempt to produce a 'generic definition' of the institution, encompassing twentieth-century developments in its character, is to be found in the works of Chamberlain, joined later by Kuhn.[44] It will be recalled that in his first edition of *Collective Bargaining* in 1951, Chamberlain proposed that all the various theories held about the nature of collective bargaining could be reduced to three. 'They are that collective bargaining is (1) a means of contracting for the sale of labour, (2) a form of industrial government, and (3) a method of management.'[45] He called them respectively the marketing, governmental and managerial theories. Although presented against a background of American institutions, his supporting arguments have a more universal application.

His marketing theory does not differ in its essentials from that of the Webbs, although Chamberlain is more concerned with the contractual aspect. Legal distinctions may be drawn but 'for most practical purposes the individual labour contact has been replaced by the collective agreement'. Consequently, collective bargaining may be viewed as 'the process which determines under what terms labour will continue to be supplied to a company by its existing employees, and by those newly hired as well'.[46] The governmental theory admits the contractual character of bargaining relationships, but sees the contract mainly as providing a constitution for industrial self-government. In the words of one authority, its principal function is to 'set up organs of government, define and limit them, provide agencies for making, executing and interpreting laws for the industry and means for their enforcement'.[47] The managerial theory, in contrast, stresses the 'functional relationship' between unions and companies; they combine 'in reaching decisions on matters in which both have vital interests'.[48] The fact that union officials disclaim any intention of usurping management's functions is immaterial, as 'collective bargaining, *by its very nature*, involves [them] . . . in the managerial role'.[49] They are 'actually *de facto* managers'.[50]

In separating these theories, Chamberlain did not suggest that they were clear-cut and mutually incompatible alternatives. Partly, he argued, they reflect different stages in the historical development of collective bargaining. Early negotiations were mainly a matter of fixing terms for the sale of labour; the agreements might consist of no more than standard piecework price lists. Later came the need for procedures for settling disputes on these and other issues between the parties, which sometimes took the form of setting up joint bodies possibly with an independent chairman; this provided a foundation for the governmental theory. Only when eventually agreements were made on subjects that entered into the internal decision-taking processes of a business enterprise was there a basis for the managerial theory of collective bargaining.

Moreover, the three theories, he said, express not only different views of what happens in collective bargaining, but also different conceptions of what *should* happen. They are supported by value judgements so that each has its own appropriate ethical justification. The marketing view–as has previously been noted–rests on the principle that collective bargaining is necessary to redress the balance of bargaining inequality between employers and employees. The principle underlying the governmental view, is 'the sharing of industrial sovereignty' which, according to Chamberlain, has two facets. The one is that employers should divide their power with unions so as to produce '*mutually* acceptable' laws of industrial self-government; the other that they should engage in a joint defence of their autonomy–'an ethical principle of self-determination bars the intervention of others into this area of private group decisions'.[51] Lastly, the managerial view is supported by the 'principle of mutuality', which 'holds that those who are integral to the conduct of an enterprise should have a voice in decisions of concern to them'.[52] It recognises that the ownership of property is not an exclusive entitlement to the exercise of authority in industry; responsibility towards other constituent groups of a business enterprise gives grounds for insisting that managerial authority should be shared with their representatives in the manner collective bargaining can achieve. One might say that, while the first theory draws attention to the trade union acting as a *labour cartel* in collective bargaining, the second sees it as introducing an autonomous and agreed *rule of law* into employer–employee relations, and the third stresses its contribution towards making management more democratic or furthering *industrial democracy*.

As collective bargaining, when fully developed, appears to do all these things claimed in its justification, it would be tempting to accept uncritically Chamberlain's trichotomy of views. Justice is done to the subject's complexity by not trying to force it into a single theoretical mould. But the problem must be faced whether it is possible to develop an eclectic and integrated view of the institution. I think it is possible. My reasons for rejecting the marketing theory of collective bargaining have already been stated. It is certainly a view which has been and still is widely held, but it is not a valid one. Chamberlain's governmental theory, on the other hand, by placing all the emphasis on the procedural rules of collective bargaining appears to be quite unnecessarily restrictive and is not incompatible with a unitary view of the institution which also includes the substantive rules made by the parties for regulating their market relations. To be sure, the relative significance which the parties attach to their procedural and substantive rules varies in different industrial relations systems and sub-systems, but collective bargaining cannot exist as an established institution without both. Chamberlain's managerial theory is, however, in many ways the most instructive, not least because of his own subsequent modifications of it.[53] I will try to show how what is valid in it can also be incorporated into a unitary view.

PENETRATION INTO MANAGEMENT

Before pursuing this further I must briefly return to the Webbs in order to be fair to them. Much of my criticism of their view of collective bargaining has been directed against their mistaken theoretical premises. The evolution of thought on collective bargaining since their time, however, reflects in part an evolution of the institution itself. Its extension from the 'workmen' or 'manual-working producers' (to whom they referred) to white-collar employees and, in some countries, to the professions is an obvious illustration. But much more important, in considering the nature of the institution, is its growing penetration into management *qua* management. In the United States its formal penetration, as expressed in the subject matter of written agreements, has probably gone further than in any other country. It is not surprising therefore that the relationship between collective bargaining and management there should have loomed so large in public and academic debate.

The most substantial study of the impact of collective bargaining on management in that country concludes that agreements have limited managerial discretion in three principal ways.

(1) By requiring that management follows rules for lay-offs, transfers, promotions, retirements, assigning overtime, setting production standards and rates.
(2) By requiring that management be 'reasonable' or 'fair' or that management act only with just cause, or after consultation with the union, or with the consent of the union.
(3) By prohibiting certain types of conduct, such as excessive overtime.[54]

233

The question is whether, as Chamberlain first suggested, this degree of penetration turns collective bargaining into a method of management and involves trade unions in the managerial function.

But why, it might be asked, should collective bargaining or joint regulation in any circumstances be equated with joint management? Even when the subjects covered by collective agreements penetrate deeply into the managerial function, the responsibility accepted by trade unions in signing them does not go beyond upholding the observance of the rules they have helped to make. Management as a result may have to conduct itself within the limits set by these rules, but otherwise its responsibility for running the business remains undivided. Schemes which provide for the representation of trade unions on boards of management, such as the arrangement for co-determination in the German coal and steel industries, are usually thought to be a different animal. Yet the managerial theory, though it raises exaggerated claims on behalf of collective bargaining, cannot be dismissed quite so readily.

A leading proposition in Chamberlain's original argument—and one that he still sustains—was that the managerial theory viewed a collective agreement as constituting 'a set of administrative standards in the operation of a business'.[55] This was so because, apart from the known standards formulated in a written agreement, there were also 'the assumed standards in matters where union interest is admitted but standards are indefinite'.[56] But when an agreement is looked upon in this way 'as providing guidance in areas of managerial discretion, its application proceeds from the intent to accomplish certain jointly conceived objectives. This is a functional conception, and when the terms of the agreement fail to achieve that function in a particular case, it is the joint objective and not the terms that must control'.[57] In a phrase, collective bargaining then becomes joint administration, and what is that, he suggests, other than joint management?

In support of this conclusion it must be conceded that, when collective bargaining applies to management, joint regulation merges more easily into joint administration. The reason lies in the 'peculiarly personal and continuous' character of authority in industry. Although there 'must be rules and enforcement of rules in a workshop', they must also 'be flexible'.

They must reside in men not in a rule book or in a judiciary. Where there is a daily use of authority there is bound to be a disputed frontier, and there is bound to be a risk of unfairness. Such disputes cannot be resolved outside industry. They are too numerous, too technical, and too personal. There can be no final judicial solution or legislative solutions for the bulk of the disputed points in industry. The relationship between authority and right is, therefore, difficult to regulate formally. It is hard to define relative duties and hard to enforce them.[58]

The labour market deals with measurable quantities: wage rates, hours of work, apprenticeship quotas, numbers of men to be taken on or dismissed. Accordingly the rules made to regulate the market processes of bargaining and competition can and, if they are to be effective, must be formulated with some precision. Management itself is less susceptible to exact regulation. An agreed code of disciplinary rules, for example, can never serve as very much more than a general guide to the decisions to be taken in particular cases. Not to take into account their special circumstances is almost certain to lead to injustice, which neither managements nor unions want. The case for the parties building up a broad understanding on 'administrative standards', instead of maintaining a strict legalistic view of their relations, is a strong one. Even so, this is still a question of attitudes which should be adopted towards rules – how specific should they be and how much 'give and take' is desirable in applying them. Though in general the process may be a more flexible one than would be appropriate in regulating wages, the need remains for both procedural and substantive rules to deal with conflict between the divergent interests of management and unions. The fallacy in Chamberlain's earlier managerial theory of collective bargaining lay in its assumption of 'jointly conceived objectives' leading to 'functional integration', but on that point he subsequently answered himself.

After revising his own ideas on the nature of the managerial function, he reached the conclusion that 'unions, in seeking to extend the range of their decision making within the enterprise, are not trespassing on [that] . . . function'.[59] This followed upon a statement that the 'unique function' of management is the 'co-ordination of the bargains of all who compose the business'.[60] Management collectively is confronted by a variety of groups wanting to fulfil their aspirations through the medium of the enter-prise: work groups on the shop floor and functional groups within the managerial hierarchy, but also external groups – the suppliers of materials and of capital, shareholders and customers. Yet only one decision can be made with respect to any issue and that decision must bind all the participants in the company's operations. Furthermore, 'each decision must be consistent and compatible with all other decisions'.[61] As distinct from a purely technical co-ordination of work, the conflicting and ever-changing demands made upon the enterprise have constantly to be reconciled anew. Management alone can assume this responsibility by engaging in a 'multilateral bargaining process'. Trade unions, along with other interested parties, 'can make life more trying for management, by making the co-ordination process more difficult', but they cannot take over this function or share it.[62]

A modern view of collective bargaining, then, must recognise that it is an institution for regulating labour management as well as labour markets. This, however, is easily accommodated within a unitary view of the nature of the institution since it implies no more than an enlargement of the subjects covered by its substantive rules and, of course, corresponding developments in its procedure. Nevertheless it is true that, when collective bargaining broadens its scope from regulating markets to regulating management, it changes its character because different demands are placed upon it. Incidentally this applies even to regulation of wages which in their economic aspect have a managerial as well as a market function. If their market function is to allocate labour as between localities, undertakings and occupations, their managerial function is to serve, by the rewarding of performance, as a positive sanction in the organisation of work. Both functions may be submitted to joint regulation by collective bargaining, but the forms, and especially the area, of regulation appropriate for the one may be inappropriate for the other.

There are still two things to be said about the nature of collective bargaining to complete the view of it developed here. One has been described by Dunlop as its 'unappreciated' social contribution.

> One of the major activities of collective bargaining involves the determination of priorities *within* each side in the bargaining process. The view that a homogeneous union negotiates with a homogeneous management or association is erroneous and mischievous. A great deal of the complexity and beauty of collective bargaining involves the process of compromise and assessment of priorities within each side. In an important sense collective bargaining typically involves three coincidental bargains—the rejection of some claims and the assignment of priorities to others within the union, an analogous process of assess-

ing priorities and trade-offs within a single management or association, and the bargaining across the table. The same processes are involved in the administration and application of the agreement.[63]

This too is an aspect of collective bargaining which the traditional view ignored–perhaps that is why it has been so little appreciated. There are only two sides to a labour market with wages being costs for employers and incomes for employees. Viewed simply in 'bargaining' terms it was easy to slip into the assumption of homogeneity of interest on each side. Once collective bargaining penetrates into management, however, the multiplicity of diverse interests of separate work groups and the functional and hierarchical conflicts of interest within management cannot possibly be disregarded. The problem of determining priorities therefore becomes much more acute.

The additional feature of collective bargaining which remains to be mentioned is an amplification of the observation that it is a 'power relationship between organisations'. Although accurate as far as it goes, this is an over-simplification of the power relationships involved in collective bargaining. Neither trade unions on the one side nor employers' associations or, for that matter, individual companies on the other have a monopoly of power on their own side. Within these organisations various groups may have sources of power, i.e. sanctions at their own command, whose use the organisations as entities may be unable or unwilling to control. This condition has to be distinguished from the faction fights or other group conflicts which may emerge in the organisation's internal government and the settling of priorities. The latter will affect their policies and decisions in negotiation but they may nevertheless act in the end as if they had a single collective will. The feature of collective bargaining that I have in mind has shown itself in such phenomena as 'fractional bargaining' in the United States[64] or in the 'pull down of authority' from full-time trade unions officials to shop stewards in Great Britain.[65]

It is causally connected with full (or high levels of) employment which has enhanced the power of separate work and union groups on the shop floor, but also with widening scope of the subjects of collective bargaining and its penetration into management. The fact that these groups have their own sanctions from the instant stoppage to bans on overtime and the withdrawal of co-operation–though diminished in some countries by legal regulation–means that they are able to negotiate independent settlements with management at various levels. Such 'bargaining' is also collective and its results may either conflict with the terms of agreements made by trade unions or supplement them to such an extent that the agreements' regulative effect is undermined. Which of these two outcomes occurs depends on how comprehensive and rigorous a regulation of employment relationships is provided by formal union agreements. All this has far-reaching implications for the theory of the structure of collective bargaining which is not my present concern. But even in defining the nature of the institution what might be called its *de facto* federal character must not be overlooked.

ARE UNIONS BARGAINING AGENTS?

Having discussed the nature of collective bargaining, I can return in conclusion to the problem posed at the outset: the relationship between a trade union and its members or, more specifically, whether that relationship can be correctly and fully expressed in the notion of its acting as a bargaining agent on their behalf. The preceding argument has questioned the validity of this notion on several counts. In the first place I have argued that it is based on a terminological confusion. In the economic meaning of the word trade unions do not 'bargain' with employers. They negotiate collective agreements with them to regulate bargaining and competition in labour markets, but also their own procedural relations and, now increasingly, managerial relations arising out of the exercise of managerial authority within the firm. Since collective agreements represent a body of jointly agreed rules of varying degrees of precision or generality, and the process of negotiation in arriving at them is best conceived as a diplomatic use of power, trade unions operate primarily as political, not economic, instititions.

This conclusion in turn has two basic implications at variance with the notion of a trade union as a bargaining agent. The first is that a union's behaviour in industry, not to speak of politics, does not merely reflect its members' interests, and still less that limited segment of their interests as sellers of labour. A union's behaviour is also influenced by the institutional interests of the organisation as championed by its officialdom, interests in its survival and growth. These include its internal stability and possibly a longer view of the

238

members' interests than they are initially prepared to take themselves, which introduces the factor of leadership. The internal politics of the trade union and of a wider labour movement exert their influence too, and so do a very wide range of other 'volitional' and 'environmental' factors. The latter include the economic environment (product as well as labour market conditions) but equally such factors as the technology of production and accepted social norms and cultural values. Moreover it is the union members' and officials' perception of this economic environment which may sometimes be decisive instead of the environment itself, and this is dependent on processes of communication.

The second implication relates to why trade unions are valued by their members. The notion of bargaining agent suggests that they are valued for their 'bargaining' achievements. If this were the case one would have to conclude on the weight and balance of existing evidence that union members were unusually prone to self-deception. Even though the empirical 'constant share' proposition may be controversial among economists, no one doubts that variations in the share of wages in the national income have had little influence on the workers' standard of living compared with the effect of growth in the national income as a whole. On the one hand, there are grave doubts whether trade unions through collective bargaining have a substantial long-run effect on wage differentials, in view of the comparative rigidity of national wage structures and the possibility of accounting for such shifts as have taken place by factors lying outside their control. Quite apart, however, from the puzzle presented by this economic mirage, which appears to dazzle the sight of union members, one has also to explain why employees should be interested in union organisation when they are working in unorganised firms on terms and conditions of employment as favourable as those negotiated by trade unions.

All these difficulties disappear once one goes out from an alternative assumption: that the value of a union to its members lies less in its economic achievements than in its capacity to protect their dignity. Viewed from this angle, employees—white-collar no less than manual workers—have an interest in union organisation, however favourable their economic circumstances or the state of the labour market, for at least two reasons. They are interested in the regulation of labour markets and of labour management because such regulation defines their rights, and consequently their status and security, and so liberates them from dependence on chance and the arbitrary will of others. Equally they are interested in participating as directly as possible in the making and administration of these rules in order to have a voice in shaping their own destiny and the decisions on which it most depends. This is not to say that members of trade unions have no interest in higher wages or shorter working hours, or that they do not put pressure on their unions to pursue these objectives. That would be manifestly absurd. But, as labour history demonstrates again and again, wages or hours movements have no more than a temporary appeal and their momentum may be spent as much by success as it is by failure. Permanent organisation could not be built on this foundation. To secure a permanent membership trade unions have to render a constant service to their members. This is made possible by their participation in job regulation, and the deeper and more extensive that participation the greater the service they can offer.

COLLECTIVE BARGAINING:
FROM DONOVAN TO DURKHEIM
(1969)

More than a year has now elapsed since the Donovan Commission issued its Report.[1] After the immediate flurry of quick judgements as the mass media met their absurdly-hasty deadlines for comment, a period of digestion has followed during which interested parties have made more considered attempts at understanding and response. In January the Government declared its own policy in a White Paper[2] containing its main proposals for an Industrial Relations Act, and proceeded immediately to establish the new Commission on Industrial Relations. Fairly general agreement has emerged in all the ensuing debate that the future of collective bargaining is the central issue, but responses have been more mixed about the Report's, and indeed the Government's, diagnosis of what is wrong with existing institutions. This is a matter of concern for the obvious reason that the nature of the diagnosis determines the nature of the prescription.

There can hardly be need to recapitulate at length the Donovan analysis. In terms which have become familiar, its rests upon the argument that Britain has two systems of industrial relations, the formal and the informal, which are in conflict. The former, of which the industry-wide agreement is the keystone, flies in the face of the facts by assuming industry-wide organisations powerful enough to impose their decisions on their members. The latter, which is increasingly the reality, rests on the wide autonomy of managers in individual enterprises and the independent power of industrial work groups. The assumptions of the formal system still exert, however, a potent influence over men's minds, and prevent the informal system from developing into an effective and orderly method of regulation. The informal system therefore remains fragmented, uncodified, often dependent on work-group custom and practice, and generally incapable of serving as the necessary replacement to
241

the formal structure of industry-wide agreements which, in many cases, no longer effectively regulate employment relations. Thus the 'pretence' of the formal system leads to 'disorder' in the informal system. Some of the more obvious results are unofficial strikes, wage drift, and inefficient utilisation of labour.

THE POPULAR CASE FOR REFORM

This analysis crystallised views towards which many academic students of the subject had been moving for some time. But such views have always had their challengers, and it comes as no surprise that in some quarters the Donovan diagnosis has met with less than full acceptance. The common premise on which one major group of critics have based their scepticism and their own prescriptions is the simple one that trade unions, far from having too little power (as the Report claimed), have too much.

Yet to judge by the criticisms, the union leaders' exercise of this power is curiously capricious. They exert it to the full when they want to hold the consumer to ransom, to obstruct necessary and urgent change in technology and organisation, and to wield threats of strike action which a majority of their members secretly deplore. Yet when other sorts of discipline over their members are required, such as restraining them from defying negotiated agreements and union rules by participating in unofficial strikes, the leaders at once suspend deployment of the power they are supposed to enjoy. Blandly they contemplate this flouting of their authority, their leadership, and their pledged word, without lifting a finger to use the control which allegedly lies so abundantly to hand.

Observers of the scene must make up their own minds whether they find this a plausible explanation of our present troubles. Without doubt interpretations of this kind underlie many influential currents of opinion. The Conservative Party's policy statement, *Fair Deal at Work*, for example, claims that in the field of industrial relations: 'Huge organisations are involved, wielding immense power over individuals and the economic and social life of the nation. Government has both the right and the duty to ensure that these bodies operate in the public interest'.[3] Given the manifest weakness of employers' associations, this merely attempts a more judicious statement of the charge that trade unions are too powerful and that governments should do much more to protect their members and society against them. The same notion of the trade union as the modern equivalent of 'the overmighty subject' informs the reservations by Andrew Shonfield and Lord Tangley to the Donovan Report. Aubrey Jones has similarly taken it as a theme in a number of speeches to demonstrate the need for a body like the National Board for Prices and Incomes to protect the interests of the consumer. Its appeal to economists, extreme liberals and extreme planners alike, is evident. The liberals see union power distorting the beneficent working of the market; the planners are impatient with union opposition to incomes policy and government controls.

Nor should it be supposed that this view is confined to members of the middle class and the professional opinion-formers. It is quite widespread even among the members of trade unions, as the findings of a National Opinion Poll showed. When asked whether unions now had too much power, 30 per cent agreed that they had, as compared with only 17 per cent who felt they had too little. As might be expected, 41 per cent answered 'about right'. Moreover, 60 per cent of union members believed that unofficial strikes should be made illegal, and 58 per cent thought that agreements between managements and unions should be legally binding. There was also a majority in favour of the policy of introducing a compulsory cooling-off period before a strike begins.[4]

It is a fair assumption that measures of this sort have considerable popular support among all classes and their general drift is that the power of trade unions should be curbed. This is not to suggest any uniformity of opinion about the remedies. There are those who seek quite frankly to weaken trade unions as much as they can and, though they may not all say so in public, believe that unions are no more than an infliction which history forces us to bear. Trade unions, it is said, were born in an age of oppression and are no longer relevant to present circumstances. This is an extreme view, but it is held. Most of those who adopt this kind of analysis of the defects of collective bargaining, however, do so in order to state a case for its legal reform. They want the law to regulate both the activities and the domestic affairs of trade unions to a much greater extent than at present. Trade unions, they argue, have acquired a position of legal privilege in this country which they no longer deserve. At the very least, they should be subject to those legal restraints and obligations which have been imposed on them in other industrial countries, notably the United States.

We are not concerned here with the merits of any of these proposals or with how the law relating to trade unions should be reformed. We are concerned only with the issue of whether a case for the reform of collective bargaining can be based on the premise of excessive trade union power. Widely held though it may be, it is suspect on three main grounds. First, it does not tally with the facts; second, it contains an inherent contradiction; and third, it rests on an inadequate and erroneous view of the nature of collective bargaining.

When we look at the evidence there is very little to support the assertion that British trade unions have become more powerful over the past two decades. This point is surely crucial, for this is the period during which the faults in our collective bargaining system have become increasingly marked. The only quantitative measure of trade union strength is density of organisation: the proportion of potential union members who are actually organised. Though total membership has increased a little over this period, overall density of organisation has declined between 1948 and 1967 from 45 to 42 per cent. But it may be objected that, despite lack of union growth, the change in the state of the labour market—what we conventionally call full employment—has made the trade unions more powerful. This, too, is a statement that must be questioned. Full employment has undoubtedly increased the bargaining power of union members at their place of work, but this very fact has been an important cause of weakness in the unions as national organisations. Indeed, their failure to control their members is one of the main charges brought against them. The weakness of such control is not due, however, to caprice among their leaders but to the changed situation at the workplace. It is further argued that the situation prevailing over most of the economy of labour scarcity and long order books has made employers more vulnerable to trade union pressure and thereby enhanced union bargaining power. Even if one grants that the threat of strike action is more potent than in the days of mass unemployment in those industries where unions make use of it, it is also true that in the more affluent society union members are not as ready to respond to the call of a strike if it is likely to be a sustained affair which seriously jeopardises their earnings. Their commitments restrain their militancy. Such considerations as these provide little foundation for the assertion that faults in the collective bargaining system have in some way been correlated with growing union power.

It can also be shown that there is an inherent contradiction, a logical inconsistency, in this view. Of relevance here is an early statement of the late Professor Ashley:

> ... the only practical alternative to strikes – peaceful collective bargaining – depends for its efficiency on the existence of strongly organised unions. But strongly organised unions, though they are indispensable instruments for enforcing treaties, are powerful weapons of attack. . . . This puts the employer in an awkward moral situation: it is almost more than can be asked of average human nature to demand that he shall rejoice at the growing power of a union; and, yet, unless it is strong, it cannot effectively maintain the peace.[5]

The present critics of the unions have to face the same awkward moral situation. They cannot have it both ways. If they want the unions to be strong enough to maintain the peace by controlling members' behaviour, they should not complain of excessive union power or propose measures that will have the effect of weakening them. To put the same point more theoretically: there are two aspects of the strength of trade unions which are rarely separated – their internal and their external strength. The first is expressed in the strength of a union's internal membership sanctions, its power as an organisation over its members, its means of securing compliance with its decisions. The second lies in the external sanctions it can bring to bear on employers in negotiations or to compel them to observe agreements. But these two systems of sanctions develop in conjunction. A union that is internally weak is normally one that is externally weak: equally the unions cannot be deprived of their external strength without weakening them internally as well. This is the contradiction in the argument of those who want to curb union power.

The third point is that this type of analysis reflects a mistaken view of the nature of collective bargaining. Andrew Shonfield, in his reservation to the main Donovan Report, asserts that 'the trade union is in the last resort a fighting organisation; its business is to be equipped to make a nuisance of itself in pursuit of the interests of its members'.[6] This is not so much wrong as a half-truth, and as a half-truth it caricatures the role of trade unions in collective bargaining.

Collective bargaining is not an unrestrained power struggle in which union leaders act like army commanders, urging the troops into total war, intent only on maximising gains and imposing the greatest possible defeat upon the employers. They are in the main cautious men keenly aware that collective bargaining is a continuing relationship within which the parties have to live together. This functional requirement leads them far more often towards restraining pressures than creating them. That, indeed, is the very essence of their profession. The other half of the truth has been expressed in a vivid phrase of C. Wright Mills when he speaks of the trade union leader acting as 'a manager of discontent'.

> He organises discontent and then he sits on it, exploiting it in order to maintain a continuous organisation. . . . He makes regular what might otherwise be disruptive, both within the industrial routine and within the union he seeks to establish and maintain.[7]

Most British employers may have relied far too long and far too much on union leaders to solve their industrial relations problems for them. This is the other side of the coin to their lack of effective personnel policies, which the Donovan Report so cogently attacked.[8] But even where managements take their own responsibilities seriously and pursue well-designed and consistent personnel policies, trade unions must have authority enough to be able to resolve what are likely to be recurrent conflicts of interest and viewpoint among their constituent groups. This is as much a part of collective bargaining as the actual exchanges between the two sides. 'A great deal of the complexity and beauty of collective bargaining', as John Dunlop has said, 'involves the process of compromise and assessment of priorities within each side'.[9] It follows that, when trade unions are not strong enough to be able to act effectively as managers of conflict, then an essential part of the mechanism of social control, on which we rely for order in industry, breaks down.

If, then, contrary to popular belief, excessive trade union power does not account for the present shortcomings of collective bargaining, what is the real case for its reform?

NORMATIVE ORDER AND COLLECTIVE BARGAINING

Pursuing our analysis at a somewhat deeper level than could reasonably have been expected from the Donovan Commission, the answer, in our view, can be summed up in terms of that condition referred to by the French sociologist, Emile Durkheim, as *anomie*. Quickly translated, this described a state of normlessless resulting from a breakdown in social regulation. The concept can be elaborated and refined in many different ways. For our present purposes we will argue that the social conditions which he characterised as a state of normlessness may be produced by an excessive proliferation of different normative systems which are unrelated and divergent. In presenting our case we take as a starting point a view of industrial relations and, in particular, of collective bargaining which places them in the general theoretical context of the functions of normative systems and the dynamics of their change. Only then can the relevance of our use of the anomie concept be established.

Every system of industrial relations is a normative system regulating employment relations; in short, a system of job regulation. A norm can be seen as 'a rule, a standard, or pattern for action',[10] and a set of integrated norms–i.e. norms consistently related according to certain principles–constitutes a normative system. Norms, however, may be either substantive or procedural, and the relationship between the two is a notable feature of any system. Applied to employment relations, examples of substantive norms would include standard wage rates, working hours, overtime and holiday arrangements, or any other rules regulating terms and conditions of employment or governing work behaviour. Examples of procedural norms, on the other hand, include the constitutional provisions of machinery for negotiation and the settlement of disputes, but equally methods used in determining differential levels of rewards, rights and privileges, or in recruiting employees and allocating them to jobs, or in promoting, supervising, disciplining and dismissing them. The distinction is between norms which directly regulate employment relations and those which do so indirectly by regulating the behaviour, the patterns for action, of the various formal and informal organisations (and their representatives) that are parties to the system.

In industrial relations, both substantive and procedural norms may be of widely varying coverage, as well as being more or less general, that is, having varying degrees of diffuseness or specificity. They may apply to a single work group, to a department, to an establishment, to a company, to an occupation nationally or over a more limited area, to a whole industry and beyond. They may be so diffuse as merely to state that dismissal should not take place 'without just cause' or that only 'reasonable' amounts of overtime should be worked, or so specific as to fix the precise rate of wages for the job or a detailed timetable in a disputes procedure. This 'network or rules', apparently so particularistic, reveals nevertheless a universal pattern of systems within systems, when at various levels integrating principles can be shown to be implicit within the multiplicity and diversity of separate norms.[11] Even in a country like Britain, where universally enforced norms embodied in legislation have played so marginal a role in industrial relations, the notion of a national system is not meaningless, for it is possible to discern some integrating principles transcending the many contrasts between and within industries.

One of those principles has been the priority accorded to collective bargaining over other methods of job regulation,[12] a principle shared by other national systems in political democracies. Despite the confusion caused by its unfortunate title, collective bargaining is among other things a rule-making or norm-creating process of a bilateral character. Employer and employee organisations, through their representatives, act as joint creators of substantive and procedural norms and frequently accept the sole, or at least the main, responsibility for their interpretation, application and enforcement. Even so, it is not the only method of furnishing a society with an adequate code of written and unwritten norms for regulating employment relations. The state may lay down certain norms and impose them on all or many employment situations either directly or through some public agency. Employers or managers may impose norms unilaterally on their employees. Trade unions may similarly practise unilateral regulation in reverse. Work groups, with or without union support, may be able in part to regulate their own employment relations, especially their own work behaviour, by imposing their norms on management. Nor should the regulating force of custom be ignored.

The reasons for the emergence of collective bargaining as the principal norm-creating institution in industrial relations can best be appreciated after some essential points on normative systems in general have been made. Their significance in human affairs is closely bound up with the concept of social order. Individuals and groups located within a stable and agreed set of norms have a number of reference points and guidelines by which they can judge, in Durkheim's words, 'between the possible and the impossible, what is just and unjust, legitimate claims and hopes and those which are immoderate'.[13] In other words, an accepted normative system provides a framework of comparisons and constraints within which otherwise unlimited aspirations can be shaped with some concern for social proportion. Although order in itself may not be the highest social good and certainly no normative system can be regarded as sacrosanct, society cannot exist without normative regulation for the maintenance of social order; it depends on such regulation for the integration and predictability of expectations and behaviour. To the extent that necessary normative regulation is lacking or is weakened and threatened with collapse, disorder becomes manifest in unpatterned behaviour leading to an undermining of integration and predictability in social action and events. In more specific terms, disorder emerges as dislocation, disruption and a variety of other symptoms associated with frustrated expectations.

Societies differ, however, in the degree of disorder that is tolerated and the areas of behaviour in which it is tolerated. For analytical purposes we may conceive of two ideal types. At the one extreme, there is a quest for such a high degree of social integration and predictability that diversity of normative patterns in almost all fields of social behaviour is very severely curtailed. The tasks of norm creation and enforcement are wholly centralised, thus preventing a free market in ideas and values and precluding the existence of autonomous groups at liberty to challenge the ruling norms. In industrial relations this implies one universal system that attempts fully to regulate employment relations on a unified and consistent basis, within work establishments, between establishments in the same industry, and between all industries and occupations. Such a comprehensive order can only be imposed by dint of *force majeure*, that is, by the coercive powers of the state. Tensions and instability may develop within the system when subject groups rebel or seek some measure of autonomy, but even the mildest forms of disorder become a threat to the state and must be suppressed.

At the opposite extreme we have the pluralistic society with the least possible statutory regulation of employment relations. Through

249

the mechanisms of freedom of contract, freedom of association, an unrestricted traffic in ideas and ideologies, combined with a strong preference for voluntary action, there develops a wide variety of relatively autonomous but inter-acting norm-creating groups and agencies. The result is a multiplicity of separate normative systems which appear to evolve in a more or less haphazard fashion. Though, as already mentioned, they may not entirely lack integrating principles, some degree of constant disorder is bound to follow. Indeed it is the necessary price of change and growth; a price that is willingly paid to avoid the authoritarian, centralised control that would be required for even an approximation to absolute order.

Between these extremes there are many variants in the patterns of normative orders. We are concerned, however, with the dynamics of change in pluralistic structures in which social and industrial conflict are accepted as legitimate and not suppressed. Here the rules and standards actually prevailing at any time will never embody the unqualified agreement of all groups within the structure. Some may wish to see their employment relations regulated by different norms. We may thus speak of these groups having normative aspirations. Power is the crucial variable determining the outcome in such a situation. One group may have been able to impose its preferred normative system upon other groups, but a subjected group can perhaps mobilise power on its own account, formulate normative aspirations, challenge the prevailing norms, and force an agreed compromise. It may then be able to secure permanent acceptance of a process of bilateral regulation, or, if it is powerful enough, unilaterally impose its own set of norms in substitution for the existing set.

Conversely, of course, a group may cherish normative aspirations which differ from the prevailing norms but lack sufficient power to challenge them. A tension then exists between norms and normative aspirations. Interests are indisputably in conflict, but the conflict remains latent since aspirations cannot receive effective expression. Only when the group is able to mobilise sufficient power to challenge the prevailing norms does the conflict become manifest. In this context the relationship between power and aspirations is a complex one. Consciousness of power tends to stimulate aspirations, though a group may possess power before they become conscious of it. Conversely, new aspirations may prompt a group to see ways of augmenting their power, or to direct their present power towards new ends.

Out of manifest conflict may come agreement, but it is important to distinguish between normative agreement and normative consensus. Groups with different normative aspirations may negotiate an agreed compromise on what the prevailing norms are to be, but this does not necessarily imply a total consensus of values and principles. This is not to say that no element of consensus is present. Clearly the agreement to compromise expresses at the very least a consensus that the game should continue, and be played moreover according to certain rules. But within this procedural consensus, different groups may reach normative compromise on substantive issues while still retaining normative aspirations which markedly diverge.

The dynamics of the process now start to become visible. Normative aspirations within a group may grow, increasing the tension between them and the prevailing norms. Consciousness of power may be among the factors which enlarge aspirations in this way. The group brings its power to bear to reduce the tension between norms and aspirations. Obviously the greater the degree of consensus between the normative system and the normative aspirations of the various groups involved, the less the overall tension and the less the invocation of power in attempts to reduce that tension.

The eruption of manifest conflict in industrial relations, as groups mobilise and exert power to change old norms and fashion new ones, has in the main been met by the method of collective bargaining. As Robert Dubin has argued, in 'a democracy . . . the continuity of the society and its stability depend upon a common set of criteria for determining when conflict becomes disorder',[14] and in industry collective bargaining is the social process that provides such a 'framework within which management and worker views of the disputed matters that lead to industrial disorder can be considered, with the aim of eliminating the causes of the disorder'.[15] In this sense it is the 'great social invention that has institutionalised industrial conflict' in much the same way as 'the electoral process and majority rule have institutionalised political conflict'. For, although when either of the parties make use of their economic power 'its immediate function' is 'the creation of industrial disorder', their 'strategic end . . . is to establish a new basis of order, a new

251

set of rules' so that 'the limits of industrial disorder come to be institutionally determined'.[16]

If, then, we seek to construct a simple model of collective bargaining as a social process we must describe the input as conflict and disorder, just as we must describe the output as rules, including their application and adjustment. So whether collective bargaining is called a conflict-resolving or a rule-making process comes to much the same thing. What matters is that historically collective bargaining has been the principal method evolved in industrial societies for the creation of viable and adaptive normative systems to keep manifest conflict in employment relations within socially tolerable bounds. This it has done because the rules it produces, as expressed in collective agreements and in unwritten understandings, are supported by a sufficiently high degree of consensus among those whose interests are most affected by their application.

If one accepts that the substance of industrial relations is job regulation–the making and administration of rules for regulating employment relations–the great attraction of collective bargaining, and the main reason for the priority accorded to it over other methods of job regulation in most democratic countries, lies in its rules being jointly agreed by representatives of the parties to employment relations. This makes for a readier acceptance and observance than when they are imposed unilaterally by one side or by some external authority such as the state. The acceptability is increased too by the continuous character of collective bargaining, which enables rules constantly to be adapted to changing needs and circumstances.

But the fact that in a given society collective bargaining is generally approved, or even rated the best method of resolving industrial conflict, does not mean that its existing institutional forms are necessarily adequate to provide sufficient normative regulation. We have seen how changes in power relations transform latent into manifest conflict, and how this may be accompanied by rising normative aspirations which effectively challenge prevailing norms. In these circumstances collective bargaining institutions which previously sufficed to maintain social order, or as much of it as was desired, may no longer be able to cope with the increased input of conflict unless they are radically reformed. This is precisely what has been happening at an accelerating rate in Britain over the post-war years, and the main effect, as we will show, has been an increasing fragmentation of normative regulation. Before we come to that part of our argument, however, we have yet to explain at a theoretical level why such fragmentation should have anomic consequences.

The preceding analysis enables us to postulate four major sources of disorder in industrial relations arising from the inter-action between normative aspirations and prevailing norms. The first of these comprises situations in which one group, against the resistance of another, seeks to change the procedural norms and nature of the system—for example by converting unilateral norm-creation and enforcement into bilateral, or by enlarging or contracting the size of the unit of regulation. The second source of disorder is a similar situation with respect to the system's substantive norms; the degree of tension between the prevailing norms and the aspirations of one or more relevant groups has become so great that it provokes challenge and conflict. The third source is an absence of regulation about certain issues on which one group at least has normative aspirations. In these circumstances problem situations come under *ad hoc*, piecemeal solutions, often arrived at only after conflict between opposing groups who have brought their divergent interests and values to bear upon the particular case. Until agreement has been reached on the need for regulation, however, the prospect of recurrent disorder persists.

When these second and third sources of disorder multiply, their very frequency and extent may, in appropriate circumstances, create the fourth source of disorder—a progressive fragmentation and breakdown of existing regulative systems. This, like our first category, leads to a change in the nature of the system—in this case, a contraction in the size of the units of regulation, often accompanied by a shift from bilateral to virtually unilateral regulation. But the ensuing disorder results, not from manifest conflict over procedural norms as such, but from the substantive consequences of the breaking up of larger units of regulation into a number of smaller and un-integrated units. In contrast to the first category, this structural change is usually uncontested; the party on whom it is imposed being unable or unwilling to resist.

In the typical situation, a normative system covering a number of different groups comes under increasing tensions for a variety of possible reasons. Perhaps it does not regulate issues about which some groups have normative aspirations. Perhaps anomalies and inconsistencies of regulation between groups within the system, or in relation to groups in other systems, are not resolved. In response to these failures of the system, those groups with sufficient power break through it and impose their own norms. In so far as they serve as reference points for other groups, either in the same system or in others, their example is followed. Extreme frustration builds up among those groups who come under the same tensions but who lack power. Meanwhile, each normative system becomes either replaced or supplemented by a number of smaller systems. This increases the likelihood of disorder, since groups governed by different normative systems are clearly likely to behave in ways which frustrate each other's expectations. Besides making predictability and integration of action difficult this may create mutual frustration, jealousy, and rivalry, leading to severe inter-group conflict. Moreover, this fragmentation of normative systems is itself a factor making for tension between norms and aspirations. Disorder feeds upon disorder.

The special gravity and intractability of our fourth source of disorder should be evident, not only on account of its cumulative character. The other three demand concessions and compromise on the part of resisting groups, possibly on issues which they have regarded as matters of principle, but order can be re-established by a readjustment or extension of existing normative systems. But when the progressive and arbitrary fragmentation of these systems has passed a certain point, nothing short of their wholesale reconstruction can remove the source of disorder. In general it can be argued that the more relatively numerous the normative systems regulating employment relations, the greater the problem of social order, since the task of finding the requisite measure of integration among the various systems becomes increasingly difficult to solve. In other words, the more regulation is fragmented, the greater the likelihood of disorder when the different groups have their expectations formed and their actions guided by unrelated and divergent sets of norms.

The threat of instability which hangs over such a situation can have the most profound and serious consequences. The proliferation of norm-creating groups and the resulting multiplicity of normative systems may produce a degree of disorder which is felt to impede and imperil vital functions of social life and government. In industrial relations the economic consequences are not confined to strikes and other dislocations of the productive process. The loss of integration and predictability is also expressed in such things as chaotic pay differentials and uncontrolled movements of earnings and labour costs. And the political consequences are decidedly no less important. Growing disorder may threaten the government's ability to govern and start to generate strong popular demands for authoritarian state intervention to restore order.

An excessive proliferation of normative systems can therefore produce social consequences that are similar to those resulting from the absence of any norms to regulate conflict. Both situations can be seen in terms of a breakdown of social regulation. Both can be described in the terms of Durkheim's characterisation of anomie.

One can express, in these terms, the fundamental problem of societies that aspire to be democratic in the sense in which this word is usually understood in the western world. They seek a balance that is notoriously difficult to maintain. They eschew such a degree of social order and integration that would require for its achievement a centralisation of norm-creation repugnant to their social values. On the other hand, the degree of permitted decentralisation of norm-creation may produce social disorder too threatening for society to tolerate, precipitating a retreat to the safety of state regulation.

The general relevance of this theoretical argument for Britain's problems is already, we hope, apparent. We must now demonstrate its specific relevance to the reform of collective bargaining.

THE BREAKDOWN OF SOCIAL REGULATION

The Donovan Commission based its case for the reform of collective bargaining on its central analytical premise of two systems in conflict. It has been criticised for exaggerating the extent of the decline of the formal system of industry-wide agreements and of the growth of the informal system of shop-floor bargaining. This is due, these critics sometimes suggest, to its having generalised too much from the experience of the engineering industries. A careful reading of the Report does not sustain these charges, for its statements are qualified and 'room for argument on the extent' of these developments is acknowledged. A more apposite, if more theoretical, criticism could be directed against its conceptual assumption of *two* systems. That the regulative force of industry-wide agreements has been under-mined by the actual behaviour of managements and work groups is not in doubt, or that this has happened to a greater or lesser extent in all but a few industries. What the Report, for presentational convenience, refers to as an informal system, however, hardly merits this title when the absence of any integrating principles is the most outstanding feature of the range of industrial behaviour described.

This is very much more than a semantic question. Our contention is that the present condition of industrial relations in Britain is better characterised as a proliferation of unrelated normative systems each resting on only a small area of agreement in place of more closely integrated systems covering much larger areas, and that the overall effect is equivalent to a progressive breakdown of social regulation. How and why has this come about?

Analysis must begin with the transformation of power relations within factories and companies that has resulted from full employ-ment over much of the economy for much of the post-war period. This ground was amply covered in the Donovan Report. In the theoretical terms we are using, the interaction between power and aspirations has given a vigorous stimulus to demands from the shop floor, and the ferment has been intensified by the accelerating pace of technological, organisational and social change. Norms have come under constant pressure for revision and emergent aspirations have revealed major gaps in normative systems by bringing into existence new issues and problems for which no regulation yet exists. Two kinds of consequence have followed. Work groups capable of mobilising the necessary power have broken through a relatively larger area of regulation and imposed a relatively smaller one more favourable to themselves. And when faced with gaps in the normative system in respect of certain of their aspirations, groups with sufficient power have introduced their own. In both situations the revision and creation of norms has been improvised and piecemeal, has rested on a very small area of agreement, and has not been related to larger units of regulation. This splintering of the normative order within the establishment and the piecemeal, hotch-potch additions to it, all determined by the accidents of power distribution rather than by agreed principles of any sort, has greatly increased the probability of disorder and loss of control within establishment and enterprise boundaries.

The Breakdown of Social Regulation

But the effects have extended far beyond those boundaries, and on these the Donovan Report touched but lightly. Order rests as much on relations between establishments, occupations, and industries as within them. Here the same forces have been at work destroying customary relations and creating new situations where no defined and accepted relations exist at all. The problem, as has been argued elsewhere,[17] is one of unrestrained competition promoting and promoted by inflation, but competition of three kinds: economic, political and social. Employers have engaged in economic competition for labour in short supply by bidding up earnings above agreed rates, thus disrupting such exiguous normative relations as may have previously existed between establishments, occupations and industries. The political relations between unions have also obliged them to compete for success by out-bidding each other in seeking to revise the norms regulating their members' wages and conditions. The third form of social competition has resulted from the conflicting values held by different groups of employees, which influence their views on the relative worth of their services or the fairness of their pay compared with other groups, and consequently their pressures on employers and unions.[18]

These forces have sharpened and brought to the forefront an issue which for much of our industrial history has been somewhat muffled –possibly with significant consequences for national class and political relations. This issue is the distribution of rewards and privileges not *between* classes, but *within* classes. It has never, of course, been true that normative systems governing employment relations had the effect of determining only the distribution of rewards and privileges as between capital and labour. Whether intentionally or as a by-product, the comparative fortunes of different groups of employees were also determined. But the post-war situation by unleashing powerful competitive forces between groups and sections among wage and lower-salary earners, makes this fact far more palpable and insistent than it has ever seemed before. The jostling for advantage between groups is currently on an unprecedented scale. There are many signs that the significance of this is not yet widely appreciated. The debate on incomes policy is often conducted within the trade union movement as if collective bargaining were simply a mechanism for pursuing social justice as between capital and labour, and its function of determining the relative fortunes of

257

different groups of labour is ignored. Indeed, incomes policy *per se* is often seen as imposing constraints that unfairly handicap the employee class, which is assumed to be a homogeneous entity.

This is not to deny for a moment that there is ample scope for debate about the practical form taken by incomes policy—about whether, for example, it should or does include attempts to regulate, however crudely, dividends, rents, and prices, and which groups should be favoured as against others. But the question of whether there should be an incomes policy at all cannot be considered as if the issue at stake were simply that of workers versus employers. This is to surrender to habits of thought that were formed in a very different context. At times in the past when a significant proportion of economic resources lay idle simply through failure of governmental knowledge and will, the belief cherished by many trade unionists that a successful wage claim for one major group could help all other groups to advance might well have some validity, in that it contributed towards an upward movement in prices and incomes which brought idle resources into use. But in a situation where all resources are fully employed, an advantage gained by a strong group may be at the absolute or relative expense of weak groups, who are more likely to be wage-earners than employers, managers and shareholders.

The competitive struggle between groups under full employment has therefore created a problem of social disorder which is new simply because at no previous period has there existed such a widespread and long-lasting opportunity for employee groups to mobilise power and express their own normative aspirations. Since the problem of disorder as we now know it is new, in the past no pressing need developed for its regulation. The present urgency of that need has obviously been intensified by Britain's international trading position, but it would exist whether we suffered balance-of-payments crises or not.

The characteristic features of this relatively anomic condition have been vividly portrayed by Durkheim. It is the cause, as he said:

> ... of the incessantly recurrent conflicts, and the multifarious disorders of which the economic world exhibits so sad a spectacle. For, as nothing restrains the active forces and assigns them limits they are bound to respect, they tend to develop haphazardly and come into collision with one another, battling and weakening themselves. To be sure, the strongest succeed in completely demolishing the weakest, or in sub-

ordinating them. But if the conquered, for a time, must suffer subordination under compulsion, they do not consent to it, and consequently this cannot constitute a stable equilibrium. Truces, arrived at after violence, are never anything but provisional, and satisfy no one. Human passions stop only before a moral power they respect. If all authority of this kind is wanting, the law of the strongest prevails, and latent or active, the state of war is necessarily chronic.[19]

Again, in another passage, Durkheim notes what happens when 'an abrupt growth of power and wealth' creates unstable conditions by upsetting the established scale of values:

The scale is upset, but a new scale cannot be immediately improvised. Time is required for the public conscience to reclassify men and things. So long as the social forces thus freed have not regained equilibrium, their respective values are unknown and so all regulation is lacking for a time. The limits are unknown between the possible and the impossible, what is just and what is unjust, legitimate claims and hopes and those which are immoderate. Consequently there is no restraint upon aspirations.[20]

The process may be described in terms of its impact upon the institutions of collective bargaining. The normative system fashioned by the evolution of collective bargaining in this country, particularly in our structure of industry-wide agreements, can no longer cope with the increased input of conflict which has been generated in post-war circumstances. That is why the system is weakened and, to some extent, in a state of collapse. That is why occasional repairs to the machine will not suffice and we need a new model. All that the Donovan Report had to say in detail about 'pretence' and 'disorder' portrays manifestations of this condition. They are typical symptoms of the breakdown of normative systems. Viewed in this context, and in the preceding framework of analysis, the idea that our collapsing systems of regulation can somehow be rehabilitated by resorting to legal enforcement of collective agreements[21] is ludicrous and merely betrays a lack of understanding of the nature of the problem. To quote Durkheim once again: 'when restraints are simply imposed by force then peace and harmony are illusory; the spirit of unrest and discontent are latent; appetites superficially restrained are ready to revolt'.[22]

The failure of leadership on both sides to adapt the institutions of regulation to cope with the rising incidence and the widening range of conflict and disorder is precisely what in many situations has led to an increase in unilateral norm-creation and enforcement by work groups. While leaders have clung to the safe known forms of established methods and familiar issues, the more favoured groups among the rank and file have supplied the dynamic for themselves.

Given that the problem has overtaken us only in the post-war period, the question needs to be asked why Britain should have had to wait until now before having to grapple with it. In other words, how can we relate current events to an historical perspective?

THE PRESENT IN HISTORICAL PERSPECTIVE

At first sight it might be supposed that the impact of the Industrial Revolution upon a traditional, predominantly rural society would precipitate a state of anomie similar to the one we are now experiencing. An old stable order crumbling under the onslaught of rapid, technological change, population shifts and the growth of towns could surely be expected to produce just the effect with which we are concerned. One necessary corrective to such an assumption is the unanimity with which economic historians now stress that industrialisation was a more gradual process than the term 'revolution' implies, with its suggestion of sudden, universal upheaval. And the more gradual a set of changes, the greater the possibility that the existing normative order can adapt by degrees without being thrown into disruption. But more factors were involved than this.

We have already noted that conflicts of interest between groups in respect of a given normative system may remain latent if the group which feels deprived or threatened lacks the power to challenge the existing norms. The history of combination among wage and salary earners in the nineteenth century shows that only a very small proportion of them were able to mobilise the necessary power. Of these, a significant number were powerful craft groups, much of whose regulative effort was directed not towards changing the norms inherited from the past but to defending them against encroachments by the employers. In other industries marked by sharp price fluctuations it was the employers who were powerful enough to take their stand on custom, and who tolerated worker combinations only if they accepted a normative sliding-scale link between price and wage movements. In many of the most important factory trades the employers' interest in regulating competition in labour markets prompted them to co-operate with unions in extending regulation by negotiated piece-price lists, thereby establishing wage norms with the minimum of disruption.

None of these situations was free from disorder. The first three of our earlier postulated sources were all present. Disorder arose over the procedural structure of the regulative system – trade unions fought to convert unilateral regulation by employers into bilateral regulation and also to enlarge the unit of regulation; employers of the craft trades sometimes found themselves doing the same with respect to craftsmen who were reluctant to abandon their own unilateral regulation. Disorder arose too over the content of substantive regulation. Disputes were waged over the prevailing norms as workers' aspirations grew, as market situations fluctuated, as technology changed, and as industries expanded or contracted. And there were battles over bringing within the normative system issues hitherto left unregulated, working hours as well as wages, for instance.

Yet outside the small sector in which organised workers were able to aspire to independent action, stability was preserved by the inability of large sections of the working population to secure a voice in the norm-creating or norm-changing process. Within these sections, disparities of power enabled employers to prescribe norms as they wished without having to take employee aspirations into account. In many situations custom was the effective regulator; albeit custom which might be trimmed and guided indirectly by the regulated trades and industries. On the other hand, where technological or market change prompted employers to break with custom their employees could put up little effective resistance. In fact, such changes in norms were gradual and small.

Even the quickening of trade-union organisation in the last quarter of the nineteenth century did not immediately change this condition of relative stability. Writing, indeed, of the whole period up to the First World War, Henry Clay points out that 'all they [the parties to negotiations] had to do was to make slight modifications and adjustments in a system of rates and conditions which was generally accepted. . . . The basis of order in industry was a system of relatively stable wage standards, defined and enforced by trade unions or by custom, to which prices and production accommodated themselves.' These standards 'tended to move together and to preserve stable ratios between them, and they may fairly be said to have constituted a system'. The maintenance of order on this basis was possible, he argues, because 'economic change was gradual and seldom catastrophic'. Adjustment in the system of rates and conditions was 'continuous but slight'. Changes were 'seldom great enough to revolutionise the position of a class of workers, or to modify seriously the relation it bore to other classes'. The problem of industrial relations prior to the First World War was therefore, in Clay's words, 'the limited problem of adapting an established system of wage standards and terms of employment by piecemeal adjustments to slowly changing needs and conditions'.[23]

Before the war, however, this comparatively stable order was already showing signs of breaking under powerful stresses and strains. The increasing input of conflict was beginning to put a burden on the system which it was not fully able to meet. The general rise in prices from the later 'nineties was one major factor. Inequalities in the bargaining strength of labour in different parts of the industrial field now resulted in differential adjustments which began to undermine the stable basis of the system of wages. The rate at which, and the extent to which, wages were adjusted to changes in the price level varied from trade to trade and district to district. The influence of trade union organisation in determining wage norms was strengthening as against that of custom. Growing aspirations towards a 'living wage'–an end to the wage cuts of the bad years–was another strain which created disorder. But other norms besides those of financial rewards were concerned. The machinery of bilateral regulation was proving unable to resolve conflict between the norms implicit in craft rules and the norms implicit in employers' attempts to introduce technological and organisational change. These forces, acting upon a very unevenly organised wage-earning class, were beginning to subject regulative systems of wage standards and other norms to strains which they had not previously been called upon to bear. Moreover, the effect was cumulative. The more that organised groups questioned the existing order, the more it seemed to unorganised groups that they must do the same if they were not to be submerged.

The seeds of disintegration in normative systems had therefore already been sown when war brought its own destructive forces to bear. The causative factors were several. They included the unprecedented rise in the price level; the rapid expansion of some industries at the expense of others, with the accompanying mass transfers of labour; the speed-up of technological and organisational change; the creation of new classes of work and of workers, with an accompanying breakdown of traditional skills; and the rapid spread of union organisation as labour scarcity brought power and awakened aspirations.

Despite government encouragement of the extension of bilateral regulation, the input of conflict was such that the machinery of collective bargaining was quite unable to cope with it, and the fabric of custom, one need hardly stress, was virtually destroyed. In response to the ensuing disorder, the state was obliged to intervene with compulsory arbitration to impose regulation and order on its own account.[24] But this authoritarian intervention came only after the pre-war basis had been violently disrupted. It did not supply the basis of a new order, but merely attempted to contain the disorder consequent on the progressive breakdown of the pre-war system.

The post-war period thus inherited a situation which was more or less guaranteed to produce disorder on a major scale. On top of all the other structural adjustments required by the transition from a wartime to a peacetime economy, there was the widespread dislocation of the pre-war order of expectations and aspirations relating to the norms of employment relations. The notion of an order of normative systems that was generally accepted and to which particular adjustments could be related was now largely destroyed. Few groups were unable to point to some other group whose relative position had not improved more than their own, so that any improvement they had secured left them unsatisfied. The habit of comparison with other related groups, which before the war acted as a restraining force by preventing a group from exploiting to the full any temporary bargaining advantage, now operated in the reverse direction by triggering off further demands.

Clay stated the problem clearly in a lecture in 1923. 'The need is not to restore the pre-war system, but to secure a post-war system with the same stability as the pre-war system'.[25] It was never secured. What initiative there had been for reconstruction after the war was soon exhausted and rested in the main on the First Report of the Whitley Committee. Despite its alleged idealism, which was little more than a statement of pious and illusory objectives, this 'was a conservative, not an innovatory document'.[26] True, it had helped to promote a further voluntary extension of industry-wide machinery for bilateral regulation in the shape of Joint Industrial Councils. It was also the basis of legislation to enlarge both the small sphere of statutory wage regulation and the peace-making powers of the government.[27] But though collective bargaining covered a wider area than before the war, by 1922 the new Ministry of Labour had 'abandoned its drive for the formation of councils'[28] and subsequently many of them collapsed or ceased to have any significant regulative function. This strengthened the demand to give legal sanction to the agreements made by the councils, or at least those relating to wages, but none of the many Bills introduced for this purpose ever passed into legislation.[29]

Above all, neither the government nor the Trades Union Congress nor the British Employers' Confederation made any gestures towards co-ordinating wage adjustments. Given the destruction of the pre-war system and the consequent absence of stable reference points by which industries could judge their own norm-fixing, the arbiter tended to become power. Employers and unions often found that manifest conflict was the only means by which uncertainty and confusion over what was the 'proper' level of rewards could be resolved. The moral authority of custom and negotiated adjustments to an accepted basis of order having been undermined, there was little which, in Durkheim's words, could restrain the 'active forces' and assign them limits they were 'bound to respect'.

Why, then, did Britain not move into the same kind of situation that she has experienced since the Second World War? The answer lies in mass unemployment and its effects on the distribution of power. As depression and then full slump wrought their effects, a degree of fragmentation in normative regulation began to reveal itself. Disorder of our fourth category now appeared. But it was fragmentation of a very different kind from the current one, with different causes, different social consequences, and different social responses to those consequences. As with our present problem, a marked feature was the loss of authority of trade unions and employers' associations, and an increase in autonomy at the establishment level. But there the parallel ends. Whereas labour scarcity in our own times has shifted power towards the work group, the mass unemployment of the inter-war period shifted it towards the employer. Decline of regulation in this context took the form of employers undermining the existing norms by imposing inferior conditions on their employees, who in many situations were unable to mobilise the power to resist. Latent conflict was extensive, but the disadvantaged groups lacked the power to make it manifest.

In both periods, therefore, the coverage of regulation was being fragmented, but differences in the locus of power resulted in profound differences in the social consequences. Fragmentation today is the cause and effect of disorder of a highly visible kind which is regarded as serious by many opinion groups with otherwise little in common. Its economic effects are palpable; much of the disorder emerging as overt conflict, dislocation and inflation. In the inter-war period, the immediate effects of fragmentation bore upon those who were least powerful and articulate, who were often unable to create disorder, and who had least access to the levers of social and political influence and publicity. The process of breakdown was far less visible, since much of the conflict it created remained latent. Its economic consequences were less palpable, diffusing themselves in destructive market competition and the aggravation of deflation. The overt consequences to other sections of society were therefore less identifiable, and less pressure was brought to bear upon government and public bodies to shore up the regulative order and machinery. Some steps were taken,[30] but they reflected nothing like the widespread intensity of concern which has been aroused by our present problem.

Such have been the different consequences, in Britain's social and political context, between a deflationary and an inflationary fragmentation of normative regulation. Yet both types of breakdown have serious consequences for social functioning. Moreover, both types result in severe inequities among work groups. Under deflationary fragmentation, a fortuitous advantage was enjoyed by those groups who worked in industries where for various reasons the authority of industry-wide regulation could be maintained. Under inflationary fragmentation, the advantage goes to small groups within enterprises who are most able to mobilise power and fight for their own hand.

The economic revival of the later 'thirties saw some strengthening of voluntary regulative powers at the level of the industry. But by 1939 there had been no attempt to move towards a basis of order that Clay had defined as requiring two things: that 'the rates must be adjusted to the normal commercial needs and possibilities of each industry, and the relations between them must be such as the workers accept as reasonable'.[31] The problem towards which the country had begun to move in the years leading up to the First World War, and which had been violently intensified by the war, had not been tackled. In a sense it lay dormant and had been postponed because mass unemployment had temporarily changed its nature. A potential inflationary breakdown of regulation was converted into a deflationary breakdown; the power of those at the base of the social hierarchy to modify normative standards in their own favour was severely limited and their aspirations languished accordingly.

But what was the prospect when the locus of power moved back to the shop floor and when aspirations were once more awakened? There was no accepted basis of order which embodied the sort of moral authority necessary if all the various autonomous groups were to locate themselves in what they felt to be a fair set of normative relations. We are now living with the outcome of this situation. During the Second World War, the combination of genuine national unity, a carefully-fostered ethic of greater social equality, and resumed–though milder and more disguised–authoritarian intervention by the state,[32] served to contain the powerful forces that were building up behind the return to labour scarcity. These restraining forces even lasted for some years into the postwar period, with its conditions of continuing national emergency and extreme economic stringency. But, with their departure, there began to develop the inflationary breakdown of regulation in which we are now caught up.

There was now, however, an additional factor at work. Hitherto, apart from that small proportion of the working population employed in the craft trades, aspirations had tended to focus predominantly on market norms–on wages and working hours. Craftsmen had always aspired to extend their own unilateral regulation far beyond this to cover many of the details of job organisation and behaviour–to cover, in other words, managerial norms relating to the organisation and deployment of the labour force. Now their example began to be followed by non-craft work groups whose shop-floor power awakened new aspirations. The established formal machinery of bilateral regulation too often failed to create the norms necessary to meet

266

these new aspirations; partly indeed it was unable to do so because they were not susceptible to regulation by standardised rules throughout an industry, and employers in any case refused to negotiate on subjects they considered to be a 'managerial prerogative'. So the opportunity to deal with them bilaterally at the level of relatively large units of regulation was missed, and it was left to work groups themselves to impose what standards they could, thereby causing the regulative order to become fragmented over the new as well as the old issues of concern and conflict.

Thus, to sum up: what is new about our current industrial relations scene results from a widespread increase in the fourth of our four sources of disorder–the fragmentation of regulative systems. In the present case, of course, fragmentation is of the inflationary kind. The first three sources are still with us–the desire of one side to change the procedural norms of the regulative system; the growth of tension between prevailing substantive norms and rising group aspirations; and demands to introduce regulation on certain issues previously left unregulated. But whereas these three, along with deflationary fragmentation, have probably been responsible for most disorder in the past, they are now powerfully supplemented by inflationary fragmentation as an important source of disorder in its own right.

RECONSTRUCTION OF NORMATIVE ORDER

At this point it is appropriate to remind ourselves of the reasons why this breakdown of normative order constitutes such a serious problem. The economic factors suffer no lack of public emphasis. They include strikes and other dislocations of the economic process, and inflationary pressures which aggravate balance-of-payments crises and force us into deliberate restraints upon economic growth. Less widely recognised are the social and political dangers. Any form of breakdown in social regulation carries the threat of provoking demands for authoritarian state intervention to prop it up by coercive means. The early signs are there to see. We have already accepted government restrictions on wage movements and collective bargaining that are unprecedented in our history. Demands are widespread for a new kind of legal framework for industrial relations which aims, not so much at reconstructing our crumbling normative order on a basis of agreement, but rather at shoring it up by means of external legal constraints on the participants—more especially on employees. It would be a profound error to interpret these demands as being necessarily the expression of some sinister or reactionary force in politics. The fact that so many trade unionists, for example, have some sympathy with them suggests that they have their roots in a widespread awareness that disorder is an issue of great concern to all sections of society.

Viewed in terms of the preceding analysis, therefore, the need for the reconstruction of normative order ranks as more fundamental than a temporary tactical requirement made necessary by an unfortunate shift in our international trading figures. It emerges, in fact, as a major problem of social regulation which may face any industrial country in greater or lesser degree according to its past and present social structure, its values, the degree of dispersive pluralism it permits itself, the penalties of postponement, and other factors which would require detailed analysis not possible here. We are deceiving ourselves if we suppose, therefore, that the need for incomes policy will disappear given the successful handling of our balance-of-payments difficulties. What is at stake is whether the whole normative framework governing the production and distribution of wealth becomes further fragmented and splintered in a manner which threatens cumulative disorder, or whether we are still capable of reconstructing larger areas of agreement upon which larger units of regulation can rest. The answer to this question has great significance, as we have seen, for political values. Failure could force us into responses which would be tantamount to a decision that Britain could no longer support its present extreme degree of pluralism, and that a measure of authoritarian state regulation must take over from an anarchic drift resulting from fragmenting regulation.

If, then, the case for reforming our collective bargaining institutions is so strong, why is the will to reform them so weak? The Government's White Paper denies 'that the Royal Commission's inquiries and surveys reveal a state of general complacency and disinclination to change',[33] but the attitude survey undertaken at the Commission's request showed in the summarising words of its Report 'widespread satisfaction with the existing arrangements'.[34] Moreover, responses from both sides of industry to its principal recommendations have hardly suggested that there will be a powerful thrust to implement them. True, many voices have been raised to say that the recommendations were not strong enough, but what this has usually meant is that the Commission did not propose a greater use of legal compulsion to curb union power. In the nature of things it will take a long time for the full strategy of the Government and, not least, of the Commission on Industrial Relations, to reveal itself in practice. A great deal will depend on how managements and unions react when they are confronted with constructive initiatives, but for the present the signs point at best to a very limited appreciation of the urgency and seriousness of the case for reform.

In seeking to understand the reasons for continued complacency there are several fairly obvious factors which little can be done about. The old normative systems may be in a state of decay, but clustered around them are all kinds of established interests which feel threatened and apprehensive about any radical reforms. Individuals in organisations on both sides of industry and at various levels of authority have grown accustomed to their well-tried routines and rituals. They dislike the prospect of changing them and plunging into the unknown. A second obstacle lies in their outworn ideologies. These serve as reinforcements of inertia because they represent intellectual and emotional defences carefully constructed to justify entrenched modes of behaviour. Such obstacles stand in the way of reforming any deeply rooted social system and are to be expected.

But the reform of collective bargaining is hampered by other conditions which are not so inevitable, and our statement of the case for reform may help to identify them. In the first place, when one looks at this case at the deepest possible level, not only the unity but the immense size of the problem of reform comes fully into view. The task of replacing the old, crumbling normative systems, on whose gradual evolution we have relied for so long, with new systems that can cope with the full range of conflict endemic to industry in its modern environment has intimidating proportions.

The first and most basic step towards the accomplishment of this task was identified with great force by the Donovan Report. The construction of agreed normative systems covering the company or plant is of crucial significance. Its importance derives from the fact that the company or plant is the only unit of regulation which can integrate the diverse and often conflicting normative aspirations of the various work groups. No external authority can create order within the enterprise. Yet order at this level is basic and necessary to order at any other level. There is no escaping the clear responsibility which resides here.

Unhappily, it is a responsibility which in most cases has still to be met. Some firms have begun the reconstruction of workplace relations but they are a very small minority of the total. The requisite managerial skills are in desperately short supply and most trade unions are ill-equipped to embark on the volume and quality of the negotiations implied. The main problem at this level is the speed of advance. The necessary agreement to support improved arrangements can usually be found, given an intelligent and genuine search for it.

Certainly there are techniques which lie to hand, requiring only the will and the wit to use and adapt them to specific circumstances. The best examples of comprehensive productivity agreements point a way towards achieving agreed normative systems covering work roles and rewards, promotion, discipline, the handling of grievances, and other aspects of job organisation and structure. More specifically in relation to financial rewards, the many varied techniques of job evaluation offer methods of grappling with the problems which are associated with normative breakdown. The report of the Prices and Incomes Board on job evaluation suggests that companies are turning increasingly to its use in order to secure 'the removal of pay anomalies', the 'introduction of order out of chaos', the 'modernisation of pay structures', and the 'definition of differentials'[35]–all of them objectives which clearly relate to the search for normative order.

Yet order at the level of the enterprise, though necessary, is not sufficient. Disorderly relations may still exist between enterprises in the same industry, and between industries. Not only is this disorder undesirable for its own sake; it will also threaten order within enterprises where this has been achieved. The need for normative agreement to extend to these higher levels of regulation is therefore inescapable. Contrary to much that has been written, the Donovan Report did not recommend or assume the disappearance of industry-wide regulation–merely its limitation to issues which experience proves it can effectively regulate. Even with respect to industry-wide regulation, however, the starting-point must be effective company regulation. A powerful stimulus to the former could come from large firms which have successfully negotiated order within their own establishments, but which find themselves vulnerable to contagious disorder from outside. To safeguard their own achievement they now need to promote the creation of orderly relations between themselves and others in the same industry.

Even in this more taxing task one need not feel completely without ideas of possible lines of development. Such firms could work through the relevant employers' association to promote agreement along with the appropriate unions on a normative framework within which members would be committed to operate. The framework might include, along with other features, industry-wide guidelines for the regulation of productivity bargaining and job evaluation techniques.[36] The aim here could be the long-term pursuit of normative agreement within the industry on ways of measuring and rewarding different kinds of work, on methods of relating changes in rewards to changes in productive techniques, on the criteria which companies should apply when concerned with general wage or salary increases, on standards of labour utilisation and definitions of work roles, on career structures and promotion criteria, on the handling of disciplinary and redundancy issues, and other matters of normative contention.

Long-term perspectives of this sort are bound to seem merely visionary when judged by the present behaviour of most employers' associations. But their present behaviour gives us no basis for predicting how they may develop as the long slow task of reconstructing normative order at the enterprise level begins to show results. If enterprises can be encouraged, stimulated, prodded or goaded into creating that order–one of the foremost tasks of the Commission on Industrial Relations–an entirely new set of company attitudes towards the role and potential usefulness of employers' associations might conceivably result. If order comes to be taken increasingly seriously at company level, managements and unions may feel obliged to recognise that order is indivisible. The more progressive and resourceful managements may find themselves moving outwards from company boundaries to protect their own achievements. One vehicle which lies to hand is the employers' association. Under this kind of reinvigoration, the association could take on renewed authority and prestige by exercising leadership and stimulus towards normative co-ordination at the industry-wide level. In the

271

process trade unions would, of course, equally strengthen their own national authority.

But the contagious disorder from outside which can undermine a hard-won stability within the company may emanate not only from other enterprises in the same industry but from other industries. However rigorously leading companies set about promoting normative order, first within their own boundaries, and then, from sheer self-protection, throughout their industry as a whole, they will continue to be vulnerable to disorder and instability in other industries which are not moving at the same pace. Chaotic and unregulated earnings structures elsewhere could impel company managements and unions alike, under the logic of the indivisibility of order, to wish that their own aspirations towards order could be furthered by the creation of stable normative systems in other industries. The presumption must be that the Donovan proposal, which the Government has accepted, to make companies publicly accountable for their collective agreements and industrial relations practices would be continuously operative in raising standards of performance. But given the inevitably uneven pace of development, any given industry which has put its house in order is likely to be aware that the stability of its own normative system is coming under threat from certain other industries which can be identified.

It would clearly be desirable for an industry or a large company so placed to bring its problem to the attention of the Government for enquiry and review. Whether it might best be referred to the Prices and Incomes Board or the Commission on Industrial Relations or some other body is a secondary question. What matters is that machinery is available to deal with this particular source of disorder, capable if necessary of creating constructive relationships with the industries that are conscious of interacting with each other. Such interaction may arise from geographical proximity or from distant comparisons of alleged like with like. The defining of these links by a suitable public agency would help to identify the location and precise consequences of the ensuing disorder. The next step would be the fashioning of normative relationships between the industries involved. There is no reason why, for example, existing or claimed relativities should not be put to the test of rational techniques of inquiry such as job evaluation, even though they cannot in the foreseeable future be applied on a national scale. 'Full and continuous application of the principle of measurement and publicity'[37] would not be without its force. On the foundations laid by this kind of public leadership a gradual extension of inter-industry normative agreement might well be built.

The whole question of normative relations between industries is crucial for two reasons. Firstly, as we have seen, it is perfectly possible for each industry to create its own stable normative system yet for damaging anomalies to exist between the different systems. Secondly, if national incomes policy is not to split our society by creating a growing demand for, and resistance to, the attempted application of compulsion, the effort must be made to reach at least some minimal agreement on normative relations between industries. Ideally, agreement would need to extend to procedural as well as substantive norms. What this means is that there is need to seek not only substantive agreement, say, on the differential patterns of rewards enjoyed by different sectors, but also procedural agreement on the criteria which are to regulate changes in those relationships.

The distinction between substantive and procedural norms is crucial for meeting the sceptic's argument that the rate and character of technical, organisational, and industrial change will defeat any effort to establish stable normative relations between industries. Do not the constantly shifting patterns of demand, the rise and fall of industries, their differing rates of growth, the ever-changing valuations placed upon skills and aptitudes, rule out any possibility of normative agreement between industries? It can be conceded at once that to raise the question of agreed normative relations between industries and occupations in modern industrial society brings out with apparently crushing force the problems which flow from continuous change and adjustment in products, techniques, markets, and rates of industrial growth and decline.

Even here, however, pessimism must not be too precipitate. It is undoubtedly true that within such an environment, agreement on substantive relations can never be enough by itself to maintain order, for rapid change requires frequent adjustments in these substantive relations. If agreement extends only to the substantive relations themselves there is a danger of a new rigidity being established, with a consequent threat of disorder whenever those relations have to undergo change. What is, in a sense, more fundamental is building up agreement on procedural norms on how substantive relations are to be regulated, which provide for flexibility and change in those relations when necessary. These would constitute accepted criteria by which changes in substantive relations between occupations, industries or sectors could be seen as legitimate by all the parties affected.

It cannot be argued that agreement on consistent principles of this kind is impossible, for without it no job evaluation scheme, for example, could be successfully applied and adapted to meet dynamic industrial situations. Nevertheless the pessimist may still refuse to be persuaded. By the very nature of things, it will be said, relationships at this level must inevitably remain those of the jungle. One method of querying this scepticism is by way of an analogy which presents a social situation similarly marked by anarchy but yet susceptible of being brought under control by the articulation of agreed norms. A fire breaks out at sea and creates panic among the passengers, who proceed to fight for places in the lifeboats. Every man's hand is against his fellow's until someone with the requisite authority restores order with the cry of 'Women and children first'. Uncontrollable though the scene at first appeared, a norm has been articulated to which all can respond. It would not have exerted its influence had it not been voiced by an authoritative source, for the readiness of each individual to heed it was determined by the readiness of all. No individual could have restrained himself if the rest had continued to fight for their own hand.

The use of analogies is strictly limited, yet this example helps to illuminate some of the characteristics of the present incomes policy situation. Distasteful though the wages jungle may be for many of those who have to fight within it, no one participant is in a position to bring about a more ordered, rational situation, since the others will not accept his authority. He must therefore fight on whether he likes it or not – or go under. Nothing less than the forceful articulation of common norms by an authoritative source can restore order. The initial state of anarchy did not prove that no common norms could be discovered to regulate behaviour. To be sure, it cannot be argued from this or any other analogy that norms will be found to restrain the struggle for self-interest at the national incomes level. The search may prove fruitless. Proof can only be furnished, however, by the persistent breakdown of sustained efforts, not by an easy acceptance of the self-fulfilling prophecies of failure.

Reconstruction of Normative Order

Perhaps we can draw from the analogy a suggestion that, while we may have to rely for normative order within each industry on the initiative and resource of leading spirits within it, the promotion of order between industries, whether on a limited or on a grand scale, is likely to depend upon vigorous initiative and stimulus from a powerful external authority. The central organisations on both the employers' and the unions' side can hardly fill this role. They are not strong enough and their members are direct participants. We must therefore look to action by the government and public agencies to convene the joint search for agreement on norms that can then be articulated and applied with full measurement and publicity, and whatever sanctions emerge as necessary.

The enormous significance of such an endeavour derives not only from the Promethean character of the task of reform. It derives also from the profundity of the central theme–that of attempting to fashion agreed normative codes regulating the production and distribution of wealth in modern industrial society–and regulating changes in that production and distribution. This constitutes nothing less than a search for a normative order compatible with the rapidity of technological and social change in our times. For the keynote of the age is unquestionably continual and accelerating change, and a congruent order must therefore embody, above all, agreed procedural norms which provide for its accommodation and orderly regulation.

Failure to evolve them through agreement with representative, voluntary institutions will mean that the consequent stresses and strains will increasingly seem to call for imposed solutions. Already we see the search for short cuts, particularly those which place the responsibility for action on other people's shoulders. The more serious the consequences of an ever-increasing anomie in industrial relations, the more tempting it is to claim and to believe that in some way legal compulsion could re-establish order. If the preceding analysis is correct these short cuts are in fact blind alleys. The law has a part to play, but it cannot enforce a regulative order where none exists.

This does not mean that sanctions have no place in the process of evolving and applying a reconstructed normative order. No system of rules can be upheld without sanctions of some kind to deter or penalise the would-be deviant whose transgression would otherwise lead to normative breakdown. Equally, however, it can be

275

said that in this field, as in many others, 'any sanctions must prove to be ineffective unless they are applied only in exceptional cases'.[38] The primary aim must therefore be to achieve as great a degree of normative agreement as possible. This is no place to discuss the probable combination and nature of public and private sanctions that would be necessary. What can be said is that the longer the process of reconstruction is delayed the more punitive they may have to be.

To avert what can only be a further source of delay leading to a further aggravation of the problem, we need to promote a widespread conviction that there is no evading this massive challenge of reconstructing new normative systems of collective bargaining, despite the immensity of the task and despite the uncertainty that must prevail on how and whether it will ever be accomplished.

TRADE UNIONS AND
THE FORCE OF TRADITION
(1969)

Trade unions are rarely out of the news these days, more often than not as an object of criticism. Public opinion polls too record a decline in their popularity and prestige. Yet most of the unions, for their part, remain remarkably indifferent to what is being thought or said about them. One reason for their apparent indifference to public opinion may be the state of public opinion itself. Organisations are much the same as individuals. They do not like being preached at, and trade unions are given far more than their fair share of sermons. They are continually being told what they must do to be saved by people who know next to nothing about them, indeed nothing at all about their internal life and what makes them tick. Inundated by ill-informed advice, often suspect in its motives, they shrug their shoulders and ignore all external criticism. Their intellectual and emotional insularity, so deeply rooted in their past, is merely reinforced.

I am prompted to begin my lecture with these remarks partly to make it quite clear that, despite its title I shall not be following the example of the preachers. I do not intend to read the trade unions yet another sermon in the tones that are now habitual in the columns of *The Economist*. But I have another motive: they help to explain my choice of subject. The quintessence of much of the criticism trade unions attract today is that, in one way or another, they are out of date—in their structure and organisation, in their attitudes and policies and, not least, in their basic beliefs. This is only another way of saying they are victims of their own traditions. The past exerts too great a force for their own good on their present behaviour.

No one could possibly deny that there is some truth in this particular line of criticism. Indeed one hears it voiced as freely and as frequently at the annual Trades Union Congress as at any gathering of employers. But what does it mean and where does it lead? Is it being suggested that the trade unions should scrap every one of their

277

traditions? If not, how does one distinguish between the good and the bad? What, in any case, is the function of tradition in such organisations and can this function be dispensed with? Above all, when a well-argued case for change has been made out, what counter-force can be created which would stand any chance of overcoming the force of tradition? How, in fact, are traditions changed?

When I was honoured by the Vice-Chancellor's invitation to deliver this Sixteenth Fawley Foundation Lecture I searched my mind for a topic that, by demonstrating the value of the scientific approach in enhancing our understanding of industrial problems, would be in keeping with the terms of the Foundation. The peculiar force of tradition in the trade union world had much to recommend it in meeting that condition. Here we have a major industrial problem which is invariably approached in a most unscientific fashion. It is commonly assumed that the force of union traditions can best be overcome by exposing them to rational criticism, especially by showing that they are incompatible with the logic of modern technology or the logic of modern economic thought. In terms of social science nothing could be less scientific than this attitude. It is, as I hope to show, equivalent to a belief in magic, a belief in the possibility of changing effects without even enquiring into causes.

THE NATURE AND SIGNIFICANCE OF TRADITION

So, in taking up my theme, let me begin at its proper beginning by considering in general the nature of tradition as a social force. Max Weber described tradition as 'belief in the everyday routine as an inviolable norm of conduct' or, in another telling phrase, as 'piety for what actually, allegedly or presumably has always existed'.[1] This description draws our attention to several important points. First of all, traditions express normative standards and therefore value judgements. They may, and often do, serve as moral defences for self-regarding group interests, but in the eyes of members of the group they are binding codes demanding on occasions the sacrifice of their individual interests. To ask any member to act against the group traditions may be the same as asking him to neglect his duty and endanger his self-respect. From this angle one can see how its traditions may be a great source of strength to any group, large or small, from the nation to the family. By furnishing the group with an accepted and shared normative code they preserve its solidarity while at the same time giving to each individual member his sense of personal worth.

In the second place, Weber reminds us that adherence to a traditional code implies no more that repeating well-established routines, a way of living which makes few demands on the mind. When we stick to tradition as our guide we are not burdened with difficult problems and choices. We have the safe and comforting knowledge that we are on the right lines if we do today what we did yesterday and expect to do tomorrow. This is as true for the group as it is for the individual and an obvious source of assurance and inner security for both.

The third point to be noted in his description is brought out by the words 'actually, allegedly or presumably'. Myth and reality are mingled in forming and sustaining the content of traditions. It is enough that members of a social group believe in the received version of their history on which its traditions are based; whether that version is true is beside the point. Traditions are therefore resistant to the challenge of historical fact. Any questioning of their validity on these grounds is likely to be ignored. But this, once again, makes them a source of strength for the group as its code cannot easily be shaken by intellectual doubt and dissension.

But there is something more to be said about the sources of the power of tradition. Traditions are not accepted simply because the routines in which they are expressed have been sanctified by the passing of time. They derive their greatest strength from the fact that they embody for the group the lessons of its corporate, social experience. The normative and binding character which traditions acquire is due to their having proved their worth as patterns of behaviour which have consistently succeeded in advancing the group's goals and values. Indeed, its traditions become the sheet anchor of the group's goals and values which may never be separately articulated.

This takes me on to another point about traditions in general that is an important key to understanding how they may be changed. In their fabric ends and means are so inter-woven as to be indistinguishable. When the traditions of a group are first being created there is a sort of experimental interplay between ends and means. Before a new group has gained much social experience it tries out various methods to promote its original aims, the aims that have brought it into being. According to their success or failure, some of these methods are retained while others are discarded. Then, as particular methods get institutionalised, the group in turn adjusts its aims to suit its methods, usually scaling down some of the grander of its earlier ambitions. Once certain patterns of behaviour have become firmly established, however, and enjoy universal approval, the period of experimentation is over. The ends-means relationship, previously in flux, solidifies into a fixed mould in which the group's traditions are cast. That is why tradition and reason so often appear to be at war. A firm belief in tradition excludes reasoning about the ends-means relationship implicit in the patterns of behaviour that it upholds.

With these thoughts in mind I would ask you next to look at the special significance of tradition for trade unions. Some of our unions can trace a continuous history back to the beginning of the last century, but even those of much more recent origin do not escape the influence of common union traditions. Often their leaders and activists have been indoctrinated with these traditions in their youth at home or at work, possibly later by a spell of membership or office in other unions. No one who knows trade unionism from the inside could possibly doubt that the appeal to tradition is a very telling argument even in unions that did not exist fifty years ago.

But why should that appeal be so effective? Does this perhaps express nothing more than a national characteristic? Would it not apply just as much to any organisation in the country? It is easy, certainly, to think of examples of organisations and institutions that display an even greater reluctance than trade unions to modify any of their traditions. Parliament itself is an outstanding example and so is the legal profession. Tradition does, of course, mean a great deal to us as a people. In this respect trade unionists are not different from anybody else. Nevertheless there are grounds for concluding that they are especially prone to take tradition as their principal guide on industrial and social behaviour.

In the first place trade unions are singularly pragmatic bodies, deeply distrusting theories and ideologies. Some of their leaders – or would-be leaders – may turn to abstract ideas for rhetorical purposes, but at bottom trade unions are only interested in results, in immediate results that their members value. As a notable American student of their history, Robert Hoxie, once said:

280

The Nature and Significance of Tradition

Everywhere they have done the thing which under the particular circumstances has seemed most likely to produce results immediately desired. Modes of action which had failed, when measured by this standard, have been rejected and other means sought. Methods that have worked have been preserved and extended, the standards of judgement being always most largely the needs and experiences of the group concerned.[2]

That is the stuff of which union traditions are made. They express in a generalised form the enduring lessons of the workers' experience in industry; the modes of behaviour which have been tried and tested, and judged to be good by the group concerned. In short, they express the group's collective wisdom, orally transmitted from generation to generation. By the same token, however, this endows the traditions with an influence on behaviour which in normal times transcends any other.

The other consideration which brings out the peculiar significance of tradition in the trade union world has been stated by Professor Turner in the preface to his study of the cotton unions:

> The character of organisations, like that of people, is very much a product of their ancestry and the circumstances of their early growth. Once these things are set, only a rather radical change in an organism's environment can usually disturb its character; and sometimes the disturbance is fatal. In people, the quality these things impart is called personality. In organisations it is called (to the extent that it is recognised) tradition. But British trade unions, more than those of most countries perhaps, are historical deposits and repositories of history. And anyone with close experience of trade unionism will be aware of the extent to which every union possesses a personality of its own.[3]

We are reminded by this passage of how misleading it can be to talk about the traditions of trade unions as if they were the same for all unions. Every union, as Turner says, possesses a separate personality which is identical with its own traditions. If we think of a union's framework of organisation—membership, officials, rule book, funds and so on—as its body, then it has something else besides. Call it spirit, soul, personality or character—this is what gives it its individuality. These character traits will not be readily apparent to the outside observer unless he studies the union's history or has other ways of gaining an understanding of its mores, but they mean a great deal to the union's active members. They are the basis of their pride in belonging to this union rather than another and lend point and significance to their activity on the union's behalf.

281

This view of tradition as giving a trade union its personality has important implications when later I come to consider how union traditions may be changed, but for the present let me register this one thought with you. We know from common experience – no doubt psychologists have a word or a number of words for it – that people are most unwilling to accept criticism, even open their minds to it, when they feel it to be an attack on their personality. Such criticism, however well intentioned, will be treated as hostile, because it threatens their identity and thus the foundations of their life. And the more cogent the criticism the greater their resentment and the firmer their rejection. We have to appreciate that organisations react similarly when their traditions are attacked from outside.

Not all traditions, it is true, are of equal worth in the eyes of their adherents. I am not suggesting that every union tradition will be treated as sacred by every trade unionist. That would be nonsense. In Tawney's words: '. . . institutions which have died as creeds sometimes continue to survive as habits'.[4] Ways of behaving that have completely lost their original meaning and survive only as empty rituals may not arouse much feeling for or against. The challenging of habits, which have lost their moral force and are merely preserved by inertia, is unlikely to evoke any violent defensive reactions. But when governments or managements are proposing to do things that will run counter to certain union traditions, they need to know whether the union members' attachment to the traditions is strong or weak; otherwise they will be acting in the dark and invite defeat.

I hope I have said enough to indicate why it can be foolhardy for any outsider to engage in a direct and wholesale attack on the traditions of trade unions if he wants to see them changed. His arguments may be factually correct and logically consistent but that will not make them persuasive. Rather the reverse. By the insider they will be seen as a threat to the cohesion and security of the group which is the more dangerous for not being easily refuted and dismissed. Has rational argument, then, no part to play in changing outmoded traditions? Only, I believe, a very limited and subsidiary part. The main lever for change must be experience. This can best be shown concretely by taking two traditions, or rather sets of traditions, in the British trade union world which retain much of their earlier force though they have in some respects lost their earlier justification. Having been a great source of strength for the unions, unmodified they now threaten to become more and more a source of weakness.

THE TRADITIONS OF CRAFT

My first example is a set of traditions that are not shared by all trade unions but continue undeniably to exert a powerful influence on the industrial behaviour of some. I refer to the traditions of craft. In this day and age it is comparatively easy to mount a devastating attack on these traditions. They were the subject of several scathing passages in the Donovan Commission's Report, which had this to say about apprenticeship:

> An apprenticeship served in the trade concerned is the normal badge of a craftsman. Whether the apprenticeship course was a good course is of secondary importance. Those run by the best industrial concerns are very good. On the other hand in very many cases training plays only a secondary part in an apprenticeship. What happens in practice is that those engaged as apprentices are put on to 'skilled' work after a few weeks' elementary training, and from then on they are doing 'skilled' work just as much as any other skilled worker. In such cases apprenticeship is a farce and provides less training than a properly constructed course lasting only a few months. There are cases also where a reasonably diligent apprentice could learn the skills involved in a few months but is prevented from actually performing skilled work while an apprentice, with the result that he is compelled, at this most formative period of his life, to spend up to five years under-employed and under-occupied in order to comply with the formal requirements of an apprenticeship.[5]

One could continue, as did the Report, to show how the 'gathering speed of technological change will make still more obsolete the craft system organised on its present lines'.[6] The folly of trying to preserve rigid craft boundaries in an era when the content of jobs and the demand for particular skills is constantly changing would seem to be self-evident. In the future it must surely 'be accepted as normal for men and women to undergo re-training and further training at intervals during their working lives so as to adapt their capabilities to new techniques'.[7] Nor is it difficult to demonstrate how craftsmen can fall victims of their own traditions. When the demand for the craft they have learnt declines, they may lack the versatility of skills and outlook to find equally remunerative employment in other fields. But the question remains, why do craft traditions survive? What accounts for their enduring force?

For an answer we must turn to labour history but further back than the inter-war years. There is more at stake here than memories among older men of prolonged unemployment in the 'twenties or the 'thirties. We are dealing with the effect of collective not personal memories; with the force of traditions that are as old as British trade unionism which was cradled nearly two centuries ago in the local trade clubs of skilled artisans. Not that the traditions of craft unionism should be confused with traditions of craftsmanship; the latter govern occupational, rather than union, behaviour. The craft union, like the craft itself, may have been originally founded on the system of apprenticeship, but the union interest in this system was mainly directed to regulating entry into the trade, not to upholding certain standards of training. Control of the supply of competitive labour was the foundation of the early craft societies, for without it no viable organisation could be sustained and none of their regulations could be enforced. This function was not formulated in advance but grew naturally out of the conditions and problems that the craftsmen had to face at the time. As the modern historians of the British trade union movement have observed:

> The traditions of apprenticeship were inherited from guild regulation and statutory enforcement, but by the middle of the nineteenth century these supports had long been withdrawn, and the system survived through custom maintained by the craftsmen and acquiesced in by the employers. It was the first objective of the societies to turn this custom into a universal and uniform rule so as to exert a firm control over the size of the labour force. There was, however, little to be gained by insistence on qualification unless certain types of work were reserved for the qualified worker. Here again the societies built on custom to delimit a preserve of craftsman's work, defined sometimes by the material, sometimes by the tools and machinery, and sometimes by the product; and this preserve was then defended against the unqualified, against changes in the techniques or organisation of production, and against encroachments by other crafts.
>
> On the basis of these fundamental rules the craft society could erect others.[8]

Every trade, or for that matter every profession, has always had an interest in making its labour scarce so as to get a better price for it, but the craft societies' motivation for control of entry ran deeper than that. It was essentially protective; protective of status as well as of standards–status symbolised by the dearly-held respectability of the printer in his top hat. Competition of unapprenticed 'illegal men' threatened the craftsmen's whole way of life and their ability to protect it depended on their capacity, through organisation, to exclude trespassers from employment. Restricting the numbers of apprentices was only one device. Closing the shops to the unorganised, the custom of patrimony establishing an hereditary succession to jobs, resisting the employment of women and several other devices, all served the main objective which was not to safeguard apprenticeship for its own sake but to control labour supply. Again and again in fact, craft unions have had to recognise alternative methods of acquiring the skills of the trade, apart from apprenticeship, in order to organise the otherwise unorganised and to bring competitive labour within the orbit of craft control.

Without dwelling any longer on a story that occupies many chapters of union history, what I have said may suffice to reveal the main lessons of experience incorporated in the traditions of craft unionism. They are centred on two things corresponding with that fixed ends-means pattern which, as I suggested earlier, is implicit in every tradition. First, the principal goal that adherence to craft traditions is expected to promote is security for the group and for the individual; lifelong security of employment in the first instance but also security in its broadest sense of an anticipated satisfaction of any established expectations. Second, the actual patterns of behaviour that the traditions impose as obligatory all turn on defending a particular preserve of work against trespass. Lines of demarcation, the frontiers of this job territory, may be matters of expediency in management's eyes, to be judged by their effects on economic performance. For craftsmen, true to their traditions, they are matters of principle. To fail to defend them is to fail in one's duties as a member of the group; just as citizens are thought to be defaulting in their patriotic duties when they refuse to defend their country's frontiers against aggression.

I must be careful, I know, not to over-simplify. Today the frontiers of the job territory of most of the so-called crafts are anything but well-defined. Nationally they are as ill-defined as the overlapping jurisdictions of different unions in this country. There are areas of work that no one outside a particular craft would perform, but there are other areas which are the preserves of different crafts in different places. But this has always been so, and it has thrown the onus of defence on the vigilance and militancy of union representatives at the place of work. Since it was usually impossible for a union nationally to enforce craft boundaries, cultivation of traditions, which would motivate every group of union members wherever they might be employed, was all the more important.

Similarly technical change, by shifting the boundaries of traditional crafts and eroding their genuine skill content, strengthens rather than weakens the force of craft traditions. Even when 'the skill gap between craftsmen and non-craftsmen becomes largely notional, or could easily be crossed by a fairly brief period of training . . . the craft remains a craft' provided union members can successfully defend the work preserve against trespass. 'Indeed the more notional the skill gap becomes, the greater the significance of their demarcation practices to the craftsmen' for they 'are then more like a sea wall which stands between the inhabitants of the island and total flood'.[9]

That is why it is mistaken to believe that technological advance, by destroying traditional crafts, will inevitably eradicate craft traditions. So far the trend has been in the opposite direction. Over the post-war years job demarcation practices have been more rigidly and rigorously enforced, especially among maintenance craftsmen in industries with the most advanced technologies. The reasons are not hard to find and introduce a new and important consideration into my argument. The influence which any tradition exerts on industrial behaviour depends not only on the strength of conviction with which it is held but also on the power of its adherents to act on their conviction. One of the most significant changes in industrial relations since the war has been the rise in the independent power of work groups. This power is strategically greatest in industries with the most advanced technologies where a single, small group of workers can disrupt production at considerable cost to the employer. It has been used by craft union groups–though not by them alone–to enhance their job security by erecting stronger defences around their job territory and, where possible, by gaining more ground.

Another approach to the problem which is equally mistaken relies on reforming trade union structure. The reasoning in this case is that by eliminating craft unions in favour of industrial unions, one would also–at least in time–succeed in destroying craft traditions. I have never been able to summon much interest in the perennial debate about industrial unionism in the British context, mainly because it is, in the worst sense of the word, academic. Short of the state taking

over the unions and imposing on them its own organisational preferences, such wholesale reconstruction is an idle dream. But were
universal industrial unionism to be a practical proposition in contemporary Britain, it would offer little prospect of changing deeply-
entrenched craft attitudes. For one thing, though there are no pure
craft unions left of any size, the force of craft traditions remains
undiminished in unions that also organise unskilled or semi-skilled
workers. Furthermore in other countries, where there are strong
industrial unions, craft interest and control have not been eliminated.
The United Automobile Workers' Union in North America is a good
example. There has never been a more self-consciously industrial
union than the UAW under Walter Reuther's leadership, yet it has
had to accept the necessity for separate bargaining arrangements,
enjoying a substantial measure of autonomy, for the skilled crafts
within its membership.[10]

Setting aside both of these non-solutions to the problem, my preceding analysis should also have shown why indiscriminate and
unsympathetic criticisms of craft traditions by those who do not
share them are unlikely to be well received by those who do. However
clever or reasonable such criticisms, they are bound to be taken by
craftsmen as an attack on their ends as well as on their means.
Questioning their demarcation practices will be seen as an implied
threat to their job security. Not to reject such criticisms out of hand
would, as they see it, be jeopardizing their own future. If rational
argument is to make any inroads in challenging traditional belief it
must be directed to inserting a wedge into the fixed ends-means
relationship to loosen it enough to permit and encourage its re-exami-
nation. Or, to drop the simile, the only questioning of craft traditions
that stands any chance of being listened to by craftsmen, let alone
accepted, must take the form of asking whether their traditional
means are now the most effective for advancing their traditional ends.
Acceptance of the ends is a necessary condition and must be made
explicit. Acceptance must also be perceived as genuine which is a
matter of trust.

To state the problem in these terms is to reveal the limits of what
can be accomplished by argument alone. Let us assume that there are
situations today where groups of craftsmen could relax their existing
demarcation practices without threatening their future job security.
How are they to be convinced that this is so? They may have first to

287

be persuaded by argument to embark on any experiment which involves them in departing from the course of action prescribed by their traditions. This has happened in the negotiation of a number of successful productivity agreements, where sufficient attention has been paid to a thorough discussion of the issues on the shop floor as well as around the negotiating table. In the end, however, the argument will only be clinched for the craftsmen by the facts of their industrial life; when these tell them that they no longer need their old defences and, what is more, that these defences are holding them back from advances they might otherwise enjoy. Even then the learning process must perforce be gradual and can easily be reversed by one unfortunate set-back. The deeply-engraved lessons of past experience can only be erased by the consistent lessons of a different experience. In a world where tradition rules, old traditions can only be conquered by creating new ones.

THE TRADITIONS OF VOLUNTARISM

If that is true for craft traditions retaining their force for no more than a waning minority of trade unionists, it applies equally but with greater significance to my second example, a set of traditions that influence the behaviour of the whole of the British trade union movement. You will know what they are when I say that they have been influencing its behaviour most noticeably and in a very dramatic fashion in 1969. Voluntarism remains, I suppose, their best available title though one should never forget that it covers not one but a bundle of related beliefs. 'In its original conception, the unifying theme of voluntarism was that workers could best achieve their goals by relying on their own voluntary associations.'[11] But if independence and self-reliance have been its positive side, the negative has been much the same as the doctrine of *laissez-faire*. Voluntarism has implied, when not outright rejection, then considerable distrust of any assistance or support coming from the state as well as resistance, of course, to hostile intervention. And that remains the unsophisticated crux of the matter in the minds of many trade unionists. In April, at the height of the conflict between the unions and the Government over its proposed interim legislation to curb unofficial strikes, *The Times* reported the Rochdale representative of the Loom Overlookers (hardly a militant body) summing up the mood of the annual

288

conference of the United Textile Workers' Association. We must tell the Government, he said, to 'get off our backs and leave us to deal with our own affairs!'[12] That, one felt, was the authentic voice of tradition and, when I read those words, I suddenly knew for sure who had lost this particular battle.

But voluntarism is, as I was saying, a complex pattern of beliefs. In my evidence to the Donovan Commission I suggested that there were at least three different principles associated with it. The first expresses a preference for collective bargaining over state regulation as alternative methods of settling wages and working conditions. The second favours keeping industrial disputes out of the courts by preserving our non-legalistic type of collective bargaining. The third principle is an insistence by the bargaining parties on their complete autonomy (the notion of 'free' collective bargaining) which leads them to resent any outside intervention in their affairs. I will not repeat my arguments for asserting that, while all of these principles now need to be qualified, it is only the third that truly belongs in the rubbish bin of history.[13] I am not discussing the changes that should be made in union traditions, but rather the much more neglected question of how union traditions can be changed. And we have in fact a classic case which illustrates, not only how in general traditions may be changed, but specifically how a trade union movement wedded to a tradition of voluntarism came to abandon it.

The case I have in mind is the effects of the New Deal and subsequent legislation on the ruling beliefs of organised labour in the United States. No union movement in the world has been more completely committed to an extreme version of voluntarism than the American Federation of Labor right up to the worst years of the Great Depression in the early 'thirties. Samuel Gompers, its President from 1886 to 1924, was the great apostle of this creed. It mattered so supremely to him that, when he felt his death approaching, he made it the subject of his testament in speaking for the last time at a Federation Convention. In the future as in the past, he said, 'base your all upon voluntary principles . . . no lasting gain has ever come from compulsion.'[14] Voluntarism for a time was even taken to the lengths of opposing old-age pensions.[15] And not until 1932 was the Federation at last persuaded to endorse unemployment insurance. As the delegates were then stampeded by John L. Lewis also into supporting a campaign for shortening the working day by law, voluntarism was twice repudiated in the same day. The *New York Times* correspondent observed groups of unhappy delegates 'who showed extreme concern' and expressed the opinion that 'before long the Federation would possibly lean further towards social legislation and go on record for health and sickness insurance'.[16]

Now all this has changed. Though the American unions may have opposed some of the present legislation which regulates their affairs, they have in the end accepted it without great demur. Most important, they take for granted that all their activities should be governed by a strong framework of legal rules. Voluntarism, in the sense of opposition on principle to legal support and regulation, is dead and done for. And the cause of its demise is not in doubt. The American unions were persuaded to abandon this tradition, not by argument, but by experience; not an experience they sought but one largely forced upon them. Though they had always asserted that this could not be so, the law, mainly in the shape of the Wagner Act, proved to be a formidable ally. By providing for compulsory recognition and bargaining in good faith it helped to promote a phenomenal rate of union growth and an associated extension in the extent and subjects of collective bargaining. True, this also changed the composition of the American labour movement, and brought into being the new industrial unions for whom the earlier traditions had little or no meaning, but the old craft unions shared in the gains and were converted by them to a different outlook.

Gompers' reply in 1921 to a suggestion that the courts be given the right of review over the expulsion of union members had been 'God save Labor from the Courts'.[17] Today we read in an article written by a former member of the staff of the AFL–CIO that in 'the protection of union members' rights, government plays a crucial role'. Since the passage of the Landrum-Griffith Act, 1959, and the Civil Rights Act, 1964: 'No longer is the union considered a private club where internal affairs are the business only of the membership; instead, the unions' functions are considered so important to the proper functioning of the economy that the public has the right to make certain that the unions' business is conducted without discrimination, honestly, and with adequate safeguards for the democratic process.'[18]

My American friends find a certain irony in the contrast presented by British labour's continued adherence to voluntarism, given the conservative character of this doctrine, and the links of many of our unions with the Labour Party and socialism. But as a union tradition it has had a different content and context in this country. Above all, if it is ever to be changed, one must understand why it retains its power. This is a question, as I have said, of those lessons of past experience that it embodies for the movement as a whole. In trying to decide what they are one must distinguish between fact and fancy.

The notion that trade unions have relied entirely on their own strength for their achievements is a very romantic and misleading view of their past; an example of how a mixture of myth and reality may be reflected in a tradition. In the nineteenth century only the craft unions were prepared to rely wholly or mainly on their industrial strength. Most of the others were very much concerned with battling for legislation to regulate working hours and to provide other forms of protection. Looking at the prevailing trends at the end of the century the Webbs firmly believed that the method of legal enactment would largely replace the method of collective bargaining. In this they may have been in error but, when one studies the subsequent growth of collective bargaining and trade unions, it is apparent that government intervention during two world wars to promote union recognition by employers played a decisive part in the process.

Much more could be said in demolishing the mythical aspects of the voluntary tradition but they do not account for its strength. They are not the real lessons of experience but merely the gloss that has been put on them for added brightness. One of those lessons from the past that belongs to the common heritage of British trade unionism stands out very clearly indeed. Winston Churchill summed it up once in addressing the House of Commons: 'It is not good for trade unions that they should be brought into contact with the courts, and it is not good for the courts.' Though in criminal cases and civil cases between man and man our courts enjoy the respect and admiration of all classes in the community, he went on to say, 'where class issues are involved it is impossible to pretend that the courts command the same degree of general confidence. On the contrary they do not, and a very large number of our population have been led to the opinion that they are, unconsciously no doubt, biased.'[19] That was in 1911. Surprisingly little has happened since that time to shift this opinion very decisively, and recent experience of judicial intervention in their affairs has only made the unions more resolutely opposed to it. Their dislike of contact with the courts, let me add in parenthesis, implies no disrespect for lawyers. They often prefer them as arbitrators or chairmen of courts of enquiry.

Trade union attitudes towards the legislature on the other hand are much less clear cut. They have had to fight for legislation to establish their essential freedoms and to regain them from adverse decisions in the courts. They have had an interest, some more than others, in protective labour legislation to supplement and support their achievements in collective bargaining. The voluntary tradition in Britain has never meant the unions' rejecting political action or social legislation. On the contrary, their commitment in both these respects is a salient feature of their traditions. Voluntarism has rather meant that political action should be treated as subordinate to industrial action and statutory regulation as inferior to regulation by collective agreement. But this is not the same as an unqualified hostility to the state and the use of compulsion. Their attitude to the courts has, I believe, been the hard core of the unions' attachment to voluntarism. For the rest, though any government intervention in union affairs will always be treated with suspicion, there is more of a readiness to examine proposals on their merits and assess the balance of possible results.

Given my premise that traditions can only be finally changed by experience, what sort of experience promises then to have any impact on the British trade unions' strong attachment to their voluntary tradition? In the first place it must obviously be an experience of state intervention that, on balance, is demonstrably beneficial to the unions and their members. Secondly, it must not carry any open or veiled threats to their security and independence. These are two basic and essential requirements. But why, you may ask, should the unions be treated by the government with such circumspection? That depends on how one sees their future and what value is placed on their role in a democratic society. I believe that we need stronger unions organising a much larger section of the community, extending their industrial influence through a growing range of subjects for negotiation (an inevitable consequence of linking pay with productivity), and commanding greater resources to improve their organisation and supporting staffs. I further believe that the unions cannot accomplish this solely by their own efforts. It will depend on their getting public support in the various ways envisaged in the Government's White Paper *In Place of Strife*.

The Traditions of Voluntarism

By now you will have guessed that I am stating my credo as a member of the Commission on Industrial Relations. It could hardly be otherwise. I would not have departed from Oxford's quiet intellectual pastures where I was grazing happily for so many years, were it not for the conviction that this new Commission represents a promising and long overdue form of public participation in industrial relations. It has not been set up, of course, only to strengthen trade unions but, first and foremost, to reform the relations between unions and employers, and between management and workers. But, by not outraging the voluntary tradition, I am hopeful that it may succeed in demonstrating the possibility of modifying that tradition to the benefit of the unions and, for that matter, the employers and the community at large.

This brings me to my final observations. My consideration of two important sets of traditions that continue to exert a powerful influence on the behaviour of British trade unions has yielded a conclusion which is something of a paradox. The changing of these traditions—and in certain respects they undoubtedly need to be changed–appears to be more the responsibility of managements and governments than of the trade unions themselves. Even well-informed and intelligent opinion finds it particularly hard to accept the validity of this conclusion. The reasons why it is true are therefore worth recapitulating in their naked simplicity.

Trade unions may be a force for progress, but in their actual functioning they are, in the literal and unusual meaning of the word, 'reactionary' bodies. They react very closely to their members and their members in the main react to their everyday industrial experience. That is how union traditions have been formed over the years to express the lessons of group experience. They can only be changed by different experience that teaches different lessons. But different experience will only be forthcoming when those who carry the final responsibility for running industry and politics, that is managements and governments, are willing and able to provide it. Or to put the whole of the argument in a nutshell: trade unions cannot determine the greater part of the experience to which their members react. I am not denying the significance of leadership in trade unions. The point is that union leaders, who have the force of mind and character to challenge outmoded traditions, cannot work miracles and make bricks without straw. Argument may be needed to induce trade unions to embark on new and uncharted courses of behaviour, as in the early days of incomes policy, but experience in the end is the main lever of permanent change.

The logic of this argument seems to me to be obvious and inexorable. Why then should it be disregarded and ignored? I can suggest some part of the explanation. Managements and governments are also the victims of their traditions and, in this country, an important strand in the traditions of both has been the belief that trade unions should solve their industrial relations problems for them. That is to say, they have regarded union leaders mainly as managers of discontent, expecting them always to get the men back to work or whatever else was needed to keep things running smoothly. The unions for their part, disinclined to belittle their own importance, have not gone out of their way to challenge this belief. Consequently, as things have got worse in recent years, there has been almost a national obsession that they could be put right by reforming the trade unions, whereas in fact the cause of union reform is most likely to be advanced by managements and governments fully accepting their own responsibilities in industrial relations. The Donovan Commission said as much but, due to this national obsession, its central message fell on deaf ears. Still, we should not despair. Modern managements and governments, are, in Max Weber's well-known categories, more bureaucratic than traditional administrations, which, as he said, 'means fundamentally the exercise of control on the basis of knowledge'.[20] They should therefore in time be open to persuasion by rational argument.

REFERENCES
ON TRADE UNIONS

1. J. T. Roper, *Trade Unionism and the New Social Order*, WEA Study Outlines No. 6, Workers' Educational Association, 1942, p. 10.
2. *The Economist*, 3 January, 1948.
3. Sidney and Beatrice Webb, *Industrial Democracy*, Longmans, 1902 edn., p. 271.
4. J. B. S. Hardman, *American Labor Dynamics*, Harcourt Brace, 1928, p. 111.
5. *ibid.*
6. *Labour Party Conference Report, 1956*, p. 82.
7. John Kenneth Galbraith, *The New Industrial State*, Hamish Hamilton, 1967, p. 262 and p. 282.
8. Perry Anderson, 'The Limits and Possibilities of Trade Union Action', *The Incompatibles* (ed. R. Blackburn and A. Cockburn), Penguin Special, 1967, pp. 264–5.
9. *ibid.*, pp. 266–7.
10. Will Herberg, 'Bureaucracy and Democracy in Labor Unions', *The Antioch Review*, Autumn 1943.
11. Michael Shanks, *The Stagnant Society*, Penguins, 1961, p. 115.
12. *Fair Deal At Work*, Conservative Political Centre, April 1968, p. 63.
13. G. D. H. Cole, *Short History of the British Working Class Movement 1789–1937*, Allen and Unwin 1937 edn., p. 12.

ON MANAGEMENT

1. Subsequently published as *The Fawley Productivity Agreements*, Faber, 1964.
2. W. E. J. McCarthy and S. R. Parker, *Shop Stewards and Workshop Relations*, Royal Commission on Trade Unions and Employers' Associations, Research Papers 10, HMSO, 1968, p. 50.
3. See Peter B. Doeringer, 'Determinants of the Structure of Industrial Type Internal Labor Markets', *Industrial and Labor Relations Review*, January 1967.
4. R. Marriott, *Incentive Payment Systems*, Staples, 1957, p. 18.
5. Sidney and Beatrice Webb, *Industrial Democracy*, Longmans, 1902 edn., pp. 286–7.
6. 'Incentive Pay Systems', *Ministry of Labour Gazette*, July 1966.
7. J. R. Crossley, 'Collective Bargaining, Wage Structure and the Labour Markets in the United Kingdom', *Wage Structure in Theory and*

Practice (ed. E. M. Hugh Jones) North Holland Publishing Co., Amsterdam, 1966.

8. S. Alderson, 'Incentives–Do they Work?' *Twentieth Century*, Summer 1964, p. 164.
9. See National Board for Prices and Incomes, *Report No. 65* (*Supplement*), Paper 1, 'A Review of the Literature on Payment by Results', Cmnd. 3627–I, HMSO, 1968.
10. See P. J. D. Cooke, 'How to Learn from Curves', *Management Today*, November 1967.
11. For a summary statement see H. Behrend, 'Financial Incentives as the Expression of a System of Beliefs', *British Journal of Sociology*, June 1959.
12. S. H. Slichter *et al.*, *The Impact of Collective Bargaining on Management*, Brookings Institution, 1960, p. 497.
13. Liesl Klein, *Multiproducts Ltd.*, HMSO, 1964, p. 143.
14. See his mimeographed paper, *Paper 1: Introduction* for the International Management Seminar on Forms of Wage and Salary Payment for High Productivity, OECD, Paris, 1967, p. 11.

INDUSTRIAL RELATIONS:
WHAT IS WRONG WITH THE SYSTEM?

1. John T. Dunlop, *Industrial Relations Systems*, Holt, 1958, p. 6. 1958, p. 6.
2. *ibid.*, pp. 13–16.
3. Occasionally agreements attach 'personal' rates to individuals which disappear with their relinquishing of the job. This device is usually employed to facilitate the transition to a more ordered wage structure.
4. See R. Maciver and C. H. Page, *Society–An Introductory Analysis*, Macmillan, 1953, p. 474.
5. Peter Drucker, *The New Society*, Heinemann, 1951, p. 27.
6. T. Lupton's study of two workshop situations (*On The Shop Floor*, Pergamon Press, 1963) showed that in one (the Wye Garment Company) the workers' social groups had no behavioural norms relating to output and earnings.
7. This implies the possibility of conflict between these ends, but not its necessity. Managerial employees, because of the identification of their career interests with the success of the enterprise, may use their informal organisation to counteract the shortcomings of its formal organisation.
8. As Drucker explains: 'Its existence does not rest on the needs and purposes of the enterprise but on the needs and purposes of the members as human beings. Management can neither make the plant community nor abolish it; it is spontaneous and irrepressible in every enterprise.' *op. cit.*, p. 263.

References

9. Although the primary unit of organisation within the plant community is often described as a 'work group' this is a complex phenomenon. Leonard R. Sayles (in *Behaviour of Industrial Work Groups*, Wiley, 1958, pp. 144–61) distinguishes 'friendship cliques, work teams and pressure or interest groups' with overlapping memberships.

10. Sidney and Beatrice Webb summed up the 'fundamental object' of trade unionism as 'the deliberate regulation of the conditions of employment in such a way as to ward off from the manual-working producers the evil effects of industrial competition'. (*Industrial Democracy*, Longmans, 1902 ed., p. 807.)

11. William M. Leiserson, *American Trade Union Democracy*, Columbia U.P., 1959, p. 17.

12. See Dunlop, *op. cit.*, pp. 16–18.

13. In the case of state regulation they may be consulted by the government and affect the content of the rules as political pressure groups, but the responsibility for authorship rests with the government.

14. This is not to be confused with unilateral regulation by union *members* in the workplace which belongs to enterprise systems of internal job regulation. This may extend over many other subjects and workers other than craftsmen.

15. For examples of these safeguards see the provisions of Section 3 of the Wages Council Act, 1959.

16. The organisation of employees is an indispensable condition. Whether employers need to be organised is a condition contingent on the structure of the industry and on the viability of plant agreements.

17. In New Zealand union membership is legally enforced and in Canada union recognition by employers. In Ceylon and in other countries collective agreements are given the force of law.

18. The Coal Mines (Minimum Wage) Act, 1912, and the Cotton Manufacturing Industry (Temporary Provisions) Act, 1934, were examples of legislation permitting the legal enforcement of substantive wage agreements. On one occasion, under the Railways Act, 1921, a procedural agreement was given statutory effect until it was replaced by revised voluntary arrangements in 1935.

19. Under the 'claims' procedure in Section 8 of the Terms and Conditions of Employment Act, 1959.

20. Strictly there are no voluntary rules if by that is meant that an individual is free to disregard them with impunity. All rules need to be upheld by sanctions or they cease to be rules. Voluntary here means the absence of legal compulsion, though the parties may have powerful sanctions of their own to enforce their autonomous rules.

21. 1961 ed., pp. 134–5.

22. In certain circumstances striking *in breach of contract* is a criminal offence for merchant seamen; for employees in the public utility industries of gas, water and electricity; and for any workers whose action causes danger to life or valuable property.

297

References

23. O. Kahn-Freund, 'Labour Law' in *Law and Opinion in England in the 20th Century*, Stevens, 1959, pp. 262–3.

24. In recent years the spread of long-term (three or two years) agreements has modified this earlier practice.

25. Conflicts of interest are disputes over *changes* in the existing provisions of collective agreements, while conflicts of right are about the application, interpretation or observance of these provisions. The latter become justiciable disputes when collective agreements are made legally binding; a reason for clearly separating them from the former.

26. Over the two post-war decades 1944–53 and 1954–63 the annual averages were respectively 2.2 and 3.9 million working days lost. (*Ministry of Labour Gazette*, April 1964, p. 145.) Even the higher figure only amounts to $1\frac{1}{2}$ working hours a year per employed person.

27. Apart from the short period from 1917 to 1919 when wages were virtually subject to state regulation.

28. In the words of the Fourth (and final) Report of the Council on Prices, Productivity and Incomes (July 1961), p. 3.

29. 'Inequalities and other anomalies are tolerated so long as they are the result of private arrangement. But Governments, rather optimistically, are expected to be consistent, and to base their administrative action on generally accepted social or moral principles.' (Henry Clay, *The Problem of Industrial Relations*, Macmillan, 1929, p. 67.)

30. In the concluding words of the Fourth Report of the Council on Prices, Productivity and Incomes, *op. cit.*, p. 29: 'The sources of opposition are . . . a strong attachment to principles learned the hard way in a world very different from the one we live in. . . . At the heart of the problem of inflation under full employment is a frame of mind.'

31. 'The Wages Structure and Some Implications for Incomes Policy', *National Institute Economic Review*, November 1962, p. 42.

32. In industries covered by the Ministry of Labour's earnings and hours inquiries. See, E. G. Whybrew, 'Overtime and the Reduction of the Working Week: A Comparison of British and Dutch Experience', *British Journal of Industrial Relations*, July 1964, p. 153.

33. H. A. Turner, *The Trend of Strikes*, Leeds U.P., 1963, pp. 18–19.

34. See Emily Clark Brown, 'Interests and Rights of Soviet Industrial Workers and the Resolution of Conflict', *Industrial and Labor Relations Review*, January 1963. 'The "collective" in any Soviet enterprise, manual and non-manual workers alike, find their conditions controlled in great detail by central decisions. Yet considerable scope remains for local decisions.' (p. 264.) 'Soviet informants often talked of how workers when dissatisfied can and do "call meetings and make a fuss" until their complaints are met.' (p. 271.)

35. As is shown by James W. Kuhn in *Bargaining in Grievance Settlement* (Columbia U.P., 1961).

36. It was an American, A. M. Ross, in *Trade Union Wage Policy* (California U.P., 1953), who first drew attention to the 'coercive com-

parisons' which 'play a large and often dominant role. . . in the determination of wages under collective bargaining.'

37. The concluding words of my contribution on 'Collective Bargaining' in *The System of Industrial Relations in Great Britain*, edited by Flanders and Clegg, Blackwell, 1954.

38. Robert Neild, 'New functions: new men?', *The Listener*, 27th August, 1964, p. 303.

39. *Bulletin*, British Employers' Confederation, 1st July, 1964, p. 1.

40. See pages 89–93.

41. Neil W. Chamberlain, *Collective Bargaining*, McGraw-Hill, 1951, p. 450.

42. *ibid.*, p. 451.

43. *ibid.*, p. 455.

44. For further discussion of the concept of 'productivity bargaining', see Allan Flanders, *The Fawley Productivity Agreements*, Faber, 1964, pp. 238–48.

45. See *op. cit.*, p. 250.

46. The Webbs' idea, that by legal enactment a universal labour code would guarantee every worker certain fundamental rights as to income, leisure and treatment in industry, may have been false prophecy for the first half of the twentieth century; it is not to be dismissed for the second. We are already moving in that direction.

THE INTERNAL SOCIAL RESPONSIBILITIES
OF INDUSTRY

1. Theodore Levitt, 'The Dangers of Social Responsibility', *Harvard Business Review*, Sept.–Oct., 1958.

2. Wallace B. Donham (in his foreword to Elton Mayo's *The Social Problems of an Industrial Civilisation*, Harvard U.P., 1945, p. ix) suggested this work showed 'that it is within the power of industrial administrations to create within industry itself a partially effective substitute for the old stabilising effect of the neighbourhood. Given stable employment, it might make of industry (as of the small town during most of our national life) a socially satisfying way of life as well as way of making a living.' Frank Tannenbaum in *A Philosophy of Labor* (Knopf, 1952, pp. 198–9) envisages a similar result being achieved by the merging of the business corporation and the trade union ('the only true society that industrialism has fostered'), so that they 'cease to be a house divided' and 'a common identity may once again come to rule the lives of men'.

3. Michael P. Fogarty, *Personnel Management*, March 1963.

4. Norman Ross, *The Democratic Firm*, Fabian Research Series 242, 1964, p. 21.

5. Many employment practices exist as workplace conventions and are

upheld by workers without any formal trade union support. Regulation of output has been shown to exist in unorganised firms.

6. T. H. Marshall, *Sociology at the Crossroads and Other Essays*, Heinemann, 1963, p. 98.
7. Frank Tannenbaum, *op. cit.*, p. 140.
8. Lord Eustace Percy in the Riddell Lecture for 1944: 'The Unknown State.'
9. Lord Denning in an Address to the Assembly of College Faculties, University College, London, *Daily Telegraph*, 27 June 1958.
10. George Goyder, *The Responsible Company*, Blackwell, 1961, p. 81.
11. C. A. R. Crosland, *The Corporation and Modern Society*, Harvard University Press, 1959, p. 274.
12. The results were published in Allan Flanders, Ruth Pomeranz and Joan Woodward, *Experiment in Industrial Democracy—A Study of the John Lewis Partnership*, Faber, 1968.
13. Wilfred Brown, *Exploration in Management*, Heinemann, 1960, Ch. XIV and p. 276.
14. W. M. Blumenthal, *Codetermination in the German Steel Industry*, Princeton University Press, 1956, p. 110.
15. 'It seems to take more power from employers than it really does.' Clark Kerr, 'The Trade Union Movement and the Redistribution of Power in Postwar Germany', *The Quarterly Journal of Economics*, November 1954, p. 558.
16. George Goyder, *op. cit.*, p. 90.
17. Neil Chamberlain, *Labor*, McGraw-Hill, 1958, pp. 226–8.
18. *ibid.*, pp. 230–1.
19. Norman Ross, *op. cit.*, p. 22.
20. Michael P. Fogarty, 'Co-Determination and Company Structure in Germany', *British Journal of Industrial Relations*, March 1964, p. 89.
21. Benjamin M. Selekman, *A Moral Philosophy for Management*, McGraw-Hill Paperbacks, 1959, p. 165.
22. Sidney and Beatrice Webb, *Industrial Democracy*, Longmans, 1902 ed., p. 850.
23. H. A. Clegg, *A New Approach to Industrial Democracy*, Blackwell, 1960, p. 119.
24. *ibid.*, p. 120.
25. *ibid.*, p. 134.
26. *ibid.*, p. 121.
27. Trist, Higgin, Murray & Pollock, *Organisational Choice*, Tavistock, 1963, p. 294.
28. Douglas McGregor, *The Human Side of Enterprise*, McGraw-Hill 1960, p. 33.
29. *ibid.*, pp. 47–8.
30. Quoted by Richard Cabot in 'Mary Parker Follett, an Appreciation', *Radcliffe Quarterly*, April 1934.

References

COLLECTIVE BARGAINING: PRESCRIPTION FOR CHANGE

1. Evidence of the Ministry of Labour, paras. 129–33, pp. 38–9. (All subsequent references to Evidence are to published written evidence submitted to the Royal Commission on Trade Unions and Employers' Associations.)
2. These proportions are based on information on the coverage of collective agreements supplied by the Ministry of Labour. They cannot be taken to indicate more than rough orders of magnitude.
3. The result may be seen in union membership. In national and local government and some of the nationalised industries more than four out of every five white-collar workers are members of trade unions, while in private manufacturing the proportion is less than one in eight (G. S. Bain, 'The Growth of White-Collar Unionism in Great Britain,' *British Journal of Industrial Relations*, November 1966, p. 321).
4. Ministry of Labour, *op. cit.*, para. 15, p. 117.
5. See p. 96.
6. The National Arbitration Tribunal and later the Industrial Disputes Tribunal, which made its last awards in 1959.
7. Evidence of the Confederation of British Industry, para. 113, p. 24.
8. 'Can Britain have a Wage Policy?' *Scottish Journal of Political Economy*, June 1958, p. 119.
9. The outstanding characteristic of the national pay structure is the rigidity of its relationships' (Guy Routh, *Occupation and Pay in Great Britain 1906–60*, Cambridge U.P., 1965, p. 147).
10. 'Is Britain a Half-time Country?', *Sunday Times*, 1 March, 1964.
11. There, following union recognition, they take the place of district and national agreements, except in cases where multi-plant company agreements are signed.
12. *Ministry of Labour Gazette*, February 1963.
13. *Financial Times*, 7th June, 1966.
14. See the section on 'Roots of Managerial Irresponsibility', especially pp. 253–5, in *The Fawley Productivity Agreements*, Faber, 1964.
15. For a fuller statement of the ideological causes see Alan Fox, 'Managerial Ideology and Labour Relations', *British Journal of Industrial Relations*, November 1966.
16. The evidence suggests that most local strikes are either over money (piecework prices, supplementary rates and bonus payments) or over dismissals, recognition, changes in work and complaints about conditions, etc. Both categories usually reflect a lack of agreed rules.
17. K. W. Wedderburn, *The Worker and the Law*, MacGibbon & Kee, 1965, p. 11.
18. See p. 112.
19. The I.L.O. comparison for the decade 1955–64 shows only West Germany, Netherlands, New Zealand, Norway, Sweden and

References

Switzerland with lower figures, while those for the United States were more than three times as great.

20. On a claim by the National Union of Vehicle Builders early in 1965 which complained of dismissals and refusal to consult union officials.

21. According to McCarthy and Clifford ('The Work of Industrial Courts of Inquiry', *British Journal of Industrial Relations*, March 1966, p. 44) there have been nine Courts out of a total seventy-five, since the passing of the 1919 Industrial Courts Act, in which union recognition has been the principal issue in dispute. The Ministry of Labour in its Evidence (paras. 27–8, p. 99) points out that in recent years '30 per cent of the differences on which conciliation takes place relate to questions of union recognition', and shows why this is often 'not a satisfactory method' for settling such disputes.

22. The text is given in the Evidence of the Ministry of Labour, pp. 133–40.

23. *ibid.*, pp. 130 f.

24. A similar suggestion is included in the Ministry of Labour's Evidence (para. 48, pp. 85 f.) but it is coupled, in my view mistakenly, with the idea that this might be one of the possible functions of a labour court.

25. As is suggested in the Ministry of Labour's Evidence (para. 49, p. 86).

26. *ibid.*, p. 117.

27. *ibid.*

28. See F. J. Bayliss, *British Wages Councils*, Blackwell, 1962, pp. 138–41, and McCormick and Turner in 'The Legal Minimum Wage, Employers and Unions: an Experiment' (*Manchester School*, September 1957) who concluded: 'The real risk of the statutory system is ... that it may make trade unions lazy' (p. 316).

29. Flanders and Clegg (ed.), *The System of Industrial Relations in Great Britain*, Blackwell, 1954, p. 63.

30. These have been clearly stated by Daniel H. Gray in *Manpower Planning*, Institute of Personnel Management, 1966.

31. Brought together and summarised in its *General Report, April 1965 to July 1966* (No. 19, Cmnd. 3087).

32. Schedule 2, para. 11, *Prices and Incomes Act*.

33. See its report on *Productivity and Pay during the Period of Severe Restraint* (No. 23, Cmnd. 3167).

34. No. 16, Cmnd. 3012. 'We consider ... that pay settlements in the bus industry should not primarily be directed to attracting more labour for the practical reason that in an area of general labour shortage pay adjustments designed to do this are likely to be ineffective. The most effective remedy for an undertaking suffering from a shortage of labour in such an area is to make better use of labour which it already has' (p. 30).

35. There would have to be different targets for men and for women. But the objective of equal pay for equal work could be approached by gradually reducing the difference in stages.

36. Including measures for redistribution between wage and non-wage incomes, but these lie outside the scope of my essay.

302

References

37. Cmnd. 3073. The statutory powers embodied in Part IV of the Prices and Incomes Act were said to be necessary 'to deter the selfish minority who are not prepared to co-operate'.
38. In his personal evidence to the Royal Commission.
39. Hilde Behrend, Harriet Lynch and Jean Davies, in *A National Survey of Attitudes to Inflation and Incomes Policy* (Occasional Papers in Social and Economic Administration, No. 7, Edutext Publications, 1966), which was taken before the standstill, found that of 581 respondents capable of some attempt at describing the Government's incomes policy, 57·6 per cent believed that it could not be successful on a voluntary basis. Their reasons for this belief were overwhelmingly that people were too selfish, greedy, or unwilling to co-operate. Given that incomes policy would not be accepted voluntarily, more people were in favour of legal enforcement than were against it. The tone of this response was supported by surveys carried out after the introduction of the standstill for the *Sunday Times* (4 September, 1966) and the *Daily Telegraph* (5 September, 1966). In both surveys, about 60 per cent of the respondents supported the standstill.
40. *A Constitution for the Socialist Commonwealth of Great Britain*, Longmans, 1920, p. 272.
41. Evidence of the Trades Union Congress, para. 134, pp.50–1.
42. Slichter *et al.*, *The Impact of Collective Bargaining on Management*, Brookings Institution, 1960, p. 497.
43. A form of measured day work designed to give a stable wage in return for a steady level of performance which retains an incentive for workers to raise their performance by means of a graded pay structure. Within limits they can choose a higher or lower wage for a higher or lower level of performance.
44. It should be noted that the distinction which is often drawn between methods or systems of payment and pay structures is at bottom artificial and misleading. The structure itself can have an incentive (or disincentive) effect on performance. One way of rewarding learning, for example, is by having a suitable graded wage structure which induces workers to acquire additional knowledge and skill in order to increase their pay by up-grading.
45. Robert Dubin, 'Constructive Aspects of Industrial Conflict', *Industrial Conflict*, McGraw-Hill, 1954, p. 44.

COLLECTIVE BARGAINING:
A THEORETICAL ANALYSIS

1. R. H. Tawney, *The Attack and Other Papers*, Allen and Unwin, 1953, p. 136.
2. Sidney and Beatrice Webb, *Industrial Democracy*, Longmans, 1902 ed., p.v.

References

3. Sidney and Beatrice Webb, *The History of Trade Unionism 1666–1920*, Longmans, 1920 ed., p. 1.
4. See particularly Ch. XIII on 'The Assumptions of Trade Unionism'.
5. *The History, op. cit.*, p. 141. The Webbs had access to the original correspondence with employers on which Nassau Senior based an unpublished, government-commissioned report in 1830. The most interesting feature of the correspondence, they said, was 'the extent to which the employers complained of the manner in which their rivals incited, and even subsidised, strikes against attempted reductions of rates. The mill owner, whose improved processes gave him an advantage in the market, found any corresponding reduction of piecework rates resisted, not only by his own operatives, but by all the other manufacturers in the district, who sometimes went so far as to publish a joint declaration that any such reduction was "highly inexpedient". The evidence, in fact, from Nassau Senior's point of view, justified his somewhat remarkable proposal to punish employers for conniving at combinations'.
6. *Industrial Democracy, op. cit.*, p. 173.
7. *ibid.*, p. 174.
8. *ibid.*, p. 179.
9. R. Maciver and C. H. Page, *Society*, Macmillan, 1953, p. 474.
10. *Industrial Democracy, op. cit.*, p. 704.
11. *ibid.*
12. *Society, op. cit.*
13. They concluded that the device of restriction of numbers had economic advantages and disadvantages, but society – they mistakenly claimed – was 'fortunately saved from so embarrassing a choice' because its 'effective use . . . is no longer practicable' (p. 713). The device of the common rule, in contrast, was 'positively conducive to national efficiency and national wealth' and in its 'universal and elaborate application . . . the economist finds a sound and consistent theory of trade unionism'. (p. 795).
14. As pointed out by W. Milne-Bailey, *Trade Unions and the State*, Allen and Unwin, 1934, p. 86.
15. The Webbs' summary of the 'fundamental object' of trade unionism, *Industrial Democracy, op. cit.*, p. 867.
16. This was the substance of their 'Trade Union Theory' in Part III of *Industrial Democracy*, although they also considered some political questions about the relationship between trade unionism and democracy in their final chapter.
17. Selig Perlman, *A Theory of the Labor Movement*, Kelley, 1949, p. 173.
18. I take this description of one of the 'essential characteristics of collective bargaining' from Frederick Harbison, in *Industrial Relations: Challenges and Responses*, ed. J. H. G. Crispo, University of Toronto Press, 1966, p. 61.
19. W. Milne-Bailey, *Trade Union Documents*, Bell, 1929, p. 211.

References

20. David L. Cole, 'Government in the Bargaining Process: The Role of Mediation', *The Annals of the American Academy of Political and Social Sciences*, January 1961, pp. 48 f.
21. *Cf.* John T. Dunlop, *Collective Bargaining: Principles and Cases*, Irwin, 1949, p. 67.
22. They claimed that where the machinery for collective bargaining has broken down 'we usually discover that this distinction has not been made'. *Industrial Democracy, op. cit.*, pp. 182–3.
23. George W. Taylor, 'Effectuating the Labor Contract through Arbitration', *Labor Relations Reports*, Vol. 21, p. 19. Quoted in *International Labour Review*, October 1960, p. 312.
24. *Industrial Democracy, op. cit.*, p. 797.
25. *Cf.* J. W. F. Rowe, '. . . the influence of custom may be said to have constituted the real basis of the trade union standard rate. The standard rate was not an original conception of trade unionism: it was essentially the means whereby principles which custom stamped as right and proper, were solidified into a system, which it was the function of trade unionism to maintain as rigidly as possible', *Wages in Practice and Theory*, Routledge, 1928, p. 156.
26. Edward H. Chamberlin on 'Labor Union Power and the Public Interest' in *The Public Stake in Union Power*, ed. P. D. Bradley, University of Virginia Press, 1959, p. 9.
27. Sumner H. Slichter, *Union Policies and Industrial Management*, Brookings Institution, 1941, p. 1.
28. Frank Tannenbaum, *A Philosophy of Labor*, Knopf, 1952, p. 145.
29. T. H. Marshall, *Sociology at the Crossroads and other essays*, Heinemann, 1963, p. 98.
30. *Industrial Democracy, op. cit.*, p. 184.
31. Concern for the viability of the institution was a central point in M. W. Reder's attempt to bridge the Dunlop–Ross controversy in 'The Theory of Union Wage Policy', reproduced in *Labor and Trade Unionism: an interdisciplinary reader*, edited by Galeson and Lipset, Wiley, 1960. He argued that *de facto* agreement on comparisons to be treated as relevant in wage negotiations was the 'hall-mark of "mature" collective bargaining', because this gave the parties terms of reference that enabled them regularly to conduct their 'bargaining duel' and yet diminish the risks of stoppage which could be costly to both. But economic limits did eventually assert themselves because: 'If the wage pattern within which a given firm finds itself is incompatible with its long-run economic survival, the firm will either break out of this pattern or disappear.' (p. 14.)
32. Arthur M. Ross, *Trade Union Wage Policy*, University of California, Press, 1948, was written in reply to John T. Dunlop, *Wage Determination under Trade Unions*, Macmillan, New York, 1944. See also Dunlop's response in the Preface to the 1950 edition of his book.
33. An excellent summary of the main arguments and conclusions to date

can be found in the first chapter of Harold M. Levinson, *Determining Forces in Collective Wage Bargaining*, Wiley, New York, 1966.

34. For a critical view see: K. G. J. C. Knowles and E. M. F. Thorne on 'Wage Rounds, 1948–1959' and Knowles and D. Robinson on 'Wage Rounds and Wage Policy', *Bulletin of the Oxford University Institute of Statistics*, February 1961 and May 1962.

35. Ross, *op. cit.*, p. 50.

36. Barbara Wootton, *The Social Foundations of Wage Policy*, Allen and Unwin, 1955, p. 68: 'Pay and prestige are closely linked; and (in spite of some exceptions) it is the rule that the high-prestige person should also be the highly paid person. . . . Once this rule is admitted as a factor in its own right, it is remarkable how effectively it explains much that, on a purely economic hypothesis, has to be explained away.'

37. Wootton, *op. cit.*, concluded that at present 'the weight of the social influences . . . falls overwhelmingly on the side of conservatism' (p. 12) and referred to them as 'static' (p. 164). J. R. Hicks in reply suggested that 'custom is the static and equality the dynamic element' in collective wage determination ('Economics Foundations of Wage Policy', *Economic Journal*, September 1955). But *outraged* custom can be a very dynamic factor. It was only a force for stability when it provided a universally accepted and unchallenged standard.

38. Levinson, *op. cit.*, p. 272. Political variables are taken to be internal and external trade union (and employer) rivalries (i.e. political competition) as with Ross. The collective bargaining situations analysed and compared are in six industries on the Pacific Coast of the United States covering the period 1945–1962. The effect of the environmental factors is considered on wage *rates* and *major fringe benefits*.

39. *ibid.*, p. 276.

40. *ibid.*, p. 269.

41. Milton Derber *et al.*, *Plant Union-Management Relations: From Practice to Theory*, University of Illinois, 1965, p. 70.

42. For a statement of how management's behaviour in collective bargaining may be influenced by its 'frame of reference' see: Alan Fox, *Industrial Sociology and Industrial Relations*, Research Papers 3, Royal Commission on Trade Unions and Employers' Associations, HMSO, 1966.

43. Neil W. Chamberlain, 'The Union Challenge to Management Control', *Industrial and Labor Relations Review*, January 1963, p. 188.

44. Neil W. Chamberlain, *Collective Bargaining*, McGraw-Hill, 1951. The second and substantially revised edition of this book appeared in 1965 with James W. Kuhn as joint author.

45. Chamberlain, 1951 edition, *op. cit.*, p. 121.

46. *ibid.*

47. William M. Leiserson, 'Constitutional Government in American Industries', *American Economic Review*, Vol. 12, Supplement, 1922, p. 61.

References

48. Chamberlain, *op. cit.*, p. 137.
49. *ibid.*, p. 130.
50. Neil W. Chamberlain, *The Union Challenge to Management Control*, Harper, 1948, p. 198. This earlier work contains the fullest exposition of the managerial theory and of the 'functional integration' of management and unions which the author then envisaged as the logical outcome of the evolution of collective bargaining.
51. Chamberlain, *Collective Bargaining, op. cit.*, pp. 128–9.
52. *ibid.*, p. 135.
53. In the second edition of *Collective Bargaining* it is renamed the 'industrial relations' concept and the earlier stress on three theories is replaced by a reference to 'three viewpoints' which 'are not necessarily conflicting'. (p. 113.)
54. Sumner H. Slichter, James J. Healy and E. Robert Livernash, *The Impact of Collective Bargaining on Management*, Brookings Institution, 1960, p. 948.
55. Chamberlain, 1951 edition, *op. cit.*, p. 153. The wording in Chamberlain and Kuhn, 1965 edition, is 'a guide for administrative action within the firm' (p. 131).
56. *ibid.*, p. 154.
57. *ibid.*, p. 157.
58. Joseph I. Roper, *Joint Consultation and Responsibility in Modern Industry*, Study Outline 19, Workers' Educational Association, 1950, pp. 34–5.
59. Neil W. Chamberlain, *Labor*, McGraw-Hill, New York, 1958, p. 232.
60. *ibid.*, p. 228.
61. *ibid.*, p. 226.
62. *ibid.*, p. 252.
63. John T. Dunlop, 'The Social Utility of Collective Bargaining', in *Challenges to Collective Bargaining*, ed. Lloyd Ulman, Prentice-Hall, 1967, p. 173.
64. See James W. Kuhn, *Bargaining in Grievance Settlement*, Columbia University Press, 1961 and for a definition of 'fractional bargaining', pp. 79–82.
65. See W. E. J. McCarthy, *The Role of Shop Stewards in British Industrial Relations*, Research Papers 1, Royal Commission on Trade Unions and Employers' Associations, HMSO, 1966; and on the 'methods and effects of shop steward bargaining', pp. 16–37.

COLLECTIVE BARGAINING:
FROM DONOVAN TO DURKHEIM

1. *Royal Commission on Trade Unions and Employers' Associations 1965–1968: Report*, Cmnd. 3623.
2. *In Place of Strife–A Policy for Industrial Relations*, Cmnd. 3888.

References

3. *Fair Deal at Work*, Conservative Political Centre, April 1968, p. 61.
4. *NOP Bulletin–July 1968 Special Supplement: Trade Unionism*, National Opinion Polls Ltd., 1968. Later polls tell a similar story. An enquiry conducted by the Opinion Research Centre of the *Sunday Times* (5 January 1969), after leakage of the Government's White Paper proposals, showed 62 per cent of a random sample of union members in favour of secret ballots before official strikes, and 57 per cent favouring the imposition of a cooling-off period on unofficial strikes, with 65 per cent supporting legally binding agreements. A survey of non-Conservative voters in England towards the end of 1968 also showed that 62 per cent of them were in favour of making unofficial strikes illegal as compared with 31 per cent against. Among 'Constant Labour' voters, i.e. those who both voted Labour in 1966 and intend to do so again at the next General Election, there was an even higher majority of 64 per cent. (*Socialist Commentary*, February 1969, p. 30).
5. W. J. Ashley, *The Adjustment of Wages*, Longmans, 1903, pp. 20 f.
6. *Report, op. cit.*, p. 291.
7. C. Wright Mills, *The New Men of Power*, Harcourt Brace, 1948, p. 9.
8. 'Many firms have no such policy and perhaps no conception of it'. *Report, op. cit.*, p. 25.
9. John T. Dunlop, 'The Social Utility of Collective Bargaining' in *Challenges to Collective Bargaining* (ed. L. Ulman), Prentice-Hall, 1967, p. 173.
10. *International Encyclopaedia of the Social Sciences*, Vol. 11, Macmillan and The Free Press, 1968, p. 204.
11. As John T. Dunlop showed in his pioneering work *Industrial Relation Systems*, Holt, 1958.
12. For other principles see pp. 94–9.
13. E. Durkheim, *Suicide*, Routledge and Kegan Paul, 1952, p. 253.
14. A. Kornhauser, R. Dubin and A. M. Ross, *Industrial Conflict*, McGraw-Hill, 1954, p. 40.
15. *ibid.*, p. 44.
16. *ibid.*, p. 45.
17. See pp. 163–5.
18. The apparently growing momentum of the demand for equal pay for women in industry is a contemporary illustration of how a stronger assertion of only partially-realised normative aspirations may generate new forms of social competition.
19. E. Durkheim, *The Division of Labour in Society*, Free Press: Collier Macmillan, 1964, p. 3.
20. *Suicide, op. cit.*, p. 253.
21. In practical terms this can mean little more than legally enforcing the 'peace obligation' in existing and largely outmoded procedural agreements.
22. *ibid.*, p. 251.

References

23. Henry Clay, *The Problem of Industrial Relations*, Macmillan, 1929, pp. 12–16.
24. By the end of the war the provisions for compulsory arbitration had resulted in what was virtually state regulation of wages.
25. *ibid.*, p. 78.
26. *ibid.*, p. 153.
27. Under the Trade Boards Act, 1918, and the Industrial Courts Act, 1919.
28. Ian G. Sharp, *Industrial Conciliation and Arbitration in Great Britain*, Allan and Unwin, 1950, p. 330. From 1921 until the Second World War only one new council was created.
29. Though two of them (in 1924 and in 1934) passed their second reading. See Sharp, *op. cit.*, pp. 333 f.
30. The Cotton Manufacturing Industry (Temporary Provisions) Act of 1934 was introduced to prevent, in the words of the prior Board of Inquiry, 'the possible collapse of the whole principle of collective bargaining' in the industry. In addition, statutory wage regulation was extended in 1938 and 1939, as a result of the establishment of new Trade Boards for the furniture, baking and rubber industries (at the request of employers and trade unions) and the passing of the Road Haulage Wages Act.
31. Clay, *op. cit.*, p. 77.
32. The provisions of the Conditions of Employment and National Arbitration Order (Order 1305) of 1940 may have been accepted by the unions as an alternative to state control of wages, but the restrictions imposed on the right to strike and lockout resulted inevitably in publicly-imposed settlements of major wage disputes and the application of a national policy.
33. *In Place of Strife*, *op. cit.*, p. 7.
34. *ibid.*, p. 33.
35. National Board for Prices and Incomes, Report No. 83, *Job Evaluation*, Cmnd. 3772, 1968, p. 12.
36. Practical examples of this model are already available in the national agreements concluded, for example, in the chemical and rubber industries.
37. Sidney and Beatrice Webb, *A Constitution for the Socialist Commonwealth of Great Britain*, Longmans, 1920, p. 272.
38. See p. 193.

TRADE UNIONS AND THE FORCE OF TRADITION

1. H. H. Gerth and C. Wright Mills (ed. and trans.), *From Max Weber – Essays in Sociology*, Routledge and Kegan Paul, 1948, p. 296.
2. R. F. Hoxie, *Trade Unionism in the United States*, Appleton, 1921, p. 34.

References

3. H. A. Turner, *Trade Union Growth, Structure and Policy*, Allen and Unwin, 1962, p. 14.
4. R. H. Tawney, *Equality*, Allen and Unwin, 1937 edn., p. 2.
5. Royal Commission on Trade Unions and Employers' Associations, 1965–1968, *Report*, Cmnd. 3623, H.M.S.O., 1968, pp. 87–8.
6. *ibid.*
7. *ibid.*
8. H. A. Clegg, Alan Fox and A. F. Thompson, *A History of British Trade Unions since 1889*, Vol. 1, Clarendon Press, 1964, p. 5.
9. Allan Flanders, *The Fawley Productivity Agreements*, Faber, 1964, p. 216.
10. Following its 1957 Convention. See, A. R. Weber (ed.) *The Structure of Collective Bargaining*, The Free Press of Glencoe, New York, 1961, p. 15.
11. Michael Rogin, 'Voluntarism: The Political Foundation of an Anti-political Doctrine', *Industrial and Labor Relations Review*, July 1962, pp. 521–2.
12. *The Times*, 19 April, 1969.
13. See pp. 173–8.
14. Louis S. Reed, *The Labor Philosophy of Samuel Gompers*, Columbia U.P., 1930, pp. 129–30.
15. Rogin, *op. cit.*, p. 531.
16. Edward Levenson, *Labor on the March*, Harpers, 1938, p. 50.
17. Reed, *op. cit.*, p. 123.
18. Peter Henle, 'Some Reflections on Organised Labor and the New Militants', *Monthly Labor Review*, July 1969, pp. 22–3.
19. W. Milne-Bailey, *Trade Union Documents*, Bell, London, 1929, pp. 380–1.
20. Max Weber, *The Theory of Social and Economic Organisation*, trans., A. M. Henderson and Talcott Parsons, Oxford U.P., 1947, p. 339.

ACKNOWLEDGEMENTS

Trade Unions in the Sixties
A lecture to a Workers' Educational Association conference first published as an article in *Socialist Commentary*, August 1961.

Trade Unions and Politics
A shortened version of the London Trades Council 1860–1960 Centenary Lecture in January 1961.

What are Trade Unions for?
A shortened version of the Second Joe Madin Memorial Lecture given at Sheffield and first published as an article in *Socialist Commentary*, December 1968.

The Fawley Experiment
A paper read to a residential course for managers at Cambridge and published as an article in *Industrial Welfare*, October 1963.

Productivity Bargaining Prospects
First published as an article entitled 'The Case for the Package Deal' in *The Times*, 9 July 1968.

Pay as an Incentive
A previously unpublished paper read to a British Institute of Management conference at Birmingham in November 1968.

Industrial Relations: What is Wrong with the System?
First published by Faber and Faber in 1965 in association with the Institute of Personnel Management. German and Japanese translations have been published by Europäische Verlagsanstalt, Frankfurt, and the Orion Press, Tokyo.

The Internal Social Responsibilities of Industry
A revised version of a paper presented to an International Seminar jointly convened at New Delhi in March 1965 by the India International Centre and the Gandhian Institute of Studies. The original paper is included in *Social Responsibilities of Business*, Manaktalas,

311

Acknowledgements

Bombay, 1966, and the revised paper appeared as an article in the *British Journal of Industrial Relations*, March 1966.

Collective Bargaining: Prescription for Change
A revised version of my written evidence submitted to the Royal Commission on Trade Unions and Employers' Associations in November 1966. First published by Faber and Faber in 1967. A Japanese translation has been published by Charles E. Tuttle Co., Inc., Tokyo.

Collective Bargaining: A Theoretical Analysis
A paper entitled 'Bargaining Theory under Modern Capitalism', presented to the First World Congress of the International Industrial Relations Association held at Geneva in September 1967. First published as an article in the *British Journal of Industrial Relations*, March 1968, and then in *Industrial Relations: Contemporary Issues* (edited by B. C. Roberts), Macmillan, 1968. A French translation appeared in *Sociologie du Travail*, January–March 1968.

Collective Bargaining: From Donovan to Durkheim
A joint article with Alan Fox first published in the *British Journal of Industrial Relations*, July 1969. A French translation appeared in *Sociologie du Travail*, July–September 1969.

Trade Unions and the Force of Tradition
The Sixteenth Fawley Foundation Lecture given at the University of Southampton in November 1969 and published by the University.

INDEX

Accountability: control of management by, 138–9, 145; extended, 140–6

Alderson, S., 296

Allen, W. W., 165, 301

Anderson, Perry, 295

Anomie defined, 247

Arbitrary dismissal, protection against, 185–6, 187

Arbitration, compulsory, 160–1

Ashley, W. J., 245, 308

Bain, G. S., 301

Baking Industry (Hours of Work) Act, 1954, 185

Balance of payments and wages, action by governments, 104–5

Bayliss, F. J., 302

Behrend, H., 296, 303

'Blue Book' (Esso Refinery), *see* Fawley experiment

Blumenthal, W. M., 300

British Productivity Council, 19

Brown, Emily Clark, 298

Brown, Wilfred, 300

Cabot, Richard, 300

Castle, Mrs. Barbara, 69

Ceylon, collective agreements in, having force of law, 297

Chamberlain, Neil (J. Kuhn), 125, 145, 230–3, 300, 306, 307

Chamberlin, Edward H., 305

Churchill, (Sir) Winston, on class issues in courts of law, 291

Civil Rights Act, 1964, U.S.A., 290

Civil Service Arbitration Tribunal, 181

Civil Service Pay Research Unit, 192

Clay, Henry, 261, 262, 298, 309

Clegg, H. A., 148–9, 150, 284, 299, 300, 302, 310

Coal Mines (Minimum Wages) Act, 1912, 297

Co-determination, 141–2, 146

Cole, G. D. H., 43, 295, 305

Collective bargaining: basis for survival of, 159; case for decentralising, 115; Chamberlain's three theories of, 230–5; connections with management, 233–8; Donovan recommendations, 45; Donovan to Durkheim, 241–76; 'free', 101; inadequate growth of, 157–61; and interests of society at large, 162–8; and job regulation, 87 *seqq.*; legislation to strengthen, 183–7; and litigation, 95–6; and normative order, 246–55; open-ended agreements, 99; *see also* Industrial relations; political character, social achievements, 220–5; prescription for change, 155–211; present in historical perspective, 260–7; and procedural disputes, 180–2; and recognition disputes, 178–80; sectional character of, 116; theoretical analysis, 213–40; three leading principles of, Great Britain, 94–99; uniformity lacking, 84; and unions 41–2, 238–40; 'voluntary' and 'compulsory' arbitration in, 97; Webbs', classical view, 213–21, 224, 226, 233; in workplace. 168–73

'Collective relations' defined, 87

Commission on Industrial Relations. 45, 293

'Common purpose' in industry, 143–5

Communists in trade unions, 18

Company law, 138–9

Conditions of Employment and National Arbitration Order, 1940, 309

Confederation of British Industry, 67, 191, 194, 301

Consultation, 60, 61, 63; *see also* Joint consultation

Contracts of Employment Act, 1963, 107

Cooke, P. J. D., 296

313

Index

Index

Taylor, George W., 305
Terms and Conditions of Employment Act, 1959, 160–1, 178, 183, 297
'Theory X' and 'Theory Y', *see* McGregor, Douglas
Thompson, A. F., 284, 310
Thorne, E. M. F., 306
'Total task–total reward', 80
Trade Boards, 102
Trade Boards Act, 1918, 309
Trades Councils, 24, 34
Trades Disputes Act, 1906, 33
Trades Union Congress, 17, 19, 24–5, 31–2, 47, 180, 187, 191–4, 198–9, 264
Trade Unions: are they bargaining agents?, 238–40; attitudes toward legislature, 291–2; communism in, 18, 31; democratic functions of, 41; Disputes Committee of, 180; Donovan Report on power of, 242 *seqq.*; enduring social achievements of, 42; extent of political commitment of, 24–37, *and see below*, political aims of; as external to business enterprise, 90; and incomes policy, 45–7; and Labour Party, 32–6; lacking in social purpose, 16–19; Marxist view of role of, 38–9; political aims, industrial aims of, 26–9, 31–2, 38–47; and public opinion, 14–15; as 're-actionary', 293–4; 'responsible' approach of, 39–40; responsibilities of, 40–1; and restrictive practices, 58–9; social purpose of, at present, 20; as 'sword of justice', 21; in 30's, 16–17; in 6o's, 13–23, 44; and tradition generally, 18–19, 277–94
Traditions, 277–94; nature and significance of, 278–83; of craft, 283–8; of voluntarism, 288–94
Trist, Higgin, Murray & Pollock, 300
Turner, H. A., 111–12, 281, 298, 302, 310

Under-employment, in context of full employment, 67, 70, 108, 162, 165–7
United Automobile Workers' Association, 287
United Textile Workers' Association, 289

Voluntarism, tradition of, 288–94; three principles associated with, 289; in U.S. unions, 289–90; voluntary principle, value of, 173–178; voluntary system (industrial relations), discredited, 83–4

Wages Council Act, 1959, 297
Wages Councils, as form of tripartite job regulation, 94; as successors to Trade Boards, 102, 157–8, 183–4
Wages: differentials, problems of, 120; wages-prices spiral, 162 *seqq.*
Wages Regulation Orders, 157, 158, 184
Wagner Act, U.S.A., 290
Webb, Sidney and Beatrice, 27–8, 75, 148, 194, 213–26, 233, 291, 295, 297, 299, 300, 303–5, 309
Weber, A. R., 310
Weber, Max, 278, 279, 294, 310
Wedderburn, K. W., 301
White collar unions, 45
Whitley Committee, 97, 263
Whybrew, E. G., 298
Woodcock, George, 38
Woodward, Joan, 300
Wootton, Barbara, 306
Work groups, 88–9
Working to rule, 112
Workplace bargaining: as post-War upsurge, 44–5; arguments in favour of, 115; 'creative', 153; fragmented by piecework, 78–9; nature of, 108–113, 168–73
Workplace relations, future of, 121–3, 195 *seqq.*
Wright-Mills, C., 246, 308, 309

317